D1405136

Lean In

FOR GRADUATES

Lean In

FOR GRADUATES

Sheryl Sandberg
with Nell Scovell

ALFRED A. KNOPF   NEW YORK   2014

THIS IS A BORZOI BOOK
PUBLISHED BY ALFRED A. KNOPF

Copyright © 2013, 2014 by Lean In Foundation

All rights reserved. Published in the United States by
Alfred A. Knopf, a division of Random House LLC, New York,
and in Canada by Random House of Canada Limited, Toronto,
Penguin Random House companies. Originally published
in hardcover in the United States, in different form,
by Alfred A. Knopf, a division of Random House LLC,
New York, in 2013.

www.aaknopf.com

Knopf, Borzoi Books, and the colophon are registered
trademarks of Random House LLC.

Library of Congress Control Number: 2014002390
ISBN 978-0-385-35367-0 (hardcover)
ISBN 978-0-385-35386-1 (eBook)

Manufactured in the United States of America
Published March 12, 2013
Expanded Edition for Graduates Published April 8, 2014

TO MY PARENTS
for raising me to believe that
anything was possible

AND TO MY HUSBAND
for making everything possible

Contents

A Letter to Graduates   xi

Introduction: Internalizing the Revolution   3

1. The Leadership Ambition Gap:
   What Would You Do If You Weren't Afraid?   15

2. Sit at the Table   34

3. Success and Likeability   49

4. It's a Jungle Gym, Not a Ladder   66

5. Are You My Mentor?   81

6. Seek and Speak Your Truth   97

7. Don't Leave Before You Leave   116

8. Make Your Partner a Real Partner   131

9. The Myth of Doing It All   153

10. Let's Start Talking About It 177

11. Working Together Toward Equality 201

Sara's Story: I Overcame My Fear and Ran for
Mayor of My Town 219

Allison's Story: We Are Not Leftover. We Are
Leaning In. 222

12. Own Who You Are *by Mellody Hobson* 225

Nola's Story: To Understand My Future, I Had to
Understand My Past 241

Matthew's Story: I Learned to Sit at the Table 244

13. Man Up and Lean In *by Kunal Modi* 247

Ursula's Story: Where I Was Didn't Define
Who I Was 257

Marie's Story: I Testified Against My Rapist 259

14. Listen to Your Inner Voice *by Rachel Simmons* 261

Ty-Licia's Story: I Learned to Be Myself 271

Mana's Story: I Spoke Out About My Eating
Disorder and Recovery 274

15. Find Your First Job *by Mindy Levy* 277

Regina's Story: Don't Deny Your Dream 296

Jessica's Story: I Negotiated for a Raise 298

16. Negotiate Your Salary *by Kim Keating* 301

Jana's Story: A Group to Boost My Confidence   318

Sindhura's Story: I Took a Risk and Stepped
on the Gas   320

17. Let's Lean In Together *by Rachel Thomas*   323

The Beginning, Not the End . . .   331

Acknowledgments   333

Notes   343

Index   391

Dear Graduate,

Congratulations! You made it!

It's time to celebrate all the hard work that led to this joyful occasion. The road to graduation is a long, steep climb, so take a moment at the summit to be proud of your accomplishments. Whether you know exactly where you're heading or feel a bit lost, everyone has this in common: you're all in for big surprises.

At my college graduation, I never would have predicted that I'd wind up working in technology. I had given up being a serious math student in ninth grade when I attended a math competition, noticed that there were no other girls, and decided that "math was for boys" (yep, pretty much the *opposite* of leaning in). Also, I graduated in June 1991— two months before the birth of the World Wide Web. It's shocking, but I made it through college with zero internet. No cell phones with cameras either, which given that I wore leg warmers and headbands is a blessing.

There's no question that the world moves faster today. This means that grabbing opportunities is more important than ever. And I don't have to tell you that you are entering a struggling economy. So along with all the excitement, most of you will also feel some uncertainty and fear.

Graduating is one of life's trickier transitions. School offers clear structure and expectations, while the real world is harder to navigate. Your community is about to scatter. Not all the skills you've acquired will transfer. As you start your adult life, you will wonder if you're making the right choices. You may also wish you had more choices.

The embarrassing truth is that I left college more concerned about my personal life than my professional life. My parents married young and repeatedly warned me that the "good ones" got snatched up in college. I believed them and even taped a poster to my dorm room wall of a frog sitting in the middle of a frilly four-poster bed, with a caption that read, "You have to kiss a lot of frogs before you find your prince." I had fun with a few frogs and, in retrospect, am amazed that anyone was willing to kiss me under that ridiculous poster. But I graduated princeless—and frogless for that matter—which left me worried about my future.

Like you, I entered the workforce during a recession. Even my friends who had jobs were nervous. I was nervous too. It took me a long time to find my way into an industry I love. It took me a longer time to find the right partner. It took me even longer to find my voice.

When I graduated, I believed that the feminists who came before me had done the hard work of demanding equality and now it was ours for the taking. In my early jobs, my peers were a balanced mix of men and women. But with each passing year, there were fewer and fewer women in the room until I was often the only one. Slowly—and sadly—it dawned on me that the promise of equality is not the same as achieving equality.

While we have far more opportunity than our mothers and grandmothers, there are still biases that work against us. It can be painful to acknowledge that our experience as individuals is inescapably linked to our gender. We long for a true meritocracy, where we are judged on our abilities alone. But the world has a way of attaching the word "female" to our achievements: "female surgeon," "female director," "female marathoner," "female senator."

Very few people, women or men, sail through their professional lives without hurdles and setbacks. But women face additional challenges, including blatant and subtle discrimination, sexual harassment, and a lack of sensible public and workforce policies. Women of color face even greater barriers. I say this not to discourage you, but to prepare you. Until we—and others—are aware of these biases, we cannot change them. While this book doesn't have all the answers, it does explore many of the issues that I wish I'd understood better when I graduated.

As you start your career, you should be aware that men are often promoted based on potential, while women are promoted on past performance.[1] You should also be aware that when men are successful, they are often better liked by both men and women, but when women are successful, they are liked less.[2] I have asked audiences around the world to raise their hands if they've been told they were too aggressive at work. Time and again, a small fraction of men raise their hands, while a great majority of women shoot a hand into the air . . . and sometimes two.

You should also be aware of the internal barriers that we often impose on ourselves. Too many women sit on the side of the room when they should be sitting at the table. Too many women lower their voices when they should be speaking up.

This is not our fault. We internalize messages that say it's wrong for us to be outspoken, aggressive, and as powerful as— or even more powerful than—men. In response, we alter our actions. A study by two Princeton researchers asked college students to compete in a video game in which players dropped bombs on opponents. When the students believed they were being monitored, the men dropped more bombs than the women. When the students believed no one was watching, the women dropped significantly more bombs than the men.[3]

We hold ourselves back not just out of fear of seeming too aggressive but also by underestimating our abilities. Ask a woman to explain why she's successful and she'll credit luck, hard work, and help from others. Ask a man the same question and he's likely to explain, or at least think, "C'mon, I'm awesome!"[4]

I know how hard it can be to believe in yourself. To this day, I struggle to feel confident. A few months after I finished writing *Lean In*—an *entire book* about how women should own their success—I was at a meeting to kick off a project with the senior Facebook team. For years, my colleague Jay Parikh and I had pushed for this project, but no one agreed with us. Then, suddenly, we had a breakthrough. I was thrilled and started the meeting by telling everyone how grateful I was for their support and how I had worried for years that I was wrong about the need for this initiative. Jay looked up, paused, and said, "I knew Sheryl and I were right and you would all come around eventually." *Really? His belief that we were right was not shaken by years of everyone disagreeing with us?*

Later that night, I was Facebook messaging with Jay, and I asked him if I could tell this story on my book tour. He said yes. I asked if I could use his name when telling the story. He said of course. He's a great guy, so I told him I would make sure he did not come across as arrogant. He typed back, "I'm not worried about that." *Again, really?*

It would be so nice to feel that level of confidence. And while it's never a good idea to be boastful, believing in your own self-worth is essential to achieving your full potential. As you begin your career, you will probably find yourself working next to a man who has Jay's deep and deserved faith in himself. If you take the chair on the side of the room, he will take the seat at the table because he knows he's awesome. So please remember that you deserve a seat at that same table . . . and that you are awesome too.

Part of believing in yourself means not worrying too much about failure. Know that your career—and your life—will have starts and stops, twists, and even U-turns. This is especially true in an economy where you may have to take the job you can get as opposed to the job you want. Focus on taking full advantage of any opportunity to develop your skills. And remember that your early years in the workforce are a great time to strengthen areas of weakness. So many of us avoid doing the things we're not good at, practically ensuring that we will never improve. If leading a project scares you, volunteer to do it. If you don't like speaking in public, start by addressing small groups. Look for ways to stretch yourself, both big and small.

My first job out of school was with the World Bank in Washington, D.C. My thesis advisor, Larry Summers, had just taken a job as chief economist and hired me to be his research assistant. At times, I was incredibly busy helping him write papers and speeches. But when he left town to deliver those speeches, I sometimes didn't have enough work to do. I would sheepishly approach some of the other economists to ask if they needed help. The response was usually "no," which I took to mean that I was literally useless. Sometimes I sat at my desk trying to look busy. Sometimes I snuck out. But over time, I stopped asking for tasks and just started doing things I thought might help. They began to see me as more capable, and after a while I was consistently busy.

While I eventually got that right, I got plenty wrong. It never even occurred to me to negotiate my first salary. I waited for someone to tell me how much money I'd be earning so I could figure out where to live. I ended up supplementing my income by teaching aerobics classes on the weekend. Yes, I turned to a world of leg lifts and leotards. There was a downside: During my first month at work, I was riding in an elevator with a group of tall middle-aged men in gray suits when one of them exclaimed, "Sheryl, I didn't recognize you with your clothes on," before exiting the elevator. The other gray suits looked down on me in shock. I quietly explained, "I teach an aerobics class," which sounded even more embarrassing. The next time the doors opened, I hurried out even though I was on the wrong floor.

Each of us makes her own way in her own time. You may not love every job you have, but you will learn from all of them. Sometimes you will have mentors to help guide the way and sometimes you will have to rely on your colleagues, friends, teachers, and family for advice. You might want to join a Lean In Circle (leanin.org/circles), which is a peer mentoring group that provides education and encouragement. When you need help—and we all do—please look for it. No one needs to navigate this world alone.

And if anyone, including that voice in the back of your head, insists you must choose between work and having a family, remember that men routinely assume they can have both. You should assume that you can too, especially since mothers now make up the majority of primary or co-breadwinners for American families.[5]

I have so many hopes for you. I hope you head into the next phase of your life with your eyes wide open. I hope you find engaging work and pursue it with gusto. I hope that if you aspire to lead, you will let nothing limit your ambition. Above all, I hope you believe in yourself.

Your life's course should not be determined by doing what's safe and easy but by reaching for what's challenging and hard: the classes that seem impossible on the first day, but you study enough to pass . . . the jobs you're not quite qualified for, but you work like crazy to acquire the skills . . . the moments when you feel alone and overwhelmed, but you are brave enough to ask for help.

This is your time. You can help create a more equal world where everyone sits at the table and all voices are heard. Generations of women are rooting for you. I am rooting for you.

So start by aiming high. Be ambitious. Seize opportunities. *Make* opportunities. Embrace leadership. Lean in.

—SHERYL

Lean In

FOR GRADUATES

Internalizing the Revolution

I GOT PREGNANT with my first child in the summer of 2004. At the time, I was running the online sales and operations groups at Google. I had joined the company three and a half years earlier when it was an obscure start-up with a few hundred employees in a run-down office building. By my first trimester, Google had grown into a company of thousands and moved into a multibuilding campus.

My pregnancy was not easy. The typical morning sickness that often accompanies the first trimester affected me every day for nine long months. I gained almost seventy pounds, and my feet swelled two entire shoe sizes, turning into odd-shaped lumps I could see only when they were propped up on a coffee table. A particularly sensitive Google engineer announced that "Project Whale" was named after me.

One day, after a rough morning spent staring at the bottom of the toilet, I had to rush to make an important client meeting. Google was growing so quickly that parking was an ongoing problem, and the only spot I could find was quite far away. I sprinted across the parking lot, which in reality meant lumbering a bit more quickly than my absurdly slow pregnancy crawl. This only made my nausea worse, and I arrived at the meeting praying that a sales pitch was the only thing that would come out of my mouth. That night, I recounted these troubles to my husband, Dave. He pointed out that Yahoo, where he worked at the time, had designated parking for expectant mothers at the front of each building.

The next day, I marched in—or more like waddled in—to see Google founders Larry Page and Sergey Brin in their office, which was really just a large room with toys and gadgets strewn all over the floor. I found Sergey in a yoga position in the corner and announced that we needed pregnancy parking, preferably sooner rather than later. He looked up at me and agreed immediately, noting that he had never thought about it before.

To this day, I'm embarrassed that I didn't realize that pregnant women needed reserved parking until I experienced my own aching feet. As one of Google's most senior women, didn't I have a special responsibility to think of this? But like Sergey, it had never occurred to me. The other pregnant women must have suffered in silence, not wanting to ask for special treatment. Or maybe they lacked the confidence or seniority to demand that the problem be fixed. Having one pregnant woman at the top—even one who looked like a whale—made the difference.

Today in the United States and the developed world, women are better off than ever. We stand on the shoulders of the women who came before us, women who had to fight for the rights that we now take for granted. In 1947, Anita Summers, the mother of my longtime mentor Larry Summers, was hired as an economist by the Standard Oil Company. When she accepted the job, her new boss said to her, "I am so glad to have you. I figure I am getting the same brains for less money." Her reaction to this was to feel flattered. It was a huge compliment to be told that she had the same brains as a man. It would have been unthinkable for her to ask for equal compensation.

We feel even more grateful when we compare our lives to those of other women around the world. There are still countries that deny women basic civil rights. Worldwide, about 4.4 million women and girls are trapped in the sex trade.[1] In places like Afghanistan and Sudan, girls receive little or no education, wives are treated as the property of their husbands, and women who are raped are routinely cast out of their homes for disgracing their families. Some rape victims are even sent to jail for committing a "moral crime."[2] We are centuries ahead of the unacceptable treatment of women in these countries.

But knowing that things could be worse should not stop us from trying to make them better. When the suffragettes marched in the streets, they envisioned a world where men and women would be truly equal. A century later, we are still squinting, trying to bring that vision into focus.

The blunt truth is that men still run the world. Of the

195 independent countries in the world, only 19 are led by women.[3] Women hold just 21 percent of seats in parliaments globally.[4] In the United States, where we pride ourselves on liberty and justice for all, the gender division of leadership roles is not much better. Women became 50 percent of the college graduates in the United States in the early 1980s.[5] Since then, women have slowly and steadily advanced, earning more and more of the college degrees, taking more of the entry-level jobs, and entering more fields previously dominated by men. Despite these gains, the percentage of women at the top of corporate America has barely budged over the past decade.[6] A meager twenty-three of the Fortune 500 CEOs are women.[7] Women hold about 15 percent of executive officer positions, 17 percent of board seats, and constitute 19 percent of our elected congressional officials.[8] The gap is even worse for women of color, who hold just 4 percent of top corporate jobs, 3 percent of board seats, and 5 percent of congressional seats.[9] While women continue to outpace men in educational achievement, we have ceased making real progress at the top of any industry. This means that when it comes to making the decisions that most affect our world, women's voices are not heard equally.

Progress remains equally sluggish when it comes to compensation. In 1970, American women were paid 59 cents for every dollar their male counterparts made. By 2010, women had protested, fought, and worked their butts off to raise that compensation to 77 cents for every dollar men made.[10] As activist Marlo Thomas wryly joked on Equal

Pay Day 2011, "Forty years and eighteen cents. A dozen eggs have gone up ten times that amount."[11]

I have watched these disheartening events from a front-row seat. I graduated from college in 1991 and from business school in 1995. In each entry-level job after graduation, my colleagues were a balanced mix of male and female. I saw that the senior leaders were almost entirely male, but I thought that was due to historical discrimination against women. The proverbial glass ceiling had been cracked in almost every industry, and I believed that it was just a matter of time until my generation took our fair share of the leadership roles. But with each passing year, fewer and fewer of my colleagues were women. More and more often, I was the only woman in the room.

Being the sole woman has resulted in some awkward yet revealing situations. Two years after I joined Facebook as chief operating officer, our chief financial officer departed suddenly, and I had to step in to complete a funding round. Since I had spent my career in operations, not finance, the process of raising capital was new and a bit scary. My team and I flew to New York for the initial pitch to private equity firms. Our first meeting was held in the kind of corporate office featured in movies, complete with a sprawling view of Manhattan. I offered an overview of our business and answered questions. So far so good. Then someone suggested that we break for a few minutes. I turned to the senior partner and asked where the women's restroom was. He stared at me blankly. My question had completely stumped him. I asked, "How long have you been in this office?" And he said, "One year." "Am I the only woman to have pitched a deal here in an entire year?" "I think so," he said, adding, "or maybe you're the only one who had to use the bathroom."

It has been more than two decades since I entered the workforce, and so much is still the same. It is time for us to face the fact that our revolution has stalled.[12] The promise of equality is not the same as true equality.

A truly equal world would be one where women ran half our countries and companies and men ran half our homes. I believe that this would be a better world. The laws of economics and many studies of diversity tell us that if we tapped the entire pool of human resources and talent, our collective performance would improve. Legendary investor Warren Buffett has stated generously that one of the reasons for his great success was that he was competing with only half of the population. The Warren Buffetts of my generation are still largely enjoying this advantage. When more people get in the race, more records will be broken. And the achievements will extend beyond those individuals to benefit us all.

The night before Leymah Gbowee won the 2011 Nobel Peace Prize for helping to lead the women's protests that toppled Liberia's dictator, she was at a book party in my home. We were celebrating the publication of her autobiography, *Mighty Be Our Powers*, but it was a somber night. A guest asked her how American women could help those who experienced the horrors and mass rapes of war in places like Liberia. Her response was four simple words:

"More women in power." Leymah and I could not have come from more different backgrounds, and yet we have both arrived at the same conclusion. Conditions for all women will improve when there are more women in leadership roles giving strong and powerful voice to their needs and concerns.[13]

This brings us to the obvious question—how? How are we going to take down the barriers that prevent more women from getting to the top? Women face real obstacles in the professional world, including blatant and subtle sexism, discrimination, and sexual harassment. Too few workplaces offer the flexibility and access to child care and parental leave that are necessary for pursuing a career while raising children. Men have an easier time finding the mentors and sponsors who are invaluable for career progression. Plus, women have to prove themselves to a far greater extent than men do. And this is not just in our heads. A 2011 McKinsey report noted that men are promoted based on potential, while women are promoted based on past accomplishments.[14]

In addition to the external barriers erected by society, women are hindered by barriers that exist within ourselves. We hold ourselves back in ways both big and small, by lacking self-confidence, by not raising our hands, and by pulling back when we should be leaning in. We internalize the negative messages we get throughout our lives—the messages that say it's wrong to be outspoken, aggressive, more powerful than men. We lower our own expectations of what we can achieve. We continue to do the majority of the housework and child care. We compromise our career goals to make room for partners and children who may not even exist yet. Compared to our male colleagues, fewer of us aspire to senior positions. This is not a list of things other women have done. I have made every mistake on this list. At times, I still do.

My argument is that getting rid of these internal barriers is critical to gaining power. Others have argued that women can get to the top only when the institutional barriers are gone. This is the ultimate chicken-and-egg situation. The chicken: Women will tear down the external barriers once we achieve leadership roles. We will march into our bosses' offices and demand what we need, including pregnancy parking. Or better yet, we'll become bosses and make sure all women have what they need. The egg: We need to eliminate the external barriers to get women into those roles in the first place. Both sides are right. So rather than engage in philosophical arguments over which comes first, let's agree to wage battles on both fronts. They are equally important. I am encouraging women to address the chicken, but I fully support those who are focusing on the egg.

Internal obstacles are rarely discussed and often underplayed. Throughout my life, I was told over and over about inequalities in the workplace and how hard it would be to have a career and a family. I rarely heard anything, however, about the ways I might hold myself back. These internal obstacles deserve a lot more attention, in part because they are under our own control. We can dismantle the hurdles in ourselves today. We can start this very moment.

I never thought I would write a book. I am not a scholar, a journalist, or a sociologist. But I decided to speak out after talking to hundreds of women, listening to their struggles, sharing my own, and realizing that the gains we have made are not enough and may even be slipping. The first chapter of this book lays out some of the complex challenges women face. Each subsequent chapter focuses on an adjustment or difference that we can make ourselves: increasing our self-confidence ("Sit at the Table"), getting our partners to do more at home ("Make Your Partner a Real Partner"), not holding ourselves to unattainable standards ("The Myth of Doing It All"). I do not pretend to have perfect solutions to these deep and complicated issues. I rely on hard data, academic research, my own observations, and lessons I have learned along the way.

This book is not a memoir, although I have included stories about my life. It is not a self-help book, although I truly hope it helps. It is not a book on career management, although I offer advice in that area. It is not a feminist manifesto—okay, it is sort of a feminist manifesto, but one that I hope inspires men as much as it inspires women.

Whatever this book is, I am writing it for any woman who wants to increase her chances of making it to the top of her field or pursue any goal vigorously. This includes women at all stages of their lives and careers, from those who are just starting out to those who are taking a break and may want to jump back in. I am also writing this for any man who wants to understand what a woman—a colleague, wife, mother, or daughter—is up against so that he can do his part to build an equal world.

This book makes the case for leaning in, for being ambitious in any pursuit. And while I believe that increasing the number of women in positions of power is a necessary element of true equality, I do not believe that there is one definition of success or happiness. Not all women want careers. Not all women want children. Not all women want both. I would never advocate that we should all have the same objectives. Many people are not interested in acquiring power, not because they lack ambition, but because they are living their lives as they desire. Some of the most important contributions to our world are made by caring for one person at a time. We each have to chart our own unique course and define which goals fit our lives, values, and dreams.

I am also acutely aware that the vast majority of women are struggling to make ends meet and take care of their families. Parts of this book will be most relevant to women fortunate enough to have choices about how much and when and where to work; other parts apply to situations that women face in every workplace, within every community, and in every home. If we can succeed in adding more female voices at the highest levels, we will expand opportunities and extend fairer treatment to all.

Some, especially other women in business, have cautioned me about speaking out publicly on these issues.

When I have spoken out anyway, several of my comments have upset people of both genders. I know some believe that by focusing on what women can change themselves— pressing them to lean in—it seems like I am letting our institutions off the hook. Or even worse, they accuse me of blaming the victim. Far from blaming the victim, I believe that female leaders are key to the solution. Some critics will also point out that it is much easier for me to lean in, since my financial resources allow me to afford any help I need. My intention is to offer advice that would have been useful to me long before I had heard of Google or Facebook and that will resonate with women in a broad range of circumstances.

I have heard these criticisms in the past and I know that I will hear them—and others—in the future. My hope is that my message will be judged on its merits. We can't avoid this conversation. This issue transcends all of us. The time is long overdue to encourage more women to dream the possible dream and encourage more men to support women in the workforce and in the home.

We can reignite the revolution by internalizing the revolution. The shift to a more equal world will happen person by person. We move closer to the larger goal of true equality with each woman who leans in.

The Leadership Ambition Gap

What Would You Do If You Weren't Afraid?

M Y GRANDMOTHER Rosalind Einhorn was born exactly fifty-two years before I was, on August 28, 1917. Like many poor Jewish families in the boroughs of New York City, hers lived in a small, crowded apartment close to their relatives. Her parents, aunts, and uncles addressed her male cousins by their given names, but she and her sister were referred to only as "Girlie."

During the Depression, my grandmother was pulled out of Morris High School to help support the household by sewing fabric flowers onto undergarments that her mother could resell for a tiny profit. No one in the community would have considered taking a boy out of school. A boy's education was the family's hope to move up the financial and social ladder. Education for girls, however, was less important both financially, since they were unlikely to contribute to the family's income, and culturally, since boys were expected to study the Torah while girls were expected to run a "proper home." Luckily for my grandmother, a local teacher insisted that her parents put her back into school. She went on not only to finish high school but to graduate from U.C. Berkeley.

After college, "Girlie" worked selling pocketbooks and accessories at David's Fifth Avenue. When she left her job to marry my grandfather, family legend has it that David's had to hire four people to replace her. Years later, when my grandfather's paint business was struggling, she jumped in and took some of the hard steps he was reluctant to take, helping to save the family from financial ruin. She displayed her business acumen again in her forties. After being diagnosed with breast cancer, she beat it and then dedicated herself to raising money for the clinic that treated her by selling knockoff watches out of the trunk of her car. Girlie ended up with a profit margin that Apple would envy. I have never met anyone with more energy and determination than my grandmother. When Warren Buffett talks about competing against only half of the population, I think about her and wonder how different her life might have been if she had been born half a century later.

When my grandmother had children of her own—my mother and her two brothers—she emphasized education for all of them. My mother attended the University of Pennsylvania, where classes were coed. When she graduated in 1965 with a degree in French literature, she surveyed a workforce that she believed consisted of two career options for women: teaching or nursing. She chose teaching. She began a Ph.D. program, got married, and then dropped out when she became pregnant with me. It was thought to be a sign of weakness if a husband needed his wife's help to support their family, so my mother became a stay-at-home parent and an active volunteer. The centuries-old division of labor stood.

Even though I grew up in a traditional home, my parents had the same expectations for me, my sister, and my brother. All three of us were encouraged to excel in school, do equal chores, and engage in extracurricular activities. We were all supposed to be athletic too. My brother and sister joined sports teams, but I was the kid who got picked last in gym. Despite my athletic shortcomings, I was raised to believe that girls could do anything boys could do and that *all* career paths were open to me.

When I arrived at college in the fall of 1987, my classmates of both genders seemed equally focused on academics. I don't remember thinking about my future career differently from the male students. I also don't remember any conversations about someday balancing work and children. My friends and I assumed that we would have both. Men and women competed openly and aggressively with one another in classes, activities, and job interviews. Just two generations removed from my grandmother, the playing field seemed to be level.

But more than twenty years after my college graduation, the world has not evolved nearly as much as I believed it would. Almost all of my male classmates work in professional settings. Some of my female classmates work full-time or part-time outside the home, and just as many are stay-at-home mothers and volunteers like my mom. This mirrors the national trend. In comparison to their male counterparts, highly trained women are scaling back and dropping out of the workforce in high numbers.[1] In turn, these diverging percentages teach institutions and mentors to invest more in men, who are statistically more likely to stay.

Judith Rodin, president of the Rockefeller Foundation and the first woman to serve as president of an Ivy League university, once remarked to an audience of women my age, "My generation fought so hard to give all of you choices. We believe in choices. But choosing to leave the workforce was not the choice we thought so many of you would make."[2]

So what happened? My generation was raised in an era of increasing equality, a trend we thought would continue. In retrospect, we were naïve and idealistic. Integrating professional and personal aspirations proved far more challenging than we had imagined. During the same years that our careers demanded maximum time investment, our biology demanded that we have children. Our partners did not share the housework and child rearing, so we found ourselves with two full-time jobs. The workplace did not evolve to give us the flexibility we needed to fulfill our responsibilities at home. We anticipated none of this. We were caught by surprise.

If my generation was too naïve, the generations that

have followed may be too practical. We knew too little, and now girls know too much. Girls growing up today are not the first generation to have equal opportunity, but they are the first to know that all that opportunity does not necessarily translate into professional achievement. Many of these girls watched their mothers try to "do it all" and then decide that something had to give. That something was usually their careers.

There's no doubt that women have the skills to lead in the workplace. Girls are increasingly outperforming boys in the classroom, earning about 57 percent of the undergraduate and 60 percent of the master's degrees in the United States.[3] This gender gap in academic achievement has even caused some to worry about the "end of men."[4] But while compliant, raise-your-hand-and-speak-when-called-on behaviors might be rewarded in school, they are less valued in the workplace.[5] Career progression often depends upon taking risks and advocating for oneself—traits that girls are discouraged from exhibiting. This may explain why girls' academic gains have not yet translated into significantly higher numbers of women in top jobs. The pipeline that supplies the educated workforce is chock-full of women at the entry level, but by the time that same pipeline is filling leadership positions, it is overwhelmingly stocked with men.

There are so many reasons for this winnowing out, but one important contributor is a leadership ambition gap. Of course, many individual women are as professionally ambitious as any individual man. Yet drilling down, the data clearly indicate that in field after field, more men than women aspire to the most senior jobs. A 2012 McKinsey survey of more than four thousand employees of leading companies found that 36 percent of the men wanted to reach the C-suite, compared to only 18 percent of the women.[6] When jobs are described as powerful, challenging, and involving high levels of responsibility, they appeal to more men than women.[7] And while the ambition gap is most pronounced at the highest levels, the underlying dynamic is evident at every step of the career ladder. A survey of college students found that more men than women chose "reaching a managerial level" as a career priority in the first three years after graduating.[8] Even among highly educated professional men and women, more men than women describe themselves as "ambitious."[9]

There is some hope that a shift is starting to occur in the next generation. A 2012 Pew study found for the first time that among young people ages eighteen to thirty-four, more young women (66 percent) than young men (59 percent) rated "success in a high-paying career or profession" as important to their lives.[10] A recent survey of millennials[11] found that women were just as likely to describe themselves as ambitious as men. Although this is an improvement, even among this demographic, the leadership ambition gap remains. Millennial women are less likely than millennial men to agree that the statement "I aspire to a leadership role in whatever field I ultimately work" describes them very well. Millennial women were also less likely than their male peers to characterize themselves as "leaders," "visionaries," "self-confident," and "willing to take risks."[12]

Since more men aim for leadership roles, it is not surprising that they obtain them, especially given all the other obstacles that women have to overcome. This pattern starts long before they enter the workforce. Author Samantha Ettus and her husband read their daughter's kindergarten yearbook, where each child answered the question "What do you want to be when you grow up?" They noted that several of the boys wanted to be president. None of the girls did.[13] (Current data suggest that when these girls become women, they will continue to feel the same way.)[14] In middle school, more boys than girls aspire to leadership roles in future careers.[15] At the top fifty colleges, less than a third of student government presidents are women.[16]

Professional ambition is expected of men but is optional—or worse, sometimes even a negative—for women. "She is *very* ambitious" is not a compliment in our culture. Aggressive and hard-charging women violate unwritten rules about acceptable social conduct. Men are continually applauded for being ambitious and powerful and successful, but women who display these same traits often pay a social penalty. Female accomplishments come at a cost.[17]

And for all the progress, there is still societal pressure for women to keep an eye on marriage from a young age. When I went to college, as much as my parents emphasized academic achievement, they emphasized marriage even more. They told me that the most eligible women marry young to get a "good man" before they are all taken. I followed their advice, and throughout college, I vetted every date as a potential husband (which, trust me, is a sure way to ruin a date at age nineteen).

When I was graduating, my thesis advisor, Larry Summers, suggested that I apply for international fellowships. I rejected the idea on the grounds that a foreign country was not a likely place to turn a date into a husband. Instead, I moved to Washington, D.C., which was full of eligible men. It worked. My first year out of college, I met a man who was not just eligible, but also wonderful, so I married him. I was twenty-four and convinced that marriage was the first—and necessary—step to a happy and productive life.

It didn't work out that way. I was just not mature enough to have made this lifelong decision, and the relationship quickly unraveled. By the age of twenty-five, I had managed to get married . . . and also divorced. At the time, this felt like a massive personal *and* public failure. For many years, I felt that no matter what I accomplished professionally, it paled in comparison to the scarlet letter D stitched on my chest. (Almost ten years later, I learned that the "good ones" were not all taken, and I wisely and very happily married Dave Goldberg.)

Like me, Gayle Tzemach Lemmon, deputy director of the Council on Foreign Relations' Women and Foreign Policy Program, was encouraged to prioritize marriage over career. As she described in *The Atlantic*, "When I was

27, I received a posh fellowship to travel to Germany to learn German and work at the *Wall Street Journal*. . . . It was an incredible opportunity for a 20-something by any objective standard, and I knew it would help prepare me for graduate school and beyond. My girlfriends, however, expressed shock and horror that I would leave my boyfriend at the time to live abroad for a year. My relatives asked whether I was worried that I'd never get married. And when I attended a barbecue with my then-beau, his boss took me aside to remind me that 'there aren't many guys like that out there.' " The result of these negative reactions, in Gayle's view, is that many women "still see ambition as a dirty word."[18]

Many have argued with me that ambition is not the problem. Women are not less ambitious than men, they insist, but more enlightened with different and more meaningful goals. I do not dismiss or dispute this argument. There is far more to life than climbing a career ladder, including raising children, seeking personal fulfillment, contributing to society, and improving the lives of others. And there are many people who are deeply committed to their jobs but do not—and should not have to—aspire to run their organizations. Leadership roles are not the only way to have profound impact.

I also acknowledge that there are biological differences between men and women. I have breast-fed two children and noted, at times with great disappointment, that this was simply not something my husband was equipped to do. Are there characteristics inherent in sex differences that make women more nurturing and men more assertive? Quite possibly. Still, in today's world, where we no longer have to hunt in the wild for our food, our desire for leadership is largely a culturally created and reinforced trait. How individuals view what they can and should accomplish is in large part formed by our societal expectations.

From the moment we are born, boys and girls are treated differently.[19] Parents tend to talk to girl babies more than boy babies.[20] Mothers overestimate the crawling ability of their sons and underestimate the crawling ability of their daughters.[21] Reflecting the belief that girls need to be helped more than boys, mothers often spend more time comforting and hugging infant girls and more time watching infant boys play by themselves.[22]

Other cultural messages are more blatant. Gymboree once sold onesies proclaiming "Smart like Daddy" for boys and "Pretty like Mommy" for girls.[23] The same year, J. C. Penney marketed a T-shirt to teenage girls that bragged, "I'm too pretty to do homework so my brother has to do it for me."[24] These things did not happen in 1951. They happened in 2011.

Even worse, the messages sent to girls can move beyond encouraging superficial traits and veer into explicitly discouraging leadership. When a girl tries to lead, she is often labeled bossy. Boys are seldom called bossy because a boy taking the role of a boss does not surprise or offend. As someone who was called this for much of my childhood, I know that it is not a compliment.

The stories of my childhood bossiness are told (and

retold) with great amusement. Apparently, when I was in elementary school, I taught my younger siblings, David and Michelle, to follow me around, listen to my monologues, and scream the word "Right!" when I concluded. I was the eldest of the neighborhood children and allegedly spent my time organizing shows that I could direct and clubs that I could run. People laugh at these accounts, but to this day I always feel slightly ashamed of my behavior (which is remarkable given that I have now written an entire book about why girls should not be made to feel this way, or maybe this partially explains my motivation).

Even when we were in our thirties, pointing out this behavior was still the best way for my siblings to tease me. When Dave and I got married, David and Michelle gave a beautiful, hilarious toast, which kicked off with this: "Hi! Some of you think we are Sheryl's younger siblings, but really we were Sheryl's first employees—employee number one and employee number two. Initially, as a one-year-old and a three-year-old, we were worthless and weak. Disorganized, lazy. We would just as soon spit up on ourselves as read the morning paper. But Sheryl could see that we had potential. For more than ten years, Sheryl took us under her wing and whipped us into shape." Everyone laughed. My siblings continued, "To the best of our knowledge Sheryl never actually *played* as a child, but really just organized other children's play. Sheryl supervised adults as well. When our parents went away on vacation, our grandparents used to babysit. Before our parents left, Sheryl protested, 'Now I have to take care of David and Michelle *and* Grandma and Grandpa too. It's not fair!' " Everyone laughed even louder.

I laughed too, but there is still some part of me that feels it was unseemly for a little girl to be thought of as so . . . domineering. *Cringe.*

From a very early age, boys are encouraged to take charge and offer their opinions. Teachers interact more with boys, call on them more frequently, and ask them more questions. Boys are also more likely to call out answers, and when they do, teachers usually listen to them. When girls call out, teachers often scold them for breaking the rules and remind them to raise their hands if they want to speak.[25]

I was recently reminded that these patterns persist even when we are all grown up. Not long ago, at a small dinner with other business executives, the guest of honor spoke the entire time without taking a breath. This meant that the only way to ask a question or make an observation was to interrupt. Three or four men jumped in, and the guest politely answered their questions before resuming his lecture. At one point, I tried to add something to the conversation and he barked, "Let me finish! You people are not good at listening!" Eventually, a few more men interjected and he allowed it. Then the only other female executive at the dinner decided to speak up—and he did it again! He chastised her for interrupting. After the meal, one of the male CEOs pulled me aside to say that he had noticed that only the women had been silenced. He told me he empathized, because as a Hispanic, he has been treated like this many times.

The danger goes beyond authority figures silencing female voices. Young women internalize societal cues about what defines "appropriate" behavior and, in turn, silence themselves. They are rewarded for being "pretty like Mommy" and encouraged to be nurturing like Mommy too. The album *Free to Be . . . You and Me* was released in 1972 and became a staple of my childhood. My favorite song, "William's Doll," is about a five-year-old boy who begs his reluctant father to buy him a traditional girl's toy. Almost forty years later, the toy industry remains riddled with stereotypes. Right before Christmas 2011, a video featuring a four-year-old girl named Riley went viral. Riley paces in a toy store, upset because companies are trying to "trick the girls into buying the pink stuff instead of stuff that boys want to buy, right?" Right. As Riley reasons, "Some girls like superheroes, some girls like princesses. Some boys like superheroes, some boys like princesses. So why do all the girls have to buy pink stuff and all the boys have to buy different color stuff?"[26] It takes a near act of rebellion for even a four-year-old to break away from society's expectations. William still has no doll, while Riley is drowning in a sea of pink. I now play *Free to Be . . . You and Me* for my children and hope that if they ever play it for *their* children, its message will seem quaint.

The gender stereotypes introduced in childhood are reinforced throughout our lives and become self-fulfilling prophecies. Most leadership positions are held by men, so women don't *expect* to achieve them, and that becomes one of the reasons they don't. The same is true with pay. Men generally earn more than women, so people *expect* women to earn less. And they do.

Compounding the problem is a social-psychological phenomenon called "stereotype threat." Social scientists have observed that when members of a group are made aware of a negative stereotype, they are more likely to perform according to that stereotype. For example, stereotypically, boys are better at math and science than girls. When girls are reminded of their gender before a math or science test, even by something as simple as checking off an M or F box at the top of the test, they perform worse.[27] Stereotype threat discourages girls and women from entering technical fields and is one of the key reasons that so few study computer science.[28] As a Facebook summer intern once told me, "In my school's computer science department, there are more Daves than girls."

The stereotype of a working woman is rarely attractive. Popular culture has long portrayed successful working women as so consumed by their careers that they have no personal life (think Sigourney Weaver in *Working Girl* and Sandra Bullock in *The Proposal*). If a female character divides her time between work and family, she is almost always harried and guilt ridden (think Sarah Jessica Parker in *I Don't Know How She Does It*). And these characterizations have moved beyond fiction. A study found that of millennial men and women who work in an organization with a woman in a senior role, only about 20 percent want to emulate her career.[29]

This unappealing stereotype is particularly unfortunate since most women have no choice but to remain in the workforce. About 41 percent of mothers are primary breadwinners and earn the majority of their family's income. Another 23 percent of mothers are co-breadwinners, contributing at least a quarter of the family's earnings.[30] The number of women supporting families on their own is increasing quickly: between 1973 and 2006, the proportion of families headed by a single mother grew from one in ten to one in five.[31] These numbers are dramatically higher in Hispanic and African-American families. Twenty-seven percent of Latino children and 52 percent of African-American children are being raised by a single mother.[32]

Our country lags considerably behind others in efforts to help parents take care of their children and stay in the workforce. Of all the industrialized nations in the world, the United States is the only one without a paid maternity leave policy.[33] As Ellen Bravo, director of the Family Values @ Work consortium, observed, most "women are not thinking about 'having it all,' they're worried about losing it all—their jobs, their children's health, their families' financial stability—because of the regular conflicts that arise between being a good employee and a responsible parent."[34]

For many men, the fundamental assumption is that they can have both a successful professional life and a fulfilling personal life. For many women, the assumption is that trying to do both is difficult at best and impossible at worst. Women are surrounded by headlines and stories warning them that they cannot be committed to both their families and careers. They are told over and over again that they have to choose, because if they try to do too much, they'll be harried and unhappy. Framing the issue as "work-life balance"—as if the two were diametrically opposed—practically ensures work will lose out. Who would ever choose work over life?

The good news is that not only can women have both families and careers, they can *thrive* while doing so. In 2009, Sharon Meers and Joanna Strober published *Getting to 50/50*, a comprehensive review of governmental, social science, and original research that led them to conclude that children, parents, and marriages can all flourish when both parents have full careers. The data plainly reveal that sharing financial and child-care responsibilities leads to less guilty moms, more involved dads, and thriving children.[35] Professor Rosalind Chait Barnett of Brandeis University did a comprehensive review of studies on work-life balance and found that women who participate in multiple roles actually have lower levels of anxiety and higher levels of mental well-being.[36] Employed women reap rewards including greater financial security, more stable marriages, better health, and, in general, increased life satisfaction.[37]

It may not be as dramatic or funny to make a movie about a woman who loves both her job and her family, but that would be a better reflection of reality. We need more portrayals of women as competent professionals and happy mothers—or even happy professionals and competent mothers. The current negative images may make us laugh, but they also make women unnecessarily fearful by presenting life's challenges as insurmountable. Our culture remains baffled: *I don't know how she does it.*

Fear is at the root of so many of the barriers that women face. Fear of not being liked. Fear of making the wrong choice. Fear of drawing negative attention. Fear of overreaching. Fear of being judged. Fear of failure. And the holy trinity of fear: the fear of being a bad mother/wife/daughter.

Without fear, women can pursue professional success and personal fulfillment—and freely choose one, or the other, or both. At Facebook, we work hard to create a culture where people are encouraged to take risks. We have posters all around the office that reinforce this attitude. In bright red letters, one declares, "Fortune favors the bold." Another insists, "Proceed and be bold." My favorite reads, "What would you do if you weren't afraid?"[38]

In 2011, Debora Spar, president of Barnard College, an all-women's liberal arts school in New York City, invited me to deliver its commencement address. This speech was the first time I openly discussed the leadership ambition gap. Standing on the podium, I felt nervous. I told the members of the graduating class that they should be ambitious not just in pursuing their dreams but in aspiring to become leaders in their fields. I knew this message could be misinterpreted as my judging women for not making the same choices that I have. Nothing could be farther from the truth. I believe that choice means choice for all of us. But I also believe that we need to do more to encourage women to reach for leadership roles. If we can't tell women to aim high at a college graduation, when can we?

As I addressed the enthusiastic women, I found myself fighting back tears. I made it through the speech and concluded with this:

> You are the promise for a more equal world. So my hope for everyone here is that after you walk across this stage, after you get your diploma, after you go out tonight and celebrate hard—you then will lean way in to your career. You will find something you love doing and you will do it with gusto. Find the right career for you and go all the way to the top.
>
> As you walk off this stage today, you start your adult life. Start out by aiming high. Try—and try hard.
>
> Like everyone here, I have great hopes for the members of this graduating class. I hope you find true meaning, contentment, and passion in your life. I hope you navigate the difficult times and come out with greater strength and resolve. I hope you find whatever balance you seek with your eyes wide open. And I hope that you—yes, you—have the ambition to lean in to your career and run the world. Because the world needs you to change it. Women all around the world are counting on you.
>
> So please ask yourself: What would I do if I weren't afraid? And then go do it.

As the graduates were called to the stage to collect their diplomas, I shook every hand. Many stopped to give me a hug. One young woman even told me I was "the baddest bitch" (which, having checked with someone later, actually did turn out to be a compliment).

I know my speech was meant to motivate them, but they actually motivated me. In the months that followed, I started thinking that I should speak up more often and more publicly about these issues. I should urge more women to believe in themselves and aspire to lead. I should urge more men to become part of the solution by supporting women in the workforce and at home. And I should not just speak in front of friendly crowds at Barnard. I should seek out larger, possibly less sympathetic audiences. I should take my own advice and be ambitious.

Writing this book is not just me encouraging others to lean in. This is me leaning in. Writing this book is what I would do if I weren't afraid.

2

Sit at the Table

A FEW YEARS AGO, I hosted a meeting for Treasury Secretary Tim Geithner at Facebook. We invited fifteen executives from across Silicon Valley for breakfast and a discussion about the economy. Secretary Geithner arrived with four members of his staff, two senior and two more junior, and we all gathered in our one nice conference room. After the usual milling around, I encouraged the attendees to help themselves to the buffet and take a seat. Our invited guests, mostly men, grabbed plates and food and sat down at the large conference table. Secretary Geithner's team, all women, took their food last and sat in chairs off to the side of the room. I motioned for the women to come sit at the table, waving them over so they would feel welcomed. They demurred and remained in their seats.

The four women had every right to be at this meeting, but because of their seating choice, they seemed like spectators rather than participants. I knew I had to say something. So after the meeting, I pulled them aside to talk. I pointed out that they should have sat at the table even without an invitation, but when publicly welcomed, they most certainly should have joined. At first, they seemed surprised, then they agreed.

It was a watershed moment for me. A moment when I witnessed how an internal barrier can alter women's behavior. A moment when I realized that in addition to facing institutional obstacles, women face a battle from within.

When I gave a TED Talk on how women can succeed in the workforce, I told this story to illustrate how women hold themselves back, literally choosing to watch from the sidelines. And yet as disappointed as I was that these women made that choice, I also deeply understood the insecurities that drew them to the side of the room and kept them glued to those chairs.

My senior year of college, I was inducted into the Phi Beta Kappa honor society. At that time, Harvard and Radcliffe had separate chapters, so my ceremony was for women only. The keynote speaker, Dr. Peggy McIntosh from the Wellesley Centers for Women, gave a talk called "Feeling Like a Fraud."[1] She explained that many people, but especially women, feel fraudulent when they are praised for their accomplishments. Instead of feeling worthy of recognition, they feel undeserving and guilty, as if a mistake has been made. Despite being high achievers, even experts in their fields, women can't seem to shake the sense that it is only a matter of time until they are found out for who they really are—impostors with limited skills or abilities.

I thought it was the best speech I had ever heard. I was leaning forward in my chair, nodding vigorously. Carrie Weber, my brilliant and totally-not-a-fraud roommate, was doing the same. At last, someone was articulating exactly how I felt. Every time I was called on in class, I was sure that I was about to embarrass myself. Every time I took a test, I was sure that it had gone badly. And every time I didn't embarrass myself—or even excelled—I believed that I had fooled everyone yet again. One day soon, the jig would be up.

At the joint reception that followed the ceremony—an after-party for nerds, so I fit right in—I told one of my male classmates about Dr. McIntosh's fantastic speech explaining how we all feel like frauds. He looked at me, confused, and asked, "Why would that be interesting?" Carrie and I later joked that the speech to the men was probably something like "How to Cope in a World Where Not Everyone Is as Smart as You."

This phenomenon of capable people being plagued by self-doubt has a name—the impostor syndrome. Both men and women are susceptible to the impostor syndrome, but women tend to experience it more intensely and be more limited by it.[2] Even the wildly successful writer and actress Tina Fey has admitted to these feelings. She once explained to a British newspaper, "The beauty of the impostor syndrome is you vacillate between extreme egomania, and a complete feeling of: 'I'm a fraud! Oh god, they're on to me! I'm a fraud!' So you just try to ride the egomania when it comes and enjoy it, and then slide through the idea of fraud. Seriously, I've just realized that almost everyone is a fraud, so I try not to feel too bad about it."[3]

For women, feeling like a fraud is a symptom of a greater problem. We consistently underestimate ourselves. Multiple studies in multiple industries show that women often judge their own performance as worse than it actually is, while men judge their own performance as better than it actually is. Assessments of students in a surgery rotation found that when asked to evaluate themselves, the female students gave themselves lower scores than the male students despite faculty evaluations that showed the women outperformed the men.[4] A survey of several thousand potential political candidates revealed that despite having comparable credentials, the men were about 60 percent more likely to think that they were "very qualified" to run for political office.[5] A study of close to one thousand Harvard law students found that in almost every category of skills relevant to practicing law, women gave themselves lower scores than men.[6] Even worse, when women evaluate themselves in front of other people or in stereotypically male domains, their underestimations can become even more pronounced.[7]

Ask a man to explain his success and he will typically credit his own innate qualities and skills. Ask a woman the same question and she will attribute her success to external factors, insisting she did well because she "worked really hard," or "got lucky," or "had help from others." Men and women also differ when it comes to explaining failure. When a man fails, he points to factors like "didn't study enough" or "not interested in the subject matter." When a woman fails, she is more likely to believe it is due to an inherent lack of ability.[8] And in situations where a man and a woman each receive negative feedback, the woman's self-confidence and self-esteem drop to a much greater degree.[9] The internalization of failure and the insecurity it breeds hurt future performance, so this pattern has serious long-term consequences.[10]

And it's not just women who are tough on themselves. Colleagues and the media are also quick to credit external factors for a woman's achievements. When Facebook filed to go public, *The New York Times* ran an article that kindly reminded me—and everyone else—that I had "been lucky" and "had powerful mentors along the way."[11] Journalists and bloggers rose up to highlight the double standard, pointing out that *The New York Times* rarely ascribed men's success to having been lucky. But the *Times* didn't say anything that I had not already told myself a thousand times. At every stage of my career, I have attributed my success to luck, hard work, and help from others.

My insecurity began, as most insecurities do, in high school. I attended a big public school in Miami—think *Fast Times at Ridgemont High*—that was far more concerned with preventing fights in the halls and keeping drugs out of the bathrooms than with academics. When I was accepted into Harvard, many of my high school classmates asked me why I would want to go to a school filled with geeks. Then they would stop short, remember who they were talking to, and sheepishly walk away without waiting for an answer, realizing they already had it.

Freshman year of college was a huge shock for me. First semester, I took a course called The Concept of the Hero in Hellenic Civilization, which was nicknamed Heroes for Zeroes. I didn't have a burning desire to study Greek mythology, but it was the easiest way to fulfill the literature requirement. The professor began the first lecture by asking which students had read these books before. I whispered to my friend next to me, "What books?" "*The Iliad* and *The Odyssey*, of course," she replied. Almost every single hand went up. Not mine. The professor then asked, "And who has read these books in the original?" "What original?" I asked my friend. "Homeric Greek," she replied. A good third of the class kept their hands up. It seemed pretty clear that I was one of the zeroes.

A few weeks later, my professor of political philosophy assigned a five-page paper. I was panicked. Five whole pages! I had only written one paper of that length in high school, and it was a year-long project. How could anyone write five pages in just one week? I stayed in every night, plugging away, and based on the time I put in, I should have gotten an A for effort. I got a C. It is virtually impossible to get a C at Harvard if the assignment is turned in. I am not exaggerating—this was the equivalent of a failing grade. I went to see my dorm proctor, who worked at the admissions office. She told me that I had been admitted to Harvard for my personality, not my academic potential. Very comforting.

I buckled down, worked harder, and by the end of the semester, I learned how to write five-page papers. But no matter how well I did academically, I always felt like I was about to get caught for not really knowing anything. It wasn't until I heard the Phi Beta Kappa speech about self-doubt that it struck me: the real issue was not that I felt like a fraud, but that I could feel something deeply and profoundly and be completely wrong.

I should have understood that this kind of self-doubt was more common for females from growing up with my brother. David is two years younger than I am and one of the people in the world whom I respect and love the most. At home, he splits child-care duties with his wife fifty-fifty; at work, he's a pediatric neurosurgeon whose days are filled with heart-wrenching life-and-death decisions. Although we had the same upbringing, David has always been more confident. Once, back in high school, we both had Saturday-night dates who canceled on us in the late afternoon. I spent the rest of the weekend moping around the house, wondering what was wrong with me. David laughed off the rejection, announcing, "That girl missed out on a great thing," and went off to play basketball with his friends. Luckily, I had my younger sister, wise and empathetic way beyond her years, to console me.

A few years later, David joined me at college. When I

was a senior and he was a sophomore, we took a class in European intellectual history together. My roommate, Carrie, also took the class, which was a huge help since she was a comparative literature major. Carrie went to all of the lectures and read all ten of the assigned books—in the original languages (and by then, I knew what those were). I went to almost all of the lectures and read all of the books—in English. David went to two lectures, read one book, and then marched himself up to our room to get tutored for the final exam. We all sat together for the test, scribbling furiously for three hours in our little blue books. When we walked out, we asked one another how it went. I was upset. I had forgotten to connect the Freudian id to Schopenhauer's conception of the will. Carrie, too, was concerned and confessed that she hadn't adequately explained Kant's distinction between the sublime and the beautiful. We turned to my brother. How did he feel about the test? "I got the flat one," he announced. "The flat one?" we asked. "Yeah," he said, "the flat A."

He was right. He did get the flat one. Actually, we all got flat A's on the exam. My brother was not overconfident. Carrie and I were overly insecure.

These experiences taught me that I needed to make both an intellectual and an emotional adjustment. I learned over time that while it was hard to shake feelings of self-doubt, I could understand that there was a distortion. I would never possess my brother's effortless confidence, but I could challenge the notion that I was constantly headed for failure.

When I felt like I was not capable of doing something, I'd remind myself that I did not fail all of my exams in college. Or even one. I learned to undistort the distortion.

We all know supremely confident people who have no right to feel that way. We also all know people who could do so much more if only they believed in themselves. Like so many things, a lack of confidence can become a self-fulfilling prophecy. I don't know how to convince anyone to believe deep down that she is the best person for the job, not even myself. To this day, I joke that I wish I could spend a few hours feeling as self-confident as my brother. It must feel so, so good—like receiving a cosmic flat one every day.

When I don't feel confident, one tactic I've learned is that it sometimes helps to fake it. I discovered this when I was an aerobics instructor in the 1980s (which meant a silver leotard, leg warmers, and a shiny headband, all of which went perfectly with my big hair). Influenced by the gospel of Jane Fonda, aerobics also meant smiling solidly for a full hour. Some days, the smile came naturally. Other days, I was in a lousy mood and had to fake it. Yet after an hour of forced smiling, I often felt cheerful.

Many of us have experienced being angry with someone and then having to pretend everything's great in public. My husband, Dave, and I have our moments, and just when we are getting into it, it will be time to go to a friend's house for dinner. We put on our "everything's great" smiles, and amazingly, after a few hours, it often is.

Research backs up this "fake it till you feel it" strategy. One study found that when people assumed a high-power pose (for example, taking up space by spreading their limbs) for just two minutes, their dominance hormone levels (testosterone) went up and their stress hormone levels (cortisol) went down. As a result, they felt more powerful and in charge and showed a greater tolerance for risk. A simple change in posture led to a significant change in attitude.[12]

I would not suggest that anyone move beyond feeling confident into arrogance or boastfulness. No one likes that in men or women. But feeling confident—or pretending that you feel confident—is necessary to reach for opportunities. It's a cliché, but opportunities are rarely offered; they're seized. During the six and a half years I worked at Google, I hired a team of four thousand employees. I did not know all of them personally, but I knew the top hundred or so. What I noticed over the years was that for the most part, the men reached for opportunities much more quickly than the women. When we announced the opening of a new office or the launch of a new project, the men were banging down my door to explain why they should lead the charge. Men were also more likely to chase a growth opportunity even before a new opening was announced. They were impatient about their own development and believed that they were capable of doing more. And they were often right—just like my brother. The women, however, were more cautious about changing roles and seeking out new challenges. I often found myself trying to persuade them to work in new areas. I have had countless conversations where women responded to this encouragement by saying, "I'm just not sure I'd be good at that." Or

"That sounds exciting, but I've never done anything like it before." Or "I still have a lot to learn in my current role." I rarely, if ever, heard these kinds of comments from men.

Given how fast the world moves today, grabbing opportunities is more important than ever. Few managers have the time to carefully consider all the applicants for a job, much less convince more reticent people to apply. And increasingly, opportunities are not well defined but, instead, come from someone jumping in to do something. That something then becomes his job.

When I first joined Facebook, I was working with a team to answer the critical question of how best to grow our business. The conversations were getting heated, with many people arguing their own positions strongly. We ended the week without consensus. Dan Rose, leader of our deal team, spent the weekend gathering market data that allowed us to reframe the conversation in analytics. His effort broke the logjam. I then expanded Dan's responsibilities to include product marketing. Taking initiative pays off. It is hard to visualize someone as a leader if she is always waiting to be told what to do.

Padmasree Warrior, Cisco's chief technology officer, was asked by *The Huffington Post*, "What's the most important lesson you've learned from a mistake you've made in the past?" She responded, "I said no to a lot of opportunities when I was just starting out because I thought, 'That's not what my degree is in' or 'I don't know about that domain.' In retrospect, at a certain point it's your ability to learn quickly and contribute quickly that matters. One of the things I tell people these days is that there is no perfect fit when you're looking for the next big thing to do. You have to take opportunities and make an opportunity fit for you, rather than the other way around. The ability to learn is the most important quality a leader can have."[13]

Virginia Rometty, IBM's first female CEO, told the audience at the 2011 *Fortune* Most Powerful Women Summit that early in her career, she was offered a "big job." She worried that she lacked the proper experience and told the recruiter that she needed to think about it. That night, she discussed the offer with her husband, who pointed out, "Do you think a man would have ever answered that question that way?"

"What it taught me was you have to be very confident," Ginni said. "Even though you're so self-critical inside about what it is you may or may not know. And that, to me, leads to taking risks."[14]

I continue to be alarmed not just at how we as women fail to put ourselves forward, but also at how we fail to notice and correct for this gap. And that "we" includes me. A few years ago, I gave a talk on gender issues to a few hundred employees at Facebook. After my speech, I took questions for as long as time permitted. Later that afternoon, I came back to my desk, where a young woman was waiting to talk to me. "I learned something today," she said. "What?" I asked, feeling good, as I figured she was about to tell me how my words had touched her. Instead, she said, "I learned to keep my hand up." She explained that toward the end of my talk, I had said that I would take only two more questions. I did so, and then she put her hand down, along with all of the other women. But several men kept their hands up. And since hands were still waving in the air, I took more questions—only from the men. Instead of my words touching her, her words hit me like a ton of bricks. Even though I was giving a speech *on gender issues*, I had been blind to one myself.

If we want a world with greater equality, we need to acknowledge that women are less likely to keep their hands up. We need institutions and individuals to notice and correct for this behavior by encouraging, promoting, and championing more women. And women have to learn to keep their hands up, because when they lower them, even managers with the best intentions might not notice.

When I first started working for Larry Summers, then chief economist at the World Bank, he was married to a tax attorney, Vicki. He was very supportive of Vicki's career and used to urge her to "bill like a boy." His view was that the men considered any time they spent thinking about an issue—even time in the shower—as billable hours. His wife and her female colleagues, however, would decide that they were not at their best on a given day and discount hours they spent at their desks to be fair to the client. Which lawyers were more valuable to that firm? To make his point, Larry told them the story of a renowned Harvard Law School professor who was asked by a judge to itemize a bill. The professor responded that he could not because he was so often thinking about two things at once.

Even now, I'm a long way from mastering the art of

feeling confident. In August 2011, *Forbes* put out its annual World's 100 Most Powerful Women list.[15] I'm savvy enough to know that the list wasn't based on a scientific formula and that magazines love these features because they generate lots of page views as readers click through each name. Still, I was shocked—no, horrified—to learn that *Forbes* ranked me as the fifth most powerful woman in the world, right after German chancellor Angela Merkel, Secretary of State Hillary Clinton, Brazilian president Dilma Rousseff, and the CEO of PepsiCo, Indra Nooyi. This put me ahead of First Lady Michelle Obama and Indian politician Sonia Gandhi. Absurd. My own mother called to say, "Well, dear, I do think you are very powerful, but I am not sure you are more powerful than Michelle Obama." *You think?*

Far from feeling powerful, I felt embarrassed and exposed. When colleagues at Facebook stopped me in the halls to say congratulations, I pronounced the list "ridiculous." When friends posted the link on Facebook, I asked them to take it down. After a few days, my longtime executive assistant, Camille Hart, summoned me into a conference room and closed the door. This was serious. She told me that I was handling the *Forbes* thing poorly and that I needed to stop subjecting anyone who brought up the list to a diatribe on its absurdity. I was showing too many people how uncomfortable I felt and revealing my insecurity. Instead, I needed to simply say, "Thank you."

We all need colleagues like Camille, who was honest enough to point out my less-than-gracious response. She was right. Whether the list was ridiculous or not, I didn't write it and I didn't have to react negatively to it. I doubt a man would have felt so overwhelmed by others' perception of his power.

I know that my success comes from hard work, help from others, and being at the right place at the right time. I feel a deep and enduring sense of gratitude to those who have given me opportunities and support. I recognize the sheer luck of being born into my family in the United States rather than one of the many places in the world where women are denied basic rights. I believe that all of us—men and women alike—should acknowledge good fortune and thank the people who have helped us. No one accomplishes anything all alone.

But I also know that in order to continue to grow and challenge myself, I have to believe in my own abilities. I still face situations that I fear are beyond my capabilities. I still have days when I feel like a fraud. And I still sometimes find myself spoken over and discounted while men sitting next to me are not. But now I know how to take a deep breath and keep my hand up. I have learned to sit at the table.

Success and Likeability

OKAY, so all a woman has to do is ignore society's expectations, be ambitious, sit at the table, work hard, and then it's smooth sailing all the way. What could possibly go wrong?

In 2003, then Columbia Business School professor Francis Flynn and New York University professor Cameron Anderson ran an experiment to test perceptions of men and women in the workplace.[1] They started with a Harvard Business School case study about a real-life entrepreneur named Heidi Roizen. The case described how Roizen became a successful venture capitalist by using her "outgoing personality . . . and vast personal and professional network [that] included many of the most powerful business leaders in the technology sector."[2] Flynn and Anderson assigned half of the students to read Heidi's story and gave the other half the same story with just one difference—they changed the name "Heidi" to "Howard."

Professors Flynn and Anderson then polled the students

about their impressions of Heidi or Howard. The students rated Heidi and Howard as equally competent, which made sense since "their" accomplishments were completely identical. Yet while students respected both Heidi and Howard, Howard came across as a more appealing colleague. Heidi, on the other hand, was seen as selfish and not "the type of person you would want to hire or work for." The same data with a single difference—gender—created vastly different impressions.

This experiment supports what research has already clearly shown: success and likeability are positively correlated for men and negatively correlated for women.[3] When a man is successful, he is liked by both men and women. When a woman is successful, people of both genders like her less. This truth is both shocking and unsurprising: shocking because no one would ever admit to stereotyping on the basis of gender and unsurprising because clearly we do.

Decades of social science studies have confirmed what the Heidi/Howard case study so blatantly demonstrates: we evaluate people based on stereotypes (gender, race, nationality, and age, among others).[4] Our stereotype of men holds that they are providers, decisive, and driven. Our stereotype of women holds that they are caregivers, sensitive, and communal. Because we characterize men and women in opposition to each other, professional achievement and all the traits associated with it get placed in the male column. By focusing on her career and taking a calculated approach to amassing power, Heidi violated our stereotypical expectations of women. Yet by behaving in the exact same manner, Howard lived up to our stereotypical expectations of men. The end result? Liked him, disliked her.

I believe this bias is at the very core of why women are held back. It is also at the very core of why women hold themselves back. For men, professional success comes with positive reinforcement at every step of the way. For women, even when they're recognized for their achievements, they're often regarded unfavorably. Journalist Shankar Vedantam once cataloged the derogatory descriptions of some of the first female world leaders. "England's Margaret Thatcher," he wrote, "was called 'Attila the Hen.' Golda Meir, Israel's first female Prime Minister, was 'the only man in the Cabinet.' President Richard Nixon called Indira Gandhi, India's first female Prime Minister, 'the old witch.' And Angela Merkel, the current chancellor of Germany, has been dubbed 'the iron frau.' "[5]

I have seen this dynamic play out over and over. When a woman excels at her job, both male and female coworkers will remark that she may be accomplishing a lot but is "not as well-liked by her peers." She is probably also "too aggressive," "not a team player," "a bit political," "can't be trusted," or "difficult." At least, those are all things that have been said about me and almost every senior woman I know. The world seems to be asking why we can't be less like Heidi and more like Howard.

Most women have never heard of the Heidi/Howard study. Most of us are never told about this downside of achievement. Still, we sense this punishment for success.

We're aware that when a woman acts forcefully or competitively, she's deviating from expected behavior. If a woman pushes to get the job done, if she's highly competent, if she focuses on results rather than on pleasing others, she's acting like a man. And if she acts like a man, people dislike her. In response to this negative reaction, we temper our professional goals. Author Ken Auletta summarized this phenomenon in *The New Yorker* when he observed that for women, "self-doubt becomes a form of self-defense."[6] In order to protect ourselves from being disliked, we question our abilities and downplay our achievements, especially in the presence of others. We put ourselves down before others can.

During the summer between my first and second year in business school, I received a letter in the mail congratulating me on becoming a Henry Ford Scholar for having the highest first-year academic record. The check was for $714.28, an odd number that immediately signaled that several students had split the prize. When we returned to school for our second year, six men let it be known that they had won this award. I multiplied my check by seven and it revealed a nearly round number. Mystery solved. There were seven of us—six men and me.

Unlike the other six winners, I didn't let my award status become general knowledge. I told only my closest friend, Stephen Paul, and knew he would keep my secret. On the surface, this decision might have worked against me, since grades at Harvard Business School are based 50 percent on class participation. Professors teach ninety-minute classes and are not allowed to write anything down, so they have to rely on their memory of class discussion. When a student makes a comment that others refer to—"If I can build on what Tom said . . ."—that helps the professor remember the critical points and who made them. Just as in real life, performance is highly dependent upon the reaction people have to one another. The other six Ford Scholars quickly became the most-quoted speakers as their academic standing gave them instant credibility. They also received early job offers from prestigious employers before the official recruiting period even began. One day in class, one of the exalted six made a comment that, to my mind, demonstrated that he had not even read the case being discussed. Everyone fawned all over him. I wondered if I was making a huge mistake not letting people know that I was the seventh student. It would have been nice to float through my second year of business school without even reading the material.

But I never really considered going public. I instinctively knew that letting my academic performance become known was a bad idea. Years later, when I learned about the Heidi/Howard case study, I understood the reason why. Being at the top of the class may have made life easier for my male peers, but it would have made my life harder.

I did not reach this conclusion in a vacuum. All through my life, culturally reinforced signals cautioned me against being branded as too smart or too successful. It starts young. As a girl, you know that being smart is good in lots of ways, but it doesn't make you particularly popular or attractive to boys. In school, I was called the "smartest girl in the class." I hated that description. Who wants to go to the prom with the smartest girl in the class? Senior year, my class voted me "most likely to succeed," along with a boy. I wasn't going to take any chances with the prom, so I convinced my friend, who worked on the yearbook, to remove my name. I got a prom date who was fun and loved sports. In fact, he loved sports so much that two days before the prom, he canceled on me to go to a basketball game, saying, "I know you'll understand since going to the playoffs is a once-in-a-lifetime opportunity." I did not point out that as a high school girl, I thought going to the prom was a once-in-a-lifetime opportunity. Luckily, I found a new date who was less of a sports fan.

I never really thought about why I went to such efforts to mute my achievements from such a young age. Then, about ten years after I graduated from business school, I was seated at dinner next to Deborah Gruenfeld, a professor of leadership and organizational behavior at Stanford, and our friendly small talk quickly turned into an intense discussion. Having studied this issue, Professor Gruenfeld was able to explain the price women pay for success. "Our entrenched cultural ideas associate men with leadership qualities and women with nurturing qualities and put women in a double bind," she said. "We believe not only that women are nurturing, but that they *should be* nurturing above all else. When a woman does anything that signals she might not be nice first and foremost, it creates a negative impression and makes us uncomfortable."[7]

If a woman is competent, she does not seem nice enough. If a woman seems really nice, she is considered more nice than competent. Since people want to hire and promote those who are both competent *and* nice, this creates a huge stumbling block for women. Acting in stereotypically feminine ways makes it difficult to reach for the same opportunities as men, but defying expectations and reaching for those opportunities leads to being judged as undeserving and selfish. Nothing has changed since high school; intelligence and success are not clear paths to popularity at any age. This complicates everything, because at the same time that women need to sit at the table and own their success, doing so causes them to be liked less.[8]

Most people, myself included, really want to be liked—and not just because it feels good. Being liked is also a key factor in both professional and personal success. A willingness to make an introduction or advocate for or promote someone depends upon having positive feelings about that person. We need to believe in her ability to do the job and get along with everyone while doing it. That's why, instinctively, many of us feel pressure to mute our accomplishments.

In October 2011, Jocelyn Goldfein, one of the engineering directors at Facebook, held a meeting with our female engineers where she encouraged them to share the progress they had made on the products they were building. Silence. No one wanted to toot her own horn. Who would want to speak up when self-promoting women are disliked? Jocelyn switched her approach. Instead of asking the women to talk about themselves, she asked them to tell one another's stories. The exercise became communal, which put everyone at ease.

Owning one's success is key to achieving more success. Professional advancement depends upon people believing that an employee is contributing to good results. Men can comfortably claim credit for what they do as long as they don't veer into arrogance. For women, taking credit comes at a real social and professional cost. In fact, a woman who explains why she is qualified or mentions previous successes in a job interview can lower her chances of getting hired.[9]

As if this double bind were not enough to navigate, gendered stereotypes can also lead to women having to do additional work without additional reward. When a man helps a colleague, the recipient feels indebted to him and is highly likely to return the favor. But when a woman helps out, the feeling of indebtedness is weaker. She's communal, right? She *wants* to help others. Professor Flynn calls this the "gender discount" problem, and it means that women are paying a professional penalty for their presumed desire to be communal.[10] On the other hand, when a man helps a coworker, it's considered an imposition and he is compensated with more favorable performance evaluations and rewards like salary increases and bonuses. Even more frustrating, when a woman declines to help a colleague, she often receives less favorable reviews and fewer rewards. But a man who declines to help? He pays no penalty.[11]

Because of these unfair expectations, women find themselves in "damned if they do" and "doomed if they don't" situations.[12] This is especially true when it comes to negotiations concerning compensation, benefits, titles, and other perks. By and large, men negotiate more than women.[13] A study that looked at the starting salaries of students graduating with a master's degree from Carnegie Mellon University found that 57 percent of the male students, but only 7 percent of the female students, tried to negotiate for a higher offer.[14] Instead of blaming women for not negotiating more, we need to recognize that women often have good cause to be reluctant to advocate for their own interests, because doing so can easily backfire.[15]

There is little downside when men negotiate for themselves. People expect men to advocate on their own behalf, point out their contributions, and be recognized and rewarded for them. For men, there is truly no harm in asking. But since women are expected to be concerned with others, when they advocate for themselves or point to their own value, both men and women react unfavorably. Interestingly, women can negotiate as well as or even more successfully than men when negotiating for others (such as their company or a colleague), because in these cases, their advocacy does not make them appear self-serving.[16] However, when a woman negotiates on her own behalf, she violates the perceived gender norm. Both male and female colleagues often resist working with a woman who has negotiated for a higher salary because she's seen as more demanding than a woman who refrained from negotiating.[17] Even when a woman negotiates successfully for herself, she can pay a longer-term cost in goodwill and future advancement.[18] Regrettably, all women are Heidi. Try as we might, we just can't be Howard.

When I was negotiating with Facebook's founder and CEO Mark Zuckerberg for my compensation, he made me an offer that I thought was fair. We had been having dinner several nights a week for more than a month and a half, discussing Facebook's mission and his vision for the future. I was ready to accept the job. No, I was *dying* to accept the job. My husband, Dave, kept telling me to negotiate, but I was afraid of doing anything that might botch the deal. I could play hardball, but then maybe Mark would not want to work with me. Was it worth it when I knew that ultimately I was going to accept the offer? I concluded it was not. But right before I was about to say yes, my exasperated brother-in-law, Marc Bodnick, blurted out, "Damn it, Sheryl! Why are you going to make less than any man would make to do the same job?"

My brother-in-law didn't know the details of my deal. His point was simply that no man at my level would consider taking the first offer. This was motivating. I went back to Mark and said that I couldn't accept, but I prefaced it by telling him, "Of course you realize that you're hiring me to run your deal teams, so you want me to be a good negotiator. This is the only time you and I will ever be on opposite sides of the table." Then I negotiated hard, followed by a nervous night wondering if I had blown it. But Mark called me the next day. He resolved the gap by improving my offer, extending the terms of my contract from four to five years and allowing me to buy into the company as well.

His creative solution not only closed the deal, but also set us up for a longer-term alignment of interests.

The goal of a successful negotiation is to achieve our objectives and continue to have people like us. Professor Hannah Riley Bowles, who studies gender and negotiations at Harvard's Kennedy School of Government, believes that women can increase their chances of achieving a desired outcome by doing two things in combination.[19] First, women must come across as being nice, concerned about others, and "appropriately" female. When women take a more instrumental approach ("This is what I want and deserve"), people react far more negatively.

There is a saying, "Think globally, act locally." When negotiating, "Think personally, act communally." I have advised many women to preface negotiations by explaining that they know that women often get paid less than men so they are going to negotiate rather than accept the original offer. By doing so, women position themselves as connected to a group and not just out for themselves; in effect, they are negotiating for all women. And as silly as it sounds, pronouns matter. Whenever possible, women should substitute "we" for "I." A woman's request will be better received if she asserts, "We had a great year," as opposed to "I had a great year."[20]

But a communal approach is not enough. According to Professor Bowles, the second thing women must do is provide a legitimate explanation for the negotiation.[21] Men don't have to legitimize their negotiations; they are expected to look out for themselves. Women, however, have to justify their requests. One way of doing this is to suggest that someone more senior encouraged the negotiation ("My manager suggested I talk with you about my compensation") or to cite industry standards ("My understanding is that jobs that involve this level of responsibility are compensated in this range"). Still, every negotiation is unique, so women must adjust their approach accordingly.

Telling a current employer about an offer from another company is a common tactic but works for men more easily than for women. Men are allowed to be focused on their own achievements, while loyalty is expected from women. Also, just being nice is not a winning strategy. Nice sends a message that the woman is willing to sacrifice pay to be liked by others. This is why a woman needs to combine niceness with insistence, a style that Mary Sue Coleman, president of the University of Michigan, calls "relentlessly pleasant."[22] This method requires smiling frequently, expressing appreciation and concern, invoking common interests, emphasizing larger goals, and approaching the negotiation as solving a problem as opposed to taking a critical stance.[23] Most negotiations involve drawn-out, successive moves, so women need to stay focused . . . and smile.

No wonder women don't negotiate as much as men. It's like trying to cross a minefield backward in high heels. So what should we do? Should we play by the rules that others created? Should we figure out a way to put on a friendly expression while not being *too* nice, displaying the right levels of loyalty, and using "we" language? I understand the paradox of advising women to change the world by adhering to biased rules and expectations. I know it is not a perfect answer but a means to a desirable end. It is also true, as any good negotiator knows, that having a better understanding of the other side leads to a superior outcome. So at the very least, women can enter these negotiations with the knowledge that showing concern for the common good, even as they negotiate for themselves, will strengthen their position.

In addition, there are huge benefits to communal effort in and of itself. By definition, all organizations consist of people working together. Focusing on the team leads to better results for the simple reason that well-functioning groups are stronger than individuals. Teams that work together well outperform those that don't. And success feels better when it's shared with others. So perhaps one positive result of having more women at the top is that our leaders will have been trained to care more about the well-being of others. My hope, of course, is that we won't have to play by these archaic rules forever and that eventually we can all just be ourselves.

We still have a long way to go. In November 2011, *San Francisco* magazine ran a story on female entrepreneurs in Silicon Valley and illustrated it by superimposing the featured women's heads onto male bodies.[24] The only body type they could imagine for successful entrepreneurship was wearing a tie or a hoodie. Our culture needs to find a robust image of female success that is first, not male, and second, not a white woman on the phone, holding a crying baby. In fact, these "bad mother with a briefcase" images are so prevalent that writer Jessica Valenti collected them in a funny and poignant blog post called "Sad White Babies with Mean Feminist Mommies."[25]

Until we can get there, I fear that women will continue to sacrifice being liked for being successful. When I first arrived at Facebook, a local blog devoted some serious pixels to trashing me. They posted a picture of me and superimposed a gun into my hand. They wrote "liar" in big red letters across my face. Anonymous sources labeled me "two-faced" and "about to ruin Facebook forever." I cried. I lost some sleep. I worried that my career was over. Then I told myself it didn't matter. Then everyone else told me it didn't matter—which only reminded me that they were reading these awful comments too. I fantasized about all sorts of rejoinders, but in the end, my best response was to ignore the attacks and do my job.

Arianna Huffington, founder of *The Huffington Post*, believes that learning to withstand criticism is a necessity for women. Early in her career, Arianna realized that the cost of speaking her mind was that she would inevitably offend someone. She does not believe it is realistic or even desirable to tell women not to care when we are attacked. Her advice is that we should let ourselves react emotionally and feel whatever anger or sadness being criticized evokes for us. And then we should quickly move on. She points to children as her role model. A child can cry one moment and run off to play the next. For me, this has been good advice. I wish I were strong enough to ignore what others say, but experience tells me I often can't. Allowing myself to feel upset, even really upset, and then move on—that's something I can do.

It also helps to lean on one another. We can comfort ourselves with the knowledge that the attacks are not personal. We can joke, as Marlo Thomas did, that "a man has to be Joe McCarthy in order to be called ruthless. All a woman needs to do is put you on hold." Real change will come when powerful women are less of an exception. It is easy to dislike senior women because there are so few. If women held 50 percent of the top jobs, it would just not be possible to dislike that many people.

Sharon Meers was motivated to write *Getting to 50/50* after observing this kind of tipping point firsthand. In the late 1990s, Amy Goodfriend was chosen to lead Goldman Sachs's U.S. derivatives team (and later became the first female partner in the Equities Division). It was a seismic event and caused four senior men to quit the group. Amy faced a lot of skepticism and criticism. Before Sharon joined the team, a male friend told her, "Amy's a bitch, but an honest bitch." Sharon found that Amy was a great boss, and over the next few years, the derivatives group was transformed under her leadership. Once there were more than five female managing directors in the division—a critical mass—the negativity and grumbling began to die down. It became normal to have female leaders, and by 2000, the stigma seemed to have dissipated. Sadly, when those senior women later left and the critical mass shrank, the faith that women could be as successful as their male peers shrank with it.

Everyone needs to get more comfortable with female leaders—including female leaders themselves. Since 1999, editor Pattie Sellers of *Fortune* magazine has overseen an annual conference that she calls the Most Powerful Women Summit. On my first night there in 2005, I was in the lounge with two close friends, Diana Farrell, then head of the McKinsey Global Institute, and Sue Decker, then CFO of Yahoo. We were talking about the name of the conference, and I mentioned that when I saw the title on Google's corporate calendar, I ran to find Camille to ask her to change the name to "*Fortune* Women's Conference." Diana and Sue laughed and said that they had done the exact same thing.

Later, Pattie explained that she and her colleagues chose this name on purpose to force women to confront their own power and feel more comfortable with that word. I still struggle with this. I am fine applying the word "powerful" to other women—the more the better—but I still shake my head in denial when it is applied to me. The nagging voice in the back of my head reminds me, as it did in business school, "Don't flaunt your success, or even let people know about your success. If you do, people won't like you."

Less than six months after I started at Facebook, Mark

and I sat down for my first formal review. One of the things he told me was that my desire to be liked by everyone would hold me back. He said that when you want to change things, you can't please everyone. If you do please everyone, you aren't making enough progress. Mark was right.

It's a Jungle Gym, Not a Ladder

BOUT A MONTH AFTER I joined Facebook, I got a call from Lori Goler, a highly regarded senior director of marketing at eBay. I knew Lori a bit socially, but she made it clear this was a business call and cut to the chase. "I want to apply to work with you at Facebook," she said. "So I thought about calling you and telling you all of the things I'm good at and all of the things I like to do. Then I figured that everyone was doing that. So instead, I want to ask you: What is your biggest problem, and how can I solve it?"

My jaw hit the floor. I had hired thousands of people over the previous decade and no one had ever said anything remotely like that. People usually focus on finding the right role for themselves, with the implication that their skills will help the company. Lori put Facebook's needs front and center. It was a killer approach. I responded, "Recruiting is my biggest problem. And, yes, you can solve it."

Lori never dreamed she would work in recruiting, but

she jumped in. She even agreed to drop down a level, since this was a new field for her and she was willing to trade seniority for acquiring new skills. Lori did a great job running recruiting and within months was promoted to her current job, leading People@Facebook. When I asked her recently if she wanted to go back to marketing someday, she responded that she believes human resources allows her to have a greater overall impact.

The most common metaphor for careers is a ladder, but this concept no longer applies to most workers. As of 2010, the average American had eleven jobs from the ages of eighteen to forty-six alone.[1] This means that the days of joining an organization or corporation and staying there to climb that one ladder are long gone. Lori often quotes Pattie Sellers, who conceived a much better metaphor: "Careers are a jungle gym, not a ladder."

As Lori describes it, ladders are limiting—people can move up or down, on or off. Jungle gyms offer more creative exploration. There's only one way to get to the top of a ladder, but there are many ways to get to the top of a jungle gym. The jungle gym model benefits everyone, but especially women who might be starting careers, switching careers, getting blocked by external barriers, or reentering the workforce after taking time off. The ability to forge a unique path with occasional dips, detours, and even dead ends presents a better chance for fulfillment. Plus, a jungle gym provides great views for many people, not just those at the top. On a ladder, most climbers are stuck staring at the butt of the person above.

A jungle gym scramble is the best description of my career. Younger colleagues and students frequently ask me how I planned my path. When I tell them that I didn't, they usually react with surprise followed by relief. They seem encouraged to know that careers do not need to be mapped out from the start. This is especially comforting in a tough market where job seekers often have to accept what is available and hope that it points in a desirable direction. We all want a job or role that truly excites and engages us. This search requires both focus and flexibility, so I recommend adopting two concurrent goals: a long-term dream and an eighteen-month plan.

I could never have connected the dots from where I started to where I am today. For one thing, Mark Zuckerberg was only seven years old when I graduated from college. Also, back then, technology and I did not exactly have a great relationship. I used Harvard's computer system only once as an undergraduate, to run regressions for my senior thesis on the economics of spousal abuse. The data was stored on large, heavy magnetic tapes that I had to lug in big boxes across campus, cursing the entire way and arriving in a sweaty mess at the sole computer center, which was populated exclusively with male students. I then had to stay up all night spinning the tapes to input the data. When I tried to execute my final calculations, I took down the entire system. That's right. Years before Mark famously crashed that same Harvard system, I beat him to it.

When I graduated from college, I had only the vaguest notion of where I was headed. This confusion was in deep contrast to my father's clear conviction of what he wanted to do from a young age. When my dad was sixteen, he felt a sharp abdominal pain during a basketball practice. My grandmother—good Jewish mother that she was—assumed it was hunger and fed him a big dinner. That made it worse. He ended up in the hospital, where he was diagnosed with acute appendicitis, but because he had eaten, they couldn't operate for twelve excruciating hours. The next morning, a surgeon removed his appendix and, along with it, the pain. My father chose his career that day, deciding that he would become a physician so he could help ease other people's suffering.

My mother shared my father's desire to help others. She was only eleven when she heard her rabbi give a sermon on the importance of civil rights and *tikkun olam*, a Hebrew phrase that means "repairing the world." She responded to the call, grabbing a tin can and knocking on doors to support civil rights workers in the South. She has remained a passionate volunteer and human rights activist ever since. I grew up watching my mother work tirelessly on behalf of persecuted Jews in the Soviet Union. She and her friend Margery Sanford would write heartfelt appeals calling for the release of political prisoners. In the evenings, my dad would join them. Thanks to the collective efforts of concerned people all over the world, many lives were saved.

Throughout my childhood, my parents emphasized the importance of pursuing a meaningful life. Dinner discussions often centered on social injustice and those fighting to make the world a better place. As a child, I never thought about what I wanted to be, but I thought a lot about what I wanted to do. As sappy as it sounds, I hoped to change the world. My sister and brother both became doctors, and I always believed I would work at a nonprofit or in government. That was my dream. And while I don't believe in mapping out each step of a career, I do believe it helps to have a long-term dream or goal.

A long-term dream does not have to be realistic or even specific. It may reflect the desire to work in a particular field or to travel throughout the world. Maybe the dream is to have professional autonomy or a certain amount of free time. Maybe it's to create something lasting or win a coveted prize. Some goals require more traditional paths; anyone who aspires to become a Supreme Court justice should probably start by attending law school. But even a vague goal can provide direction, a far-off guidepost to move toward.

With an eye on my childhood dream, the first job I took out of college was at the World Bank as research assistant to Larry Summers, who was serving a term as chief economist. Based in Washington, D.C., the Bank's mission is to reduce global poverty. I spent my first nine months in the stacks of the Bank library on the corner of Nineteenth and Pennsylvania, looking up facts and figures for Larry's papers and speeches. Larry then generously arranged for me to join an India health field mission to get a closer look at what the Bank actually did.

Flying to India took me into an entirely different world. The team was working to eradicate leprosy, which was endemic in India's most remote and poorest regions. The conditions were appalling. Due to the stigma of the disease, patients were often exiled from their villages and ended up lying on dirt floors in awful places that passed for clinics. Facts and figures could never have prepared me for this reality. I have the deepest respect for people who provide hands-on help to those in crises. It is the most difficult work in the world.

I returned to D.C. with a plan to attend law school, but Lant Pritchett, an economist in Larry's office who has devoted his life to the study of poverty, persuaded me that business school would be a better alternative. I headed back to Cambridge. I tried to stay socially conscious by joining the highly unpopular Nonprofit Club. I also spent my second year studying social marketing—how marketing can be used to solve social problems—with Professor Kash Rangan. One of the cases we worked on concerned the shortage of organ donations, which results in eighteen deaths each day in the United States alone. I never forgot this case, and seventeen years later, Facebook worked with organ registries around the world to launch a tool to encourage donor registration.

After business school, I took a job as a consultant at McKinsey & Company in Los Angeles. The work never entirely suited me, so I stayed for only a year and then moved back to D.C. to join Larry, who was now deputy secretary of the Treasury Department. At first, I served as his special assistant. Then, when he was named secretary, I became his chief of staff. My job consisted of helping

Larry manage the operations of the department and its $14 billion budget. It gave me the opportunity to participate in economic policy at both a national and an international level. I also ran point on some smaller projects, including the administration's proposal to promote the development of vaccines for infectious diseases.

During my four years at Treasury, I witnessed the first technology boom from a distance. Its impact was obvious and appealing even beyond being able to wear jeans to work. Technology was transforming communication and changing lives not just in the United States and developed countries, but everywhere. My long-term dream instinct kicked in. When President Clinton's administration ended, I was out of a job and decided to move to Silicon Valley. In retrospect, this seems like a shrewd move, but in 2001, it was questionable at best. The tech bubble had burst, and the industry was still reeling from the aftershocks. I gave myself four months to find a job but hoped it would take fewer. It took almost a year.

My Silicon Valley job search had some highs, like getting to meet my business crush, eBay CEO Meg Whitman. It also had some lows, like meeting with a high-level executive who started my interview by stating that her company would never even consider hiring someone like me because government experience could not possibly prepare anyone to work in the tech industry. It would have been so cool to have thanked her for being honest and walked out of her office. But alas, I was never cool. I sat there hemming and hawing until every last molecule of oxygen had been sucked from the room. True to her word, she never even considered hiring me.

Fortunately, not everyone shared her view. Eric Schmidt and I had met several times during my Treasury years, and I went to see him just after he became CEO of the then relatively unknown Google. After several rounds of interviews with Google's founders, they offered me a job. My bank account was diminishing quickly, so it was time to get back to paid employment, and fast. In typical—and yes, annoying—MBA fashion, I made a spreadsheet and listed my various opportunities in the rows and my selection criteria in the columns. I compared the roles, the level of responsibility, and so on. My heart wanted to join Google in its mission to provide the world with access to information, but in the spreadsheet game, the Google job fared the worst by far.

I went back to Eric and explained my dilemma. The other companies were recruiting me for real jobs with teams to run and goals to hit. At Google, I would be the first "business unit general manager," which sounded great except for the glaring fact that Google had no business units and therefore *nothing* to actually manage. Not only was the role lower in level than my other options, but it was entirely unclear what the job was in the first place.

Eric responded with perhaps the best piece of career advice that I have ever heard. He covered my spreadsheet with his hand and told me not to be an idiot (also a great piece of advice). Then he explained that only one criterion mattered when picking a job—fast growth. When companies grow quickly, there are more things to do than there are people to do them. When companies grow more slowly or stop growing, there is less to do and too many people to not be doing them. Politics and stagnation set in, and everyone falters. He told me, "If you're offered a seat on a rocket ship, you don't ask what seat. You just get on." I made up my mind that instant. Google was tiny and disorganized, but it was a rocket ship. And even more important to me, it was a rocket ship with a mission I believed in deeply.

Over the years, I have repeated Eric's advice to countless people, encouraging them to reduce their career spreadsheets to one column: potential for growth. Of course, not everyone has the opportunity or the desire to work in an industry like high tech. But within any field, there are jobs that have more potential for growth than others. Those in more established industries can look for the rocket ships within their companies—divisions or teams that are expanding. And in careers like teaching or medicine, the corollary is to seek out positions where there is high demand for those skills. For example, in my brother's field of pediatric neurosurgery, there are some cities with too many physicians, while others have too few. My brother has always elected to work where his expertise would be in demand so he can have the greatest impact.

Just as I believe everyone should have a long-term dream, I also believe everyone should have an eighteen-month plan. (I say eighteen months because two years seems too long and one year seems too short, but it does not have to be any exact amount of time.) Typically, my eighteen-month plan sets goals on two fronts. First and most important, I set targets for what my team can accomplish. Employees who concentrate on results and impact are the most valuable—like Lori, who wisely focused on solving Facebook's recruiting problem before focusing on herself. This is not just thinking communally—the expected and often smart choice for a woman—but simply good business.

Second, I try to set more personal goals for learning new skills in the next eighteen months. It's often painful, but I ask myself, "How can I improve?" If I am afraid to do something, it is usually because I am not good at it or perhaps am too scared even to try. After working at Google for more than four years, managing well over half of the company's revenues, I was embarrassed to admit that I had never negotiated a business deal. Not one. So I gathered my courage and came clean to my boss, Omid Kordestani, then head of sales and business development. Omid was willing to give me a chance to run a small deal team. In the very first deal I attempted, I almost botched the whole thing by making an offer to our potential partner before fully understanding their business. Fortunately, my team included a talented negotiator, Shailesh Rao, who stepped in to teach me the obvious: letting the other side make the first offer is often crucial to achieving favorable terms.

Everyone has room to improve. Most people have a style in the workplace that overshoots in one direction—too aggressive or too passive, too talkative or too shy. In that first deal, I said too much. This was not a shock to anyone who knows me. Once I identified this weakness, I sought help to correct it. I turned to Maureen Taylor, a communications coach, who gave me an assignment. She told me that for one week I couldn't give my opinion unless asked. It was one of the longest weeks of my life. If I had bitten my tongue each time I started to express my opinion, I would have had no tongue left.

Trying to overcorrect is a great way to find middle ground. In order for me to speak the right amount in a meeting, I have to feel as if I am saying very little. People who are shy will have to feel like they are saying way too much. I know a woman who naturally talks softly and forces herself to "shout" in business meetings just to speak at an average volume. Overriding our natural tendencies is very difficult. In all the years I've been trying, I can only think of a few times when someone said to me, "Sheryl, I wish you had spoken up more in that meeting." Omid did it once and I hugged him.

Eric turned out to be absolutely right about Google, and I will always be grateful to him and to Larry Page and Sergey Brin for taking a chance on me. My eighteen-month plan at the company extended into six and a half years, and I learned more than I ever could have hoped while working with true visionaries. But eventually I felt that it was time to make a move on the jungle gym.

In my personal life, I am not someone who embraces uncertainty. I like things to be in order. I file documents in colored folders (yes, still) and my enthusiasm for reorganizing my closet continually baffles Dave. But in my professional life, I have learned to accept uncertainty and even embrace it. Risk—and a great deal of luck—landed me at Google. That worked out so well that I decided to embrace risk again, which led me to Facebook. At the time, other companies were willing to hire me as CEO, but I joined Facebook as COO. At first, people questioned why I would take a "lower level" job working for a twenty-three-year-old. No one asks me that anymore. As I did when I joined Google, I prioritized potential for fast growth and the mission of the company above title.

I have seen both men and women miss out on great opportunities by focusing too much on career levels. A friend of mine had been working as a lawyer for four years when she realized that instead of shooting for partner, she'd rather join a company in a sales or marketing role. One of her clients was willing to hire her in this new capacity but wanted her to start at the ground level. Since she could afford the temporary pay cut, I urged her to make the jump, but she decided against taking a job that put her "back four years." I understood how painful it was for her to lose hard-earned ground. Still, my argument was that if she was going to work for the next thirty years, what difference does going "back" four years really make? If the other path made her happier and offered her a chance to learn new skills, that meant she was actually moving forward.

In many cases, women need to be more open to taking risks in their careers.[2] When I left Google to join Facebook, as a percentage of my team, fewer women tried to follow me. As they had been all along, the men were more interested in new and, as we say in tech, higher beta opportunities—where the risks were great but the potential rewards even greater. Many of the women on my team eventually showed interest in joining Facebook, but not until a few years later, when the company was more established. The cost of stability is often diminished opportunities for growth.

Of course, there are times in life when being risk averse is a good thing; adolescent and adult males drown in much greater numbers than adolescent and adult females.[3] But in business, being risk averse can result in stagnation. An analysis of senior corporate management appointments found that women are significantly more likely than men to continue to perform the same function even when they take on new duties. And when female managers move up, they are more likely to do so internally instead of switching to a different company.[4] At times, staying in the same functional area and in the same organization creates inertia and limits opportunity to expand. Seeking out diverse experiences is useful preparation for leadership.

I understand the external pressures that force women to play it safe and stay put. Gender stereotypes can make it hard to move into positions traditionally held by men. Women are also more likely to accommodate a partner's career than the other way around.[5] A job change that includes moving to another city may be a nonstarter for a woman in a relationship. The result is the unfortunate tautology that the tendency to stay put leads to staying put.

Being risk averse in the workplace can also cause women to be more reluctant to take on challenging tasks. In my experience, more men look for stretch assignments and take on high-visibility projects, while more women hang back. Research suggests that this is particularly true for women in environments that emphasize individual performance or when women are working closely with men.[6]

One reason women avoid stretch assignments and new challenges is that they worry too much about whether they currently have the skills they need for a new role. This can become a self-fulfilling prophecy, since so many abilities are acquired on the job. An internal report at Hewlett-Packard revealed that women only apply for open jobs if they think they meet 100 percent of the criteria listed. Men apply if they think they meet 60 percent of the requirements.[7] This difference has a huge ripple effect. Women need to shift from thinking "I'm not ready to do that" to thinking "I want to do that—and I'll learn by doing it."

My first day at work at the World Bank, Larry Summers asked me to perform some calculations. I was at a loss on how to proceed, so I turned to Lant Pritchett for help. "Just put it into Lotus 1–2–3," he advised. I told him that I didn't know how to do that. "Wow," he exclaimed. "I can't believe you've gotten this far, or even how you can understand basic economics, without knowing how to use Lotus." I went home convinced that I was going to get fired. The next day, Lant sat me down. My heart was pounding. But instead of firing me, he taught me how to use the program. That's a great boss.

Women are also more reluctant to apply for promotions even when deserved, often believing that good job performance will naturally lead to rewards.[8] Carol Frohlinger and Deborah Kolb, founders of Negotiating Women, Inc., describe this as the "Tiara Syndrome," where women "expect that if they keep doing their job well someone will notice them and place a tiara on their head."[9] In a perfect meritocracy, tiaras would be doled out to the deserving, but I have yet to see one floating around an office. Hard work and results *should* be recognized by others, but when they aren't, advocating for oneself becomes necessary. As discussed earlier, this must be done with great care. But it must be done.

Taking risks, choosing growth, challenging ourselves, and asking for promotions (with smiles on our faces, of course) are all important elements of managing a career. One of my favorite quotes comes from author Alice Walker, who observed, "The most common way people give up their power is by thinking they don't have any."

Do not wait for power to be offered. Like that tiara, it might never materialize. And anyway, who wears a tiara on a jungle gym?

Are You My Mentor?

WHEN I WAS a child, one of my favorite books was *Are You My Mother?*, the story of a baby bird that emerges from its shell to discover an empty nest. The hatchling heads off in search of its missing mother, asking a kitten, a hen, a dog, and a cow the burning question "Are you my mother?" Each animal responds, "No." The hatchling grows more desperate, eventually shouting, "Are you my mother?" at a car, a boat, a plane, and even a steam shovel, which can only respond with a loud "Snort!" Stuck in the shovel's jaws, the hatchling appears doomed until, miraculously, the shovel lifts the bird back to its nest. The mother returns and the hatchling announces, "You are a bird, and you are my mother."

This children's book poignantly mirrors the professional question "Are you my mentor?" If someone has to ask the question, the answer is probably no. When someone finds the right mentor, it is obvious. The question becomes a statement. Chasing or forcing that connection rarely works, and yet I see women attempt this all the time. When I give speeches or attend meetings, a startling number of women introduce themselves and, in the same breath, ask me to be their mentor. I cannot recall a single man asking me to do the same (although men have asked me to mentor their wives or girlfriends).

The question is a total mood killer—the equivalent of turning to a pensive date and asking, "What are you thinking?" Every senior woman I have talked to about this is deluged with the same request. Their reaction is unanimous: "Oh, I never know what to say when people I don't know ask me to be their mentor." The interaction is flattering, but awkward. Even media mogul Oprah Winfrey, who has taught so much to an entire generation, admits that she feels uncomfortable when someone asks her to be a mentor. She once explained, "I mentor when I see something and say, 'I want to see that grow.' "

In part, we've brought this on ourselves. For the past decade, talk of mentorship and sponsorship has been topic number one at any women's career seminar. It is the focus of blogs, newspaper articles, and research reports. Many of these young women are responding to the often repeated advice that if they want to scale the corporate ladder, they need to find mentors (people who will advise them) as well as sponsors (people who will use their influence to advocate for them).[1]

The emphasis on finding a mentor became especially clear to me when I went back to speak at Harvard Business School in the spring of 2011. I was invited by Dean Nitin

Nohria, who joined me onstage and conducted the interview. His first questions centered on Facebook and what it was like to work for Mark. I told him that I loved it, except on days when coworkers said things like, "Sheryl, can you look at this? We need to know what old people will think of this feature." We discussed the Arab Spring and a slew of other timely topics. Dean Nohria then asked me a question about women in the workforce. I'm not sure what possessed me, but I turned to look at the audience, paused, and answered with brutal honesty. "If current trends continue, fifteen years from today, about one-third of the women in this audience will be working full-time and almost all of you will be working for the guy you are sitting next to."

Dead silence in the large auditorium. I continued, "I'm sorry if this sounds harsh or surprises anyone, but this is where we are. If you want the outcome to be different, you will have to do something about it."

On that strained note, Dean Nohria ended the interview and turned to the audience for a Q&A. A number of men leapt to the microphone and posed thoughtful, big-picture questions like "What did you learn at Google that you are applying at Facebook?" and "How do you run a platform company and ensure stability for your developers?" Then two women rose to the microphone. The first asked, "Do you think it's okay to work for a company that competes with the company you worked for before business school?" The second asked, "How can I get a mentor?" My heart sank.

The men were focusing on how to manage a business

and the women were focusing on how to manage a career. The men wanted answers and the women wanted permission and help. I realized that searching for a mentor has become the professional equivalent of waiting for Prince Charming. We all grew up on the fairy tale "Sleeping Beauty," which instructs young women that if they just wait for their prince to arrive, they will be kissed and whisked away on a white horse to live happily ever after. Now young women are told that if they can just find the right mentor, they will be pushed up the ladder and whisked away to the corner office to live happily ever after. Once again, we are teaching women to be too dependent on others.

To be clear, the issue is not whether mentorship is important. It is. Mentorship and sponsorship are crucial for career progression. Both men and women with sponsors are more likely to ask for stretch assignments and pay raises than their peers of the same gender without sponsors.[2] Unfortunately for women, men often have an easier time acquiring and maintaining these relationships.[3] One recent study shows that men are significantly more likely than women to be sponsored and that those with sponsors are more satisfied with their rates of advancement.[4]

Because it is harder for young women to find mentors and sponsors, they are taking a more active role in seeking them out. And while normally I applaud assertive behavior, this energy is sometimes misdirected. No matter how crucial these connections are, they probably won't develop from asking a virtual stranger, "Will you be my mentor?"

The strongest relationships spring out of a real and often earned connection felt by both sides.

I've been lucky to have strong mentors and sponsors over the course of my career. The acknowledgments in this book include a long list of people who have been generous enough to guide and advise me. During my junior year of college, I took Larry Summers's public sector economics class. He offered to supervise my senior thesis—something very few Harvard professors volunteer to do for undergraduates. Larry has been a major part of my life ever since. I met Don Graham, chairman of the Washington Post Company, more than fifteen years ago when I was working in D.C., and he has helped me navigate some of my most challenging professional situations. If it hadn't been for Paley Center CEO Pat Mitchell's encouragement and support, I might never have spoken publicly about women in the workplace. These three, among so many others, have encouraged me, made introductions, and taught me by example. Their wisdom helped me avoid mistakes—and clean up the ones I wasn't smart enough to avoid.

In turn, I have tried to mentor others, including friends of friends, and as I get older, children of friends. I get so much joy out of watching the career of Emily White, who started working with me right out of college and now runs mobile partnerships for Facebook. When I first met Bryan Schreier, he had never worked in a tech company or traveled abroad, but he displayed unusually strong leadership and analytical skills. I hired him to help build Google's global operations, and he exceeded every expectation. Years later, when he wanted to pursue a new career as an investor, I introduced him to his current partners at Sequoia Capital. He is now a highly successful early stage venture capitalist, and I can see the impact he has on the companies he advises. I am fortunate to have Emily and Bryan and so many other talented people in my life.

Studies show that mentors select protégés based on performance and potential.[5] Intuitively, people invest in those who stand out for their talent or who can really benefit from help. Mentors continue to invest when mentees use their time well and are truly open to feedback. It may turn into a friendship, but the foundation is a professional relationship. Given this, I believe we have sent the wrong message to young women. We need to stop telling them, "Get a mentor and you will excel." Instead, we need to tell them, "Excel and you will get a mentor."

Clara Shih is a superb example. I met Clara about five years ago at a conference and was immediately impressed by her ideas about social media. She went on to write a thoughtful book on the subject and founded Hearsay Social, a software company that helps businesses manage their social media presence. Every so often, Clara would contact me, always with an interesting point or a thoughtful question. She never asked to get together to "catch up." She never asked a question that she could have found the answer to on her own. When I was leaving the Starbucks board of directors in 2012, I gave them a few names of social media experts who might join in my place and included Clara. She was only twenty-nine years old at the time, but she was invited to join the board.

While asking a stranger to be a mentor rarely, if ever, works, approaching a stranger with a pointed, well-thought-out inquiry can yield results. Garrett Neiman stopped me after I gave a speech at Stanford to explain that he had founded CollegeSpring, a nonprofit that provides SAT tutoring and college counseling to low-income students. He wanted to meet with me and made it clear that he only needed a few minutes of my time to ask for introductions to some people who could help expand his organization. He had done his homework and knew that I care deeply about education. In our first meeting and in every interaction we've had since, Garrett has been respectful of my time. He is crisp, focused, and gracious. And he always follows up to let me know the results of our discussion.

Capturing someone's attention or imagination in a minute can be done, but only when planned and tailored to that individual. Leading with a vague question such as "What is Facebook's culture like?" shows more ignorance than interest in the company, since there are hundreds of articles that provide this answer. Preparation is especially important when looking for a job. When I left the Treasury Department, former chief of staff Josh Steiner gave me great advice about asking for advice. He told me to figure out what I wanted to do *before* I went to see the people who had the ability to hire me. That way I would not waste my one shot seeking general guidance, but would be able to discuss specific opportunities that they could offer.

Mentorship is often a more reciprocal relationship than it may appear, especially in situations where people are already working at the same company. The mentee may receive more direct assistance, but the mentor receives benefits too, including useful information, greater commitment from colleagues, and a sense of fulfillment and pride. Sociologists and psychologists have long observed our deep desire to participate in reciprocal behavior. The fact that humans feel obligated to return favors has been documented in virtually all societies and underpins all kinds of social relationships.[6] The mentor/mentee relationship is no exception. When done right, everybody flourishes.

Erin Burnett, now a well-known CNN journalist, credits Willow Bay, a veteran TV correspondent and editor, for mentoring her when she first started out. Willow was a brand-new anchor of *Moneyline* but did not have deep financial experience. Erin had worked at Goldman Sachs, which made her an ideal person for Willow to hire as an assistant. Erin impressed Willow with her ambition, work ethic, and talent. Meanwhile, Erin got to watch a savvy, established journalist up close and personal. Each benefited from the other's expertise.

Justin Osofsky caught my attention at Facebook years ago when we were getting ready for our first senior-level meeting with the Walt Disney Company. Each of our teams, including sales, business development, and marketing, had submitted ideas for the partnership, but no one was coordinating, which left our presentation disjointed and unwieldy. Rather than just submitting his section,

Justin took the initiative to pull the group together and integrate all the ideas. I have been "mentoring" him ever since, which in his case means that I often turn to Justin to solve problems. This helps the company and creates ongoing opportunities for him.

Getting the attention of a senior person with a virtuoso performance works, but it's not the only way to get a mentor. I have seen lower-level employees nimbly grab a moment after a meeting or in the hall to ask advice from a respected and busy senior person. The exchange is casual and quick. After taking that advice, the would-be mentee follows up to offer thanks and then uses that opportunity to ask for more guidance. Without even realizing it, the senior person becomes involved and invested in the junior person's career. The word "mentor" never needs to be uttered. The relationship is more important than the label.

The label itself is open to interpretation. For years, I kept an eye on an enormously talented young woman on my team at Google and advised her each time she had a major decision to make. I never used the word "mentor," but I invested a lot of time in her development. So I was surprised one day when she stated flatly that she had "never had a mentor or anyone really looking out" for her. I asked what a mentor meant to her. She explained that it would be someone she spoke to for at least an hour every week. I smiled, thinking, *That's not a mentor—that's a therapist.*

Few mentors have time for excessive hand-holding. Most are dealing with their own high-stress jobs. A mentee who is positive and prepared can be a bright spot in a day.

For this same reason, mentees should avoid complaining excessively to a mentor. Using a mentor's time to validate feelings may help psychologically, but it's better to focus on specific problems with real solutions. Most people in the position to mentor are quite adept at problem solving. Give them a problem to solve. Sometimes high-potential women have a difficult time asking for help because they don't want to appear stumped. Being unsure about how to proceed is the most natural feeling in the world. I feel that way all the time. Asking for input is not a sign of weakness but often the first step to finding a path forward.

Mentoring and sponsoring relationships often form between individuals who have common interests or when the junior members remind the more senior members of themselves.[7] This means that men will often gravitate toward sponsoring younger men, with whom they connect more naturally. Since there are so many more men at the top of every industry, the proverbial old-boy network continues to flourish. And since there are already a reduced number of women in leadership roles, it is not possible for the junior women to get enough support unless senior men jump in too. We need to make male leaders aware of this shortage and encourage them to widen their circle.

It's wonderful when senior men mentor women. It's even better when they champion and sponsor them. Any male leader who is serious about moving toward a more equal world can make this a priority and be part of the solution. It should be a badge of honor for men to sponsor women. And since we know that different perspectives improve performance, companies should foster and reward this behavior.

Of course, there are some tricky issues to be solved here, including the perceived sexual context of male-female relationships. Once during my Treasury years, Larry Summers and I traveled together to South Africa, where we holed up in the living room of his hotel suite to work on his speech on fiscal policy for the next day. Jet-lagged and oblivious to the time change, we suddenly noticed it was 3:00 a.m. We both knew it would look awful if anyone saw me leaving his hotel suite at that time. We discussed the options. Maybe he should check to see if anyone was in the hall? Then we realized we were stuck because there is no difference between trying not to be seen leaving someone's hotel room late at night and *actually* leaving someone's hotel room late at night. I strode into the (luckily) empty hall and made it to my room undetected.

Junior women and senior men often avoid engaging in mentoring or sponsoring relationships out of fear of what others might think. A study published by the Center for Work-Life Policy and the *Harvard Business Review* reported that 64 percent of men at the level of vice president and above are hesitant to have a one-on-one meeting with a more junior woman. For their part, half of the junior women avoided close contact with senior men.[8] This evasiveness must end. Personal connections lead to assignments and promotions, so it needs to be okay for men and women to spend informal time together the same way men can. A senior man and junior man at a bar is seen as mentoring. A senior man and a junior woman at a bar can also be mentoring . . . but it looks like dating. This interpretation holds women back and creates a double bind. If women try to cultivate a close relationship with a male sponsor, they risk being the target of workplace gossip. If women try to get to the top without a sponsor's help, their careers will often stall. We cannot assume that interactions between men and women have a sexual component. And everyone involved has to make sure to behave professionally so women—and men—feel safe in all settings.

At Goldman Sachs in the late 1990s, management committee partner Bob Steel recognized this perception problem and came up with an admirable solution. The father of three daughters, Steel told a training class that he had a "breakfast or lunch only policy" with employees because he felt uncomfortable going out to dinner with female employees and wanted to make access equal. Sharon Meers worked at Goldman at the time and said Steel's decision caused a bit of a stir, but she thought his candor was heroic. Anything that evens out the opportunities for men and women is the right practice. Some will get there by adopting a no-dinner policy; others may adopt a dinner-with-anyone policy. In either case, we need practices that can be applied evenly.

Many companies are starting to move from informal mentoring that relies on individual initiative to more formal programs. When taken seriously, these formal mentorship/sponsorship programs can be remarkably successful. Structured programs also take the pressure off junior women from having to ask the difficult "Are you my mentor?" question. One study showed that women who found mentors through formal programs were 50 percent more likely to be promoted than women who found mentors on their own.[9] The most effective formal programs help educate men about the need to mentor women and establish guidelines for appropriate behavior. These programs can be a great way to help normalize the senior man/junior woman model.

Official mentorship programs are not sufficient by themselves and work best when combined with other kinds of development and training. Deloitte's Leading to WIN Women's Initiative is a good example. Deloitte had already established a program to support female employees, who still remained underrepresented at the highest levels of the company. This prompted Chet Wood, CEO of Deloitte Tax, to ask, "Where are all the women?" In response, Deloitte launched a leadership development program in 2008. The program targeted senior women in the tax division who were close to promotion. The women were assigned sponsors, received executive coaching, shadowed members of the executive committee, and took on global assignments. Of the twenty-one members of the inaugural group, eighteen have since been promoted.

As helpful as these formal programs can be, they are not always offered, and in some situations, senior people are not available to give guidance. The good news is that guidance can come from all levels. When I first joined Facebook, one of my biggest challenges was setting up the necessary business processes without harming the freewheeling culture. The company operated by moving quickly and tolerating mistakes, and lots of people were nervous that I would not just ruin the party but squash innovation. Naomi Gleit had joined Facebook right out of college several years earlier. As one of Facebook's earliest employees, she had a deep understanding of how the company worked. Naomi and I became close. I bet most people, including Naomi herself, probably assumed that I was mentoring her. But the truth is she mentored me. She helped me implement the changes that needed to be made and jumped in to stop me from getting things wrong. Naomi always told me the truth, even if she thought it would be hard for me to hear. She still does this for me today.

Peers can also mentor and sponsor one another. There is a saying that "all advice is autobiographical." Friends at the same stage of their careers may actually provide more current and useful counsel. Several of my older mentors advised me against taking a job at Google in 2001. Yet almost all my peers understood the potential of Silicon Valley. Peers are also in the trenches and may understand problems that superiors do not, especially when those problems are generated by superiors in the first place.

As an associate at McKinsey & Company, my first assignment was on a team that consisted of a male senior engagement manager (SEM) and two other male associates, Abe Wu and Derek Holley. When the SEM wanted to talk to Abe or Derek, he would walk over to their desks. When he wanted to talk to me, he would sit at his desk and shout, "Sandberg, get over here!" with the tone one might use to call a child or, even worse, a dog. It made me cringe every time. I never said anything, but one day Abe and Derek started calling each other "Sandberg" in that same loud voice. The self-absorbed SEM never seemed to notice. They kept it up. When having too many Sandbergs got confusing, they decided we needed to differentiate. Abe started calling himself "Asian Sandberg," Derek dubbed himself "good-looking Sandberg," and I became "Sandberg Sandberg." My colleagues turned an awful situation into one where I felt protected. They stood up for me and made me laugh. They were the best mentors I could have had.

Since when it rains, it pours, on that same project, the senior client leader wanted to fix me up with his son. He declared this intention in front of his team over and over. I knew he meant it as a compliment, but it undermined my professional authority. How could I get my clients to take me seriously if their boss was constantly reminding everyone that I was his son's age—oh, and that I should date him? One day, I gathered my courage and asked to speak to him in private. I told him (nicely) that I did not think it was appropriate for him to keep bringing up his son. He laughed it off and kept doing it.

Having tried to deal with the situation myself, I went to my manager—the same "Sandberg"-shouting SEM. He listened to my complaint and then told me that I should think about what I was "doing to send these signals." Yup, it was my fault. I told the two other Sandbergs, who were outraged. They encouraged me to go over the SEM's head and talk to the senior partner, Robert Taylor. Robert understood my discomfort immediately. He explained that sometimes those of us who are different (he is African American) need to remind people to treat us appropriately. He said he was glad I told the client no on my own and that the client should have listened. He then talked to the client and explained that his behavior had to stop. He also spoke with my SEM about his insensitive response. I could not have been more grateful for Robert's protection. I knew exactly how that baby bird felt when he finally found his mother.

6

Seek and Speak Your Truth

M Y FRIEND Betsy Cohen was pregnant with her second child when her toddler, Sam, became curious about where the baby was in her body. "Mommy," he asked, "are the baby's arms in your arms?" "No, the baby is in my tummy," she replied. "Are the baby's legs in your legs?" "No, the whole baby is in my tummy." "Really, the whole baby is in your tummy? Are you sure?" "Yes, the whole baby is in my tummy." "Then, Mommy, what's growing in your butt?"

This kind of honesty is common from children and virtually unheard-of from adults. As kids grow up, we teach them to be polite, watch what they say, not hurt others' feelings. This is not a bad thing. As a former pregnant "whale," I'm glad that most people keep some observations to themselves. But as we learn to speak appropriately, we lose something in authenticity.

Authentic communication is not always easy, but it is the basis for successful relationships at home and real effectiveness at work. Yet people constantly back away from honesty to protect themselves and others. This reticence causes and perpetuates all kinds of problems: uncomfortable issues that never get addressed, resentment that builds, unfit managers who get promoted rather than fired, and on and on. Often these situations don't improve because no one tells anyone what is really happening. We are so rarely brave enough to tell the truth.

Being honest in the workplace is especially difficult. All organizations have some form of hierarchy, which means that someone's performance is assessed by someone else's perception. This makes people even less likely to tell the truth. Every organization faces this challenge, no matter how flat it tries to be. At Facebook, we work hard to be nonhierarchical. Everyone sits at open desks in big open spaces—no offices, cubes, or partitions for any of us. We hold a company-wide Q&A every Friday where anyone can ask a question or make a comment. When people disagree with decisions, they post to the company-wide Facebook group. Still, I would be an idiot, or not telling myself the truth, if I thought that my coworkers always felt free to criticize me, Mark, or even their peers.

When psychologists study power dynamics, they find that people in low-power positions are more hesitant to share their views and often hedge their statements when they do.[1] This helps explain why for many women, speaking honestly in a professional environment carries an additional set of fears: Fear of not being considered a team player. Fear of seeming negative or nagging. Fear that constructive criticism will come across as just plain old criticism. Fear that by speaking up, we will call attention to ourselves, which might open us up to attack (a fear brought to us by that same voice in the back of our head that urges us not to sit at the table).

Communication works best when we combine appropriateness with authenticity, finding that sweet spot where opinions are not brutally honest but delicately honest. Speaking truthfully without hurting feelings comes naturally to some and is an acquired skill for others. I definitely needed help in this area. Fortunately, I found it.

When Dave was at Yahoo, he attended a management training program taught by Fred Kofman, a former MIT professor and author of *Conscious Business*. Dave hates training of any kind, and the human resources team at Yahoo had to force him to attend the two-day session. When he came home after the first day, he surprised me by describing the training as "not too bad." By the end of the second day, he started quoting Fred and making observations about our communication. I was in shock; this guy must be *good*. So I called Fred, introduced myself, and said, "I don't know what you do, but I want you to do it for my team at Google."

Fred showed up at Google, and his teachings changed my career and my life. He is one of the most extraordinary thinkers on leadership and management I have ever encountered. Many of the concepts discussed in this chapter originated with him and reflect his belief that great leadership is "conscious" leadership.

I learned from Fred that effective communication starts with the understanding that there is my point of view (my truth) and someone else's point of view (his truth). Rarely is there one absolute truth, so people who believe that they speak *the* truth are very silencing of others. When we recognize that we can see things only from our own perspective, we can share our views in a nonthreatening way. Statements of opinion are always more constructive in the first person "I" form. Compare these two statements: "You never take my suggestions seriously" and "I feel frustrated that you have not responded to my last four e-mails, which leads me to believe that my suggestions are not that important to you. Is that so?" The former can elicit a quick and defensive "That's not true!" The latter is much harder to deny. One triggers a disagreement; the other sparks a discussion. I wish I could always maintain this perspective in all my communications. I don't—but I continue to try.

Truth is also better served by using simple language. Office-speak often contains nuances and parentheticals that can bury not just the lead but the entire point. Comedies like *Office Space* ring true for a reason. People fear insulting others, especially the boss, so they hedge. Rather than stating, "I disagree with our expansion strategy," they say, "While I think there are many good reasons why we are opening this new line of business and I feel confident that the management team has done a thorough ROI analysis, I am not sure we have completely thought through all of the downstream effects of taking this step forward at this time." Huh? With all of these caveats, it's hard to decipher what the speaker actually thinks.

When communicating hard truths, less is often more. A few years ago, Mark Zuckerberg decided to learn Chinese. To practice, he spent time with a group of Facebook employees who were native speakers. One might think that Mark's limited language skills would have kept these conversations from being substantively useful. Instead, they gave him greater insight into what was going on in the company. For example, one of the women was trying to tell Mark something about her manager. Mark didn't understand so he said, "Simpler, please." Then she spoke again, but he still didn't understand, so he had to ask her to simplify further. This happened a few more times. Eventually, she got frustrated and just blurted out, "My manager is bad!" She was still speaking Chinese, but simply enough that Mark understood. If more people were this clear, the performance of many organizations would improve dramatically.

The ability to listen is as important as the ability to speak. From the time my siblings and I were very young, whenever we had arguments, our mother taught us—or more like forced us—to mirror each other, which means restating the other person's point before responding to it. For example, one day my sister and I were fighting over a lollipop. "Sheryl ate the last lollipop!" Michelle screamed. "But she had a lollipop yesterday and I didn't!" I screamed back, making an *excellent* point. My mother sat us down facing each other. I was not allowed to explain how gravely inequitable the lollipop allocation was until I acknowledged my sister's feelings. "Michelle, I understand that you are upset because I ate the last lollipop and you wanted it." As painful as this was at the time, reflecting someone's viewpoint clarifies the disagreement and becomes a starting point for resolution. We all want to be heard, and when we focus on showing others that we are listening, we actually become better listeners. I now do this with my children. And while they probably dislike the process as much as I did when I was their age, I love hearing my son explain to my daughter, "I'm sorry you're upset because you lost at Monopoly, but I'm older than you so I should win." Not bad for a seven-year-old. (Although Fred would caution my son to take out the "but" and everything after, since it tends to deny the preceding statement. Imagine someone saying, "I really like you, but . . .")

Being aware of a problem is the first step to correcting it. It is nearly impossible to know how our actions are perceived by others. We can try to guess what they're thinking, but asking directly is far more effective. With real knowledge, we can adjust our actions and avoid getting tripped up. Still, people rarely seek enough input. A few years ago, Tom Brokaw interviewed me for a piece on Facebook. Tom is a magnificent interviewer, and I felt that I stumbled through some of my answers. After we wrapped, I asked him how I could have done better. He seemed surprised by my question, so I asked him again. He then told me that in his entire career, I was only the second person to ask him for feedback.

The strategy of soliciting input broadly was first demonstrated for me by Robert Rubin, secretary of the Treasury when I joined the department in 1996. During my first week there, I was invited to a meeting on restructuring the IRS. About ten senior staffers were sitting at the table when we entered. Since I knew nothing about the topic, I took a seat in the back corner of the room (yup, not even close to the table). Toward the end of the meeting, Secretary Rubin suddenly turned and asked, "Sheryl, what do you think?" I was stunned silent—my mouth opened but nothing came out. When he saw how shocked I was, Secretary Rubin explained why he had put me on the spot: "Because you're new and not fully up to speed on how we do things, I thought you might see something we were missing." Apparently not in my case. But Secretary Rubin sent a powerful message to all of us about the value of soliciting ideas from every corner (literally).

Secretary Rubin was also aware of the dangers of blindly following leaders, or in his case, being blindly followed. Before becoming Treasury secretary, Rubin served as co-chairman of the board of Goldman Sachs. At the end of his first week as co-chairman, he noticed that Goldman was heavily invested in gold. He asked someone why the firm had taken such a big position. The startled employee answered, "That was you, sir." "Me?" Rubin replied. Apparently, the day before he had been taking his initial tour of the trading floor and commented, "Gold looks interesting." This got repeated as "Rubin likes gold," and someone spent millions of dollars to please the new boss.

More than a decade later, I experienced my own "Rubin likes gold" moment. When I joined Facebook, I faced a dilemma: I needed to bolster the business side of the company while respecting its unconventional culture. Most corporations love PowerPoint presentations, so I encouraged people *not* to prepare them for meetings with me, but instead to come with a simple list of topics. I repeated this frequently, but every meeting seemed to include a detailed PowerPoint presentation anyway. After more than two years of frustration, I announced that although I hated making rules, I was making one: no more PowerPoint in my meetings.

A few weeks later, as I was getting ready to speak to our global sales team, Kirsten Nevill-Manning, a skilled human resources leader at Facebook, came to find me. Kirsten thought I should know that everyone in Europe was upset with me. *Really? I angered an entire continent?* She explained that client meetings were very difficult without PowerPoint and asked why I would make such a stupid rule. I explained that I had intended the rule to apply only to presentations to *me*. But just as the Goldman team heard "Gold = good," the Facebook team heard "PowerPoint = bad." I got onstage in front of our entire sales team and apologized for the misunderstanding. I also let them know that if they hear a bad idea, even one they believe is coming from me or Mark, they should either fight it or ignore it.

As hard as it is to have an honest dialogue about business decisions, it is even harder to give individuals honest feedback. This is true for entry-level employees, senior leaders, and everyone in between. One thing that helps is to remember that feedback, like truth, is not absolute. Feedback is an opinion, grounded in observations and experiences, which allows us to know what impression we make on others. The information is revealing and potentially uncomfortable, which is why all of us would rather offer feedback to those who welcome it. If I make an observation or recommendation and someone reacts badly—or even just visibly tenses up—I quickly learn to save my comments for things that really matter. This is why I so admire Molly Graham's approach. Molly joined Facebook in 2008 and held a number of jobs throughout the company in communications, human resources, and mobile products. She performed extraordinarily well in all of these very different roles, not just because she is uniquely talented but because she is always learning. One day, she and I hosted a tricky client meeting. She navigated the discussion effectively, and after the clients left, I praised her effort. She paused and said, "Thanks, but you must have ideas for me on what more I could have done."

"How can I do better?" "What am I doing that I don't know?" "What am I *not* doing that I don't see?" These questions can lead to many benefits. And believe me, the truth hurts. Even when I have solicited feedback, any judgment can feel harsh. But the upside of painful knowledge is so much greater than the downside of blissful ignorance.

Requesting advice can also help build relationships. At Facebook, I knew that the most important determinant of my success would be my relationship with Mark. When I joined, I asked Mark for a commitment that he would give me feedback every week so that anything that bothered him would be aired and discussed quickly. Mark not only said yes but immediately added that he wanted it to be reciprocal. For the first few years, we stuck to this routine and voiced concerns big and small every Friday afternoon. As the years went by, sharing honest reactions became part of our ongoing relationship. Now we do so in real time rather than waiting for the end of the week. I wouldn't suggest that all relationships need this much feedback—there is such a thing as asking for too much—but for us, it has been critically important.

I have also learned the hard way that being open to hearing the truth means taking responsibility for mistakes. In my first week as chief of staff at Treasury, I had the chance to work directly with the heads of the department bureaus. There is a right and a wrong way to start a working relationship. I chose the wrong way. My first call was to Ray Kelly, who was then commissioner of the U.S. Customs Service and a former New York City police commissioner. Instead of reaching out to offer assistance, I called Commissioner Kelly with a request from the secretary. The impression I made was that my job was to demand and his job was to listen. It was a mistake. Ray's response was quick and clear. "[Expletive], Sheryl," he explained. "Just because I'm not in Larry Summers's [expletive] thirty-year-old brain trust doesn't mean that I don't know what I'm doing! If Secretary Summers wants something from me, tell him to [expletive] call me himself!" Then he hung up the phone. I thought, *This is not going well.* My first week on the job and I'd angered a man who knows a thing or two about firearms.

After I stopped shaking, I realized that Commissioner Kelly had done me a huge favor. His "feedback" was extremely helpful and delivered in a way that I would never forget. I reassessed my outreach strategy. With the other bureau chiefs, I initiated conversation by asking what I could do to help them achieve *their* goals. It's no surprise that they reacted more positively and with far fewer expletives. And after I employed my "What have I done for you lately?" approach, they were far more eager to return the favor.

As often as I try to persuade people to share their honest views, it is still a challenge to elicit them. When I started building my team at Google, I interviewed every candidate before we made an offer. Even when the team had grown to about one hundred people, I still spoke with each finalist. One day at a meeting of my direct reports, I offered to stop interviewing, fully expecting everyone to insist that my input was an essential part of the process. Instead, they applauded. They all jumped in to explain—*in unison*—that my insistence on speaking personally to every candidate had become a huge bottleneck. I had no idea that I had been holding the team back and was upset that no one had told me. I spent a few hours quietly fuming, which, given that I have no poker face, was probably obvious to everyone. Then I realized that if my colleagues had kept this to themselves, I was clearly not communicating that I was open to their input. Miscommunication is always a two-way street. If I wanted more suggestions, I would have to take responsibility for making that clear. So I went back to my team and agreed that I would not interview anymore. And more important, I told them that I wanted their input early and often.

Another way I try to foster authentic communication is to speak openly about my own weaknesses. To highlight just one, I have a tendency to get impatient about unresolved situations. My reaction is to push for people to resolve them quickly, in some cases before they realistically can. David Fischer and I have worked closely together for fifteen years at Treasury, Google, and Facebook. He jokes that he can tell from my tone of voice whether he should bother to complete a task or if I'm about to just do it myself. I acknowledge my impatience openly and ask my colleagues to let me know when I need to chill out. By mentioning this myself, I give others permission to bring up my impatience—and joke about it too. My colleagues will say to me, "Sheryl, you asked us to tell you when you get nervous and push the teams too hard. I think you're doing that now." But if I never said anything, would anyone at Facebook walk up to me and announce, "Hey, Sheryl, calm down! You're driving everyone nuts!" Somehow I doubt it. They would think it. They might even say it to one another. But they wouldn't say it to me.

When people are open and honest, thanking them publicly encourages them to continue while sending a powerful signal to others. At a meeting with about sixty Facebook engineers, I mentioned that I was interested in opening more Facebook offices around the world, especially in one particular region. Since the group included members of the security team, I asked what they were most worried about. Without being called on, Chad Greene blurted out, "Opening a Facebook office in that region." He explained why it wouldn't work and why I was dead wrong in front of the entire group. I loved it. We had never met before, and I will never forget that strong introduction. I ended the meeting by thanking Chad for his candor and then posted the story on Facebook to encourage the rest of the company to follow his example. Mark feels the same way. At a summer barbecue four years ago, an intern told Mark that he should work on his public speaking skills. Mark thanked him in front of everyone and then encouraged us to extend him a full-time job offer.

Humor can be an amazing tool for delivering an honest message in a good-natured way. A recent study even found that "sense of humor" was the phrase most frequently used to describe the most effective leaders.[2] I have seen humor get results so many times. After working in the Obama White House, Marne Levine joined Facebook to run global public policy. Marne is polished, professional, and highly competent. During her first week at her job, she needed a colleague from another team to finish drafting a few paragraphs for an upcoming congressional testimony.

The colleague was dragging his heels. He kept coming to Marne to ask questions, which she would duly answer, then she would wait, but still no paragraphs. When he came to her again with yet another question, she turned to him with a huge smile and said, "I am going to answer all of your questions. I really am. But right now, the only thing that is going to keep me from falling down on the floor and having a heart attack right in front of you is for you to get out of your chair, go back to your desk, and write the paragraphs we need for Congress." It worked beautifully.

A colleague at Google, Adam Freed, and I were frustrated by someone at work who was making our jobs very difficult. I met with her several times and earnestly explained that I felt that she was second-guessing our every move and preventing progress. During each heartfelt discussion, she would listen and nod and thank me for raising the matter. I would leave feeling better. Then the situation would get worse. Adam took a totally different approach. He invited her to lunch. They met at the Google café, chatted a bit, and then he looked at her and jokingly asked, "Why do you hate me?" Where I had failed repeatedly, Adam broke through. She asked why he would make that joke, which gave him a chance to explain in a way she was able to hear.

Unfortunately, our sense of humor sometimes fails us when we need it most. When I get emotional, it's very hard for me to treat a problem lightly. I had been at Google about three months when an uncomfortable situation erupted. I had started at the company reporting to Eric Schmidt but was transitioning to work for Omid Kordestani. During that process, Omid and I had a major misunderstanding. I went to discuss it with him, intending to explain calmly why I was upset, but as soon as I started talking, I burst into tears. I was horrified to be crying in front of my new boss whom I barely knew—which just made more tears flow. But I got lucky. Omid was patient and reassuring, insisting, "Everyone gets upset at work. It's okay."

Most women believe—and research suggests—that it is not a good idea to cry at work.[3] It is never something that I plan to do and is hardly recommended in *The Seven Habits of Highly Effective People*, but on those rare occasions when I have felt really frustrated, or worse, betrayed, tears have filled my eyes. Even as I have gotten older and more experienced, it still happens every so often.

I had been working at Facebook for almost a year when I learned that someone had said something about me that was not just false, but cruel. I started telling Mark about it and, despite my best efforts, started to cry. He assured me that the accusation was so untrue that no one could possibly believe it. And then he asked, "Do you want a hug?" I did. It was a breakthrough moment for us. I felt closer to him than ever before. I then recounted this story publicly, figuring that it might make it easier for others who have faced unwanted tears. The press reported the incident as "Sheryl Sandberg cried on Mark Zuckerberg's shoulder," which is not exactly what happened. What happened was that I expressed my feelings and Mark responded with compassion.

Sharing emotions builds deeper relationships. Motivation comes from working on things we care about. It also comes from working with people we care about. To really care about others, we have to understand them—what they like and dislike, what they feel as well as think. Emotion drives both men and women and influences every decision we make. Recognizing the role emotions play and being willing to discuss them makes us better managers, partners, and peers.

I did not always understand this. I used to think that being professional meant being organized and focused and keeping my personal life separate. Early on at Google, Omid and I would have a one-on-one meeting each week. I would enter his office with a typed agenda and get right to it. I thought I was being so efficient, but my colleague Tim Armstrong (who later became CEO of AOL) kindly pulled me aside one day to give me some advice. He told me that I should take a moment to connect with Omid before diving in. Since Omid and I were the only people in those meetings, it was clear who had mentioned this to Tim. I made the adjustment and started asking Omid how he was before leaping into my to-do list. It was a good lesson. An all-business approach is not always good business.

It has been an evolution, but I am now a true believer in bringing our whole selves to work. I no longer think people have a professional self for Mondays through Fridays and a real self for the rest of the time. That type of separation probably never existed, and in today's era of individual expression, where people constantly update their Facebook status and tweet their every move, it makes even less sense.

Instead of putting on some kind of fake "all-work persona," I think we benefit from expressing our truth, talking about personal situations, and acknowledging that professional decisions are often emotionally driven. I should have learned this lesson years earlier. When I was graduating from business school in 1995, Larry Summers offered me a job at Treasury. I wanted the job desperately, but there was an issue: I did not want to move back to D.C., where my soon-to-be ex-husband lived. One of the hardest calls I've ever had to make was to tell Larry that I could not accept the job. Larry pressed me on why, and I thought about telling him that I really wanted to try consulting in Los Angeles. Instead, I opened up. I explained that I was getting divorced and wanted to move far away from D.C., which held too many painful memories. Larry argued that it was a big city, but it didn't seem big enough for me. A year later, when enough time had passed and I felt ready to return to D.C., I called Larry and asked if the opportunity was still available. It was one of the easiest calls I have ever made, in part because I had been honest the year before. If I had told Larry that I was passing on the job for professional reasons, I would have appeared impulsive when I reversed that decision. Since the real reason was personal, sharing it honestly was the best thing to do.

People often pretend that professional decisions are not affected by their personal lives. They are afraid to talk about their home situations at work as if one should never interfere with the other, when of course they can and do. I know many women who won't discuss their children at work out of fear that their priorities will be questioned. I hope this won't always be the case.

My sister-in-law, Amy Schefler, had a college roommate, Abby Hemani, who is a partner in one of Boston's most prestigious law firms. The line between personal and professional was erased for Abby when her seven-month-old daughter was diagnosed with Dravet syndrome, a rare and severe form of epilepsy. Abby explained that her mostly male partners got used to seeing her cry at the office and their response was heartwarming. "It was as if they envisioned me as one of their own daughters and wanted to comfort me," she said. Abby insists that her public emotion improved her work situation both by turning her colleagues into a source of support and by leading to more flexible hours. "I know several men at my firm who have had similar experiences with sick children, but they didn't feel they could be as forthcoming as I was," she said. "So, in the end, I think my female manner of relating served me well."

Not every workplace and every colleague will be as generous and caring. But I do think we are moving toward at least blurring the line between personal and professional. Increasingly, prominent thinkers in the field of leadership studies like Marcus Buckingham are challenging traditional notions of leadership. Their research suggests that presenting leadership as a list of carefully defined qualities (like strategic, analytical, and performance oriented) no longer holds. Instead, true leadership stems from individuality that is honestly and sometimes imperfectly expressed.[4]

They believe leaders should strive for authenticity over perfection. This shift is good news for women, who often feel obliged to suppress their emotions in the workplace in an attempt to come across as more stereotypically male. And it's also good news for men, who may be doing the exact same thing.

I had the opportunity to see the power of authentic communication in a leader firsthand when I served on the board of Starbucks. Howard Schultz was CEO of Starbucks from 1987 through 2000, and during his tenure, the company grew from just a few stores into a global retail powerhouse. Howard stepped down as CEO in 2000, and over the next eight years Starbucks' performance faltered. When Howard returned as CEO in 2008, he held a meeting with all of the company's global managers in New Orleans. He openly admitted that the company was in serious trouble. Then he allowed his emotions to show, tearing up as he confessed that he felt that he had let down his employees and their families. The entire company rose to the challenge. Starbucks turned around and delivered its highest revenue and earnings a few years later.

Maybe someday shedding tears in the workplace will no longer be viewed as embarrassing or weak, but as a simple display of authentic emotion. And maybe the compassion and sensitivity that have historically held some women back will make them more natural leaders in the future. In the meantime, we can all hasten this change by committing ourselves to both seek—and speak—our truth.

Don't Leave Before You Leave

A FEW YEARS AGO, a young woman at Facebook came to my desk and asked if she could speak to me privately. We headed into a conference room, where she began firing off questions about how I balance work and family. As the questions came faster and faster, I started to wonder about her urgency. I interrupted to ask if she had a child. She said no, but she liked to plan ahead. I inquired if she and her partner were considering having a child. She replied that she did not have a husband, then added with a little laugh, "Actually, I don't even have a boyfriend."

It seemed to me that she was jumping the gun—*big-time*—but I understood why. From an early age, girls get the message that they will have to choose between succeeding at work and being a good mother. By the time they are in college, women are already thinking about the trade-offs they will make between professional and personal goals.[1] When asked to choose between marriage and career, female college students are twice as likely to choose marriage as their male classmates.[2] And this concern can start even younger. Peggy Orenstein, the author of *Cinderella Ate My Daughter*, related the story of a five-year-old girl who came home distraught from her after-school program and told her mother that both she and the boy she had a crush on wanted to be astronauts. When her mother asked why that was a problem, the little girl replied, "When we go into space together, who will watch our kids?" At five, she thought the most challenging aspect of space travel would be dependable child care.

As I've mentioned, I'm a big believer in thoughtful preparation. Everywhere I go, I carry a little notebook with my to-do list—*an actual notebook* that I write in with *an actual pen*. (In the tech world, this is like carrying a stone tablet and chisel.) But when it comes to integrating career and family, planning too far in advance can close doors rather than open them. I have seen this happen over and over. Women rarely make one big decision to leave the workforce. Instead, they make a lot of small decisions along the way, making accommodations and sacrifices that they believe will be required to have a family. Of all the ways women hold themselves back, perhaps the most pervasive is that they leave before they leave.

The classic scenario unfolds like this. An ambitious and successful woman heads down a challenging career path with the thought of having children in the back of her mind. At some point, this thought moves to the front of her mind, typically once she finds a partner. The woman considers how hard she is working and reasons that to make room for a child she will have to scale back. A law associate might decide not to shoot for partner because someday she hopes to have a family. A teacher might pass on leading curriculum development for her school. A sales representative might take a smaller territory or not apply for a management role. Often without even realizing it, the woman stops reaching for new opportunities. If any are presented to her, she is likely to decline or offer the kind of hesitant "yes" that gets the project assigned to someone else. The problem is that even if she were to get pregnant immediately, she still has nine months before she has to care for an actual child. And since women usually start this mental preparation well before trying to conceive, several years often pass between the thought and conception, let alone birth. In the case of my Facebook questioner, it might even be a decade.

By the time the baby arrives, the woman is likely to be in a drastically different place in her career than she would have been had she not leaned back. Before, she was a top performer, on par with her peers in responsibility, opportunity, and pay. By not finding ways to stretch herself in the years leading up to motherhood, she has fallen behind. When she returns to the workplace after her child is born, she is likely to feel less fulfilled, underutilized, or unappreciated. She may wonder why she is working for someone (usually a man) who has less experience than she does. Or she may wonder why she does not have the exciting new project or the corner office. At this point, she probably scales her ambitions back even further since she no longer believes that she can get to the top. And if she has the financial resources to leave her job, she is more likely to do so.

The more satisfied a person is with her position, the less likely she is to leave.[3] So the irony—and, to me, the tragedy—is that women wind up leaving the workforce precisely because of things they did to *stay in* the workforce. With the best of intentions, they end up in a job that is less fulfilling and less engaging. When they finally have a child, the choice—for those who have one—is between becoming a stay-at-home mother or returning to a less-than-appealing professional situation.

Joanna Strober, co-author of *Getting to 50/50*, credits a compelling job for her decision to return to the workforce after becoming a mother. "When I first started working, there were lots of scary stories about female executives who ignored their kids or weren't home enough," she told me. "Everyone in our office talked about one executive whose daughter supposedly told her that when she grew up she wanted to be a client because they got all the attention. I found these stories so depressing that I gave up before even really starting down the partner track. However, when five years later I was in a job I really loved, I found myself wanting to return to work after a few weeks of maternity leave. I realized those executives weren't scary at all. Like me, they loved their kids a lot. And, like me, they also loved their jobs."

There are many powerful reasons to exit the workforce. Being a stay-at-home parent is a wonderful, and often necessary, choice for many people. Not every parent needs, wants, or should be expected to work outside the home. In addition, we do not control all of the factors that influence us, including the health of our children. Plus, many people welcome the opportunity to get out of the rat race. No one should pass judgment on these highly personal decisions. I fully support any man or woman who dedicates his or her life to raising the next generation. It is important and demanding and joyful work.

What I am arguing is that the time to scale back is when a break is needed or when a child arrives—not before, and certainly not years in advance. The months and years leading up to having children are not the time to lean back, but the critical time to lean in.

Several years ago, I approached an employee at Facebook to manage an important new project. She seemed flattered at first but then became noticeably hesitant. She told me that she wasn't sure she should take on more responsibility. Obviously, something else was going on, so I quietly asked, "Are you worried about taking this on because you're considering having a child sometime soon?" A few years earlier, I would have been afraid to ask this question. Managers are not supposed to factor childbearing plans into account in hiring or management decisions. Raising this topic in the workplace would give most employment lawyers a heart attack. But after watching so many talented women pass on opportunities for unspoken reasons, I started addressing this issue directly. I always give people the option of not answering, but so far, every woman I have asked has appeared grateful for a chance to discuss the subject. I also make it clear that I am only asking for one reason: to make sure they aren't limiting their options unnecessarily.

In 2009, we were recruiting Priti Choksi to join Facebook's business development team. After we extended an offer, she came in to ask some follow-up questions about the role. She did not mention lifestyle or hours, but she was the typical age when women have children. So as we were wrapping up, I went for it. "If you think you might not take this job because you want to have a child soon, I am happy to talk about this." I figured if she didn't want to discuss it, she would just keep heading for the door. Instead, she turned around, sat back down, and said, "Let's talk." I explained that although it was counterintuitive, right before having a child can actually be a great time to take a new job. If she found her new role challenging and rewarding, she'd be more excited to return to it after giving birth. If she stayed put, she might decide that her job was not worth the sacrifice. Priti accepted our offer. By the time she started at Facebook, she was already expecting. Eight months later, she had her baby, took four months off, and came back to a job she loved. She later told me that if I had not raised the topic, she would have turned us down.

Like so many women, Caroline O'Connor believed that someday she'd have to choose between career and family. That day came sooner than she expected. Caroline was finishing up at Stanford's Institute of Design when she was offered the chance to start a company at the same time that she learned she was pregnant. Her knee-jerk reaction was to think that she could not do both. But then she decided to question this assumption. "I began thinking of my dilemma as I would a design challenge," O'Connor wrote. "Rather than accepting that launching a successful start-up and having a baby are utterly incompatible, I framed it as a question and then set about using tools I've developed as a designer to begin forming an answer." O'Connor gathered data from dozens of mothers about their experiences and coping mechanisms. She did fieldwork on sleep deprivation by taking a night shift with foster infants. She concluded that with a team culture that drew support from her husband and friends, it would be possible to proceed with both. O'Connor now refers to herself as "a career-loving parent," a nice alternative to "working mom."[4]

Given life's variables, I would never recommend that every woman lean in regardless of circumstances. There have been times when I chose not to. In the summer of 2006, a tiny start-up called LinkedIn was looking for a new CEO, and Reid Hoffman, LinkedIn's founder, reached out to me. I thought it was a great opportunity, and after five years in the same position at Google I was ready for a new challenge. But the timing was tricky. I was thirty-seven years old and wanted to have a second child. I told Reid the truth: regrettably, I had to pass because I didn't think I could handle both a pregnancy and a new job. His reaction was incredibly kind and supportive. He tried to talk me into it, even volunteering to work full-time at the company to support me during that period, but it was hard to see a path through.

For some women, pregnancy does not slow them down at all, but rather serves to focus them and provides a firm deadline to work toward. My childhood friend Elise Scheck looks back fondly on being pregnant, saying she has never felt so productive. She not only worked her usual hours as an attorney but organized her house and put five years of photos into albums. For others, like me, pregnancy is very difficult, making it impossible to be as effective as normal. I tried writing e-mails while hovering over the toilet, but the situation didn't lend itself to effective multitasking. Because I had already been through this with my first pregnancy, I knew what I was in for. I turned down Reid's offer and got pregnant—and extremely nauseated—a few months later.

Any regrets I had about not taking that job evaporated when, about seven months after my daughter was born, Mark offered me the opportunity to join Facebook. The timing was still not ideal. As many people had warned, and I quickly discovered to be true, having two children was more than double the work of having one. I was not looking for new challenges but simply trying to get through each day. Still, Dave and I recognized that if I waited until the timing was exactly right, the opportunity would be gone. My decision to take the job was personal, as these decisions always are. And there were days in my first six months at Facebook when I wondered whether I'd made the right choice. By the end of my first year, I knew I had . . . for me.

The birth of a child instantly changes how we define ourselves. Women become mothers. Men become fathers. Couples become parents. Our priorities shift in fundamental ways. Parenting may be the most rewarding experience, but it is also the hardest and most humbling. If there were a right way to raise kids, everyone would do it. Clearly, that is not the case.

One of the immediate questions new parents face is who will provide primary care for a child. The historical choice has been the mother. Breast-feeding alone has made this both the logical and the biological choice. But the advent of the modern-day breast pump has changed the equation. At Google, I would lock my office door and pump during conference calls. People would ask, "What's that sound?" I would respond, "What sound?" When they would insist that there was a loud beeping noise that they could hear on the phone, I would say, "Oh, there's a fire truck across the street." I thought I was pretty clever until I realized that others on the call were sometimes in the same building and knew there was no fire truck. *Busted.*

Despite modern methods that can minimize the impact of biological imperatives, women still do the vast majority of child care. As a result, becoming a parent decreases workforce participation for women but not men.[5] Forty-three percent of highly qualified women with children are leaving careers, or "off-ramping," for a period of time.[6]

Women who are the most likely to leave the workforce

are concentrated at opposite ends of the earning scale, married to men who earn the least and the most. In 2006, only 20 percent of mothers whose husbands' earnings landed in the middle (between the twenty-fifth and seventy-fifth percentiles) were out of the labor force. In contrast, a whopping 52 percent of mothers with husbands in the bottom quarter and 40 percent of mothers with husbands in the top 5 percent were out of the labor force.[7] Obviously, their reasons for staying home are vastly different. Mothers married to the lowest-earning men struggle to find jobs that pay enough to cover child-care costs, which are increasingly unaffordable. Over the past decade, child-care costs have risen twice as fast as the median income of families with children.[8] The cost for two children (an infant and a four-year-old) to go to a day-care center is greater than the annual median rent payment in every state in the country.[9]

Women married to men with greater resources leave for a variety of reasons, but one important factor is the number of hours that their husbands work. When husbands work fifty or more hours per week, wives with children are 44 percent more likely to quit their jobs than wives with children whose husbands work less.[10] Many of these mothers are those with the highest levels of education. A 2007 survey of Harvard Business School alumni found that while men's rates of full-time employment never fell below 91 percent, only 81 percent of women who graduated in the early 2000s and 49 percent of women who graduated in the early 1990s were working full-time.[11] Of Yale alumni who had reached their forties by 2000, only 56 percent of the women remained in the workforce, compared with 90 percent of the men.[12] This exodus of highly educated women is a major contributor to the leadership gap.

While it's hard to predict how an individual will react to becoming a parent, it's easy to predict society's reaction. When a couple announces that they are having a baby, everyone says "Congratulations!" to the man and "Congratulations! What are you planning on doing about work?" to the woman. The broadly held assumption is that raising their child is her responsibility. In more than thirty years, this perception has changed very little. A survey of the Princeton class of 1975 found that 54 percent of the women foresaw work-family conflict compared to 26 percent of the men. The same survey of the Princeton class of 2006 found that 62 percent of the women anticipated work-family conflict compared to only 33 percent of the men. Three decades separate the studies and still nearly twice as many women as men enter the workforce anticipating this stumbling block. Even in 2006, 46 percent of the men who anticipated this conflict expected their spouse to step off her career track to raise their children. Only 5 percent of the women believed their spouse would alter his career to accommodate their child.[13]

Personal choices are not always as personal as they appear. We are all influenced by social conventions, peer pressure, and familial expectations. On top of these forces, women who can afford to drop out of the workplace often receive not just permission but encouragement to do so from all directions.

Imagine that a career is like a marathon—a long, grueling, and ultimately rewarding endeavor. Now imagine a marathon where both men and women arrive at the starting line equally fit and trained. The gun goes off. The men and women run side by side. The male marathoners are routinely cheered on: "Lookin' strong! On your way!" But the female runners hear a different message. "You know you don't have to do this!" the crowd shouts. Or "Good start—but you probably won't want to finish." The farther the marathoners run, the louder the cries grow for the men: "Keep going! You've got this!" But the women hear more and more doubts about their efforts. External voices, and often their own internal voice, repeatedly question their decision to keep running. The voices can even grow hostile. As the women struggle to endure the rigors of the race, spectators shout, "Why are you running when your children need you at home?"

Back in 1997, Debi Hemmeter was a rising executive at Sara Lee who aspired to someday lead a major corporation like her role model, Pepsi-Cola North America CEO Brenda Barnes. Even after starting a family, Debi continued to pursue her career at full speed. Then one day when Debi was on a business trip, she opened her hotel door to find *USA Today* with the startling headline "Pepsi Chief Trades Work for Family." The subhead elaborated: "22-Year Veteran Got Burned Out." In that moment, Debi said she felt her own ambitions shift. As Debi told me, "It seemed like if this extraordinary woman couldn't make it work, who could? Soon after, I was offered a big job at a bank and I turned it down because my daughter was just a year old and I didn't think I could do it. Almost a decade later, I took a similar job and did it well, but I lost a decade. I actually saved that clipping and still have it today. It's a reminder of what I don't want another generation to go through."

If a female marathoner can ignore the shouts of the crowd and get past the tough middle of the race, she will often hit her stride. Years ago, I met an investment banker in New York whose husband worked in public service. She told me that over the years all of her female friends in banking quit, but because she was her family's primary breadwinner, she had to stick it out. There were days when she was jealous and wished she could leave, days when there was just too much to do or too much crap to put up with. But she did not have that option. Eventually, she landed in a position that had less crap and more impact. Now when she looks back, she is glad that even in the hard times, she continued in her career. Today, she has a close relationship with her children and now that they have grown up and moved away, she's especially grateful to have a fulfilling job.

Although pundits and politicians, usually male, often claim that motherhood is the most important and difficult work of all, women who take time out of the workforce pay a big career penalty. Only 74 percent of professional women will rejoin the workforce in any capacity, and only 40 percent will return to full-time jobs.[14] Those who do rejoin will often see their earnings decrease dramatically. Controlling for education and hours worked, women's average annual earnings decrease by 20 percent if they are out of the workforce for just one year.[15] Average annual earnings decline by 30 percent after two to three years,[16] which is the average amount of time that professional women off-ramp from the workforce.[17] If society truly valued the work of caring for children, companies and institutions would find ways to reduce these steep penalties and help parents combine career and family responsibilities. All too often rigid work schedules, lack of paid family leave, and expensive or undependable child care derail women's best efforts. Governmental and company policies such as paid personal time off, affordable high-quality child care, and flexible work practices would serve families, and society, well.

One miscalculation that some women make is to drop out early in their careers because their salary barely covers the cost of child care. Child care is a huge expense, and it's frustrating to work hard just to break even. But professional women need to measure the cost of child care against their future salary rather than their current salary. Anna Fieler describes becoming a mom at thirty-two as "the time when the rubber hit the road." A rising star in marketing, Anna was concerned that her after-tax salary barely covered her child-care expenses. "With husbands often making more than wives, it seems like higher ROI to just invest in *his* career," she told me. But she thought about all the time and money she had already invested in *her* career and didn't see how walking away made economic sense either. So she made what she called "a leap of blind faith" and stayed in the workforce. Years later, her income is many times greater than when she almost withdrew. Wisely, Anna and other women have started to think of paying for child care as a way of investing in their families' future. As the years go by, compensation often increases. Flexibility typically increases, too, as senior leaders often have more control over their hours and schedules.

And what about men who want to leave the workforce? If we make it too easy for women to drop out of the career marathon, we also make it too hard for men. Just as women feel that they bear the primary responsibility of caring for their children, many men feel that they bear the primary responsibility of supporting their families financially. Their self-worth is tied mainly to their professional success, and they frequently believe that they have no choice but to finish that marathon.

Choosing to leave a child in someone else's care and return to work is a difficult decision. Any parent who has done this, myself included, knows how heart wrenching it can be. Only a compelling, challenging, and rewarding job will begin to make that choice a fair contest. And even after a choice is made, parents have every right to reassess along the way.

Anyone lucky enough to have options should keep them open. Don't enter the workforce already looking for the exit. Don't put on the brakes. Accelerate. Keep a foot on the gas pedal until a decision must be made. That's the only way to ensure that when that day comes, there will be a real decision to make.

8

Make Your Partner a Real Partner

BEING A MOTHER has been an amazing experience for me. Giving birth was not. After nine months of serious nausea, I could not wait to move on to the next phase. Unfortunately, my son was in no such rush. When my due date arrived, my OB decided I should be induced. My parents and my sister, Michelle, joined me and Dave at the hospital. Some say it takes a village to raise a child, but in my case, it took a village just to get the child out of me. My hours in labor went on . . . and on . . . and on. For my supporters, excitement gave way to boredom. At one point, I needed help through a contraction but couldn't get anyone's attention because they were all on the other side of the room, showing family photos to my doctor. It has been a running joke in my family that it's hard to hold anyone's attention for too long. Labor was no exception to that rule.

After three and half hours of pushing, my son finally emerged, weighing nine pounds, seven ounces. Half of that weight was in his head. My sister is a pediatrician and has attended hundreds of deliveries. She kindly did not tell me until much later that mine was one of the hardest she had ever witnessed. It was all worth it when my son was pronounced healthy and the nausea that I had felt for nine straight months vanished within an hour. The worst was over.

The next morning, I got out of bed in my hospital room, took one step, and fell to the floor. Apparently I had yanked my leg back so hard during labor that I had pulled a tendon. I was on crutches for a week. Being unable to stand added a degree of difficulty to my first week of motherhood but also provided one unforeseen benefit: Dave became the primary caregiver for our newborn. Dave had to get up when the baby cried, bring him to me to be fed, change him, and then get him back to sleep. Normally, the mother becomes the instant baby-care expert. In our case, Dave taught me how to change a diaper when our son was eight days old. If Dave and I had planned this, we would have been geniuses. But we didn't and we aren't.

In fact, we should have planned a lot more. When I was six months pregnant, a Ph.D. candidate interviewed me by phone for her dissertation on working couples. She began by asking, "How do you do it all?" I said, "I don't. I don't even have a child," and suggested that she interview someone who actually did. She said, "You're just a few months away from having a baby, so surely you and your husband have thought about who is going to pick up your child if he is sick at school? Who is going to arrange for child care?" And so on. I couldn't answer a single one of her questions. By the end of the call, I was in full panic, overwhelmed by how truly unprepared Dave and I were to handle these responsibilities. As soon as Dave walked in the door that night, I pounced. "Ohmigod!" I said. "We are just a few months away from having a baby, and we have never talked about any of this!" Dave looked at me like I was crazy. "What?" he said. "This is *all* we talk about."

In dissecting this discrepancy, Dave and I figured out that we had spent a lot of time talking about how we would do things, but almost always in the abstract. So Dave was right that we had discussed parenthood often, and I was right that the discussion had not been that practical. Part of the problem was that our inexperience made it hard even to know what specifics to cover. We had very little idea what we were in for.

I also think that we were in denial about the tremendous shift in our lives that was rapidly approaching. Dave and I were not even working in the same city when I got pregnant (although just to be clear, we were in the same place when I *got* pregnant). Dave had founded a company, Launch Media, in L.A. and sold it to Yahoo years earlier. Yahoo's headquarters were in Northern California, where I lived and worked, but Dave's team remained in Los Angeles, where he lived and worked. When we started dating, we decided to base our life together in the Bay Area, so Dave began commuting, typically spending Monday through Thursday in Southern California and then flying north to spend weekends with me. This pattern continued even after we were married.

After the birth of our son, Dave began flying back and forth several times a week. It was great that we had the ability for him to commute, but it was far from ideal. Even though he was making an exhausting effort to be with me and our baby, he was still gone a lot. Since I was with the baby full-time, the great majority of child care fell to me. The division of labor felt uneven and strained our marriage. We hired a nanny, but she couldn't solve all our problems; the emotional support and shared experience that a spouse provides cannot be bought. After a few short months of parenthood, we had already fallen into traditional, lopsided gender roles.

We were not unique. In the last thirty years, women have made more progress in the workforce than in the home. According to the most recent analysis, when a husband and wife both are employed full-time, the mother does 40 percent more child care and about 30 percent more housework than the father.[1] A 2009 survey found that only 9 percent of people in dual-earner marriages said that they shared housework, child care, and breadwinning evenly.[2] So while men are taking on more household responsibilities, this increase is happening very slowly, and we are still far from parity.[3] (Perhaps unsurprisingly, same-sex couples divide household tasks much more evenly.)[4]

Public policy reinforces this gender bias. The U.S. Census Bureau considers mothers the "designated parent," even when both parents are present in the home.[5] When mothers care for their children, it's "parenting," but when fathers care for their children, the government deems it a "child care arrangement."[6] I have even heard a few men say that they are heading home to "babysit" for their children. I have never heard a woman refer to taking care of her own children as "babysitting." A friend of mine ran a team-building exercise during a company retreat where people were asked to fill in their hobbies. Half of the men in the group listed "their children" as hobbies. *A hobby?* For most mothers, kids are not a hobby. Showering is a hobby.

My friends Katie and Scott Mitic flip this pattern. Katie and Scott are both Silicon Valley entrepreneurs who work full-time. About a year ago, Scott traveled to the East Coast for work. He was starting a late-morning meeting when his phone rang. His team only heard one side of the conversation. "A sandwich, carrot sticks, a cut-up apple, pretzels, and a cookie," Scott said. He hung up smiling and explained that his wife was asking what she should put in the kids' lunch boxes. Everyone laughed. A few months later, Scott was back east with the same work colleagues. They were in a cab late that morning when Scott's phone rang. His team listened in disbelief as he patiently repeated the lunch list all over again: "A sandwich, carrot sticks, a cut-up apple, pretzels, and a cookie."

When Scott tells this story, it's sweet and funny. But take this same story and switch the genders and it loses its charm. That's just reality for most couples. Scott and Katie buck expectations with their division of household duties. There's an epilogue to their story. Scott went on a third trip and discovered that Katie forgot to make the kids' lunches altogether. She realized her slipup midmorning and solved the problem by having a pizza delivered to the school cafeteria. Their kids were thrilled, but Scott was not. Now when he travels, he packs lunches in advance and leaves notes with specific instructions for his wife.

There may be an evolutionary basis for one parent knowing better what to put in a child's lunch. Women who breast-feed are arguably baby's first lunch box. But even if mothers are more naturally inclined toward nurturing, fathers can match that skill with knowledge and effort. If women want to succeed more at work and if men want to succeed more at home, these expectations have to be challenged. As Gloria Steinem once observed, "It's not about biology, but about consciousness."[7]

We overcome biology with consciousness in other areas. For example, storing large amounts of fat was necessary to survive when food was scarce, so we evolved to crave it and consume it when it's available. But in this era of plenty, we no longer need large amounts of fuel in reserve, so instead of simply giving in to this inclination, we exercise and limit caloric intake. We use willpower to combat biology, or at least we try. So even if "mother knows best" *is* rooted in biology, it need not be written in stone. A willing mother and a willing father are all it requires. Yes, someone needs to remember what goes into the lunch box, but as Katie will attest, it does not have to be Mom.

As women must be more empowered at work, men must

be more empowered at home. I have seen so many women inadvertently discourage their husbands from doing their share by being too controlling or critical. Social scientists call this "maternal gatekeeping," which is a fancy term for "Ohmigod, that's not the way you do it! Just move aside and let me!"[8] When it comes to children, fathers often take their cues from mothers. This gives a mother great power to encourage or impede the father's involvement. If she acts as a gatekeeper mother and is reluctant to hand over responsibility or, worse, questions the father's efforts, he does less.

Whenever a married woman asks me for advice on co-parenting with a husband, I tell her to let him put the diaper on the baby any way he wants as long as he's doing it himself. And if he gets up to deal with the diaper before being asked, she should smile even if he puts that diaper on the baby's head. Over time, if he does things his way, he'll find the correct end. But if he's forced to do things *her* way, pretty soon she'll be doing them herself.

Anyone who wants her mate to be a true partner must treat him as an equal—and equally capable—partner. And if that's not reason enough, bear in mind that a study found that wives who engage in gatekeeping behaviors do five more hours of family work per week than wives who take a more collaborative approach.[9]

Another common and counterproductive dynamic occurs when women assign or suggest tasks to their partners. She is delegating, and that's a step in the right direction. But sharing responsibility should mean sharing responsibility. Each partner needs to be in charge of specific activities or it becomes too easy for one to feel like he's doing a favor instead of doing his part.

Like many pieces of advice, letting a partner take responsibility and do his share in his own way is easy to say and hard to do. My brother, David, and sister-in-law, Amy, were very aware of this tension when they first became parents. "There were many times when our daughter was more easily consoled by me," Amy said. "It's really hard to listen to your baby cry while your struggling husband with no breasts tries desperately and sometimes awkwardly to comfort her. David was insistent that rather than handing the baby to me when she was crying, we allow him to comfort her even if it took longer. It was harder in the short run, but it absolutely paid off when our daughter learned that Daddy could take care of her as well as Mommy."

I truly believe that the single most important career decision that a woman makes is whether she will have a life partner and who that partner is. I don't know of one woman in a leadership position whose life partner is not fully—and I mean fully—supportive of her career. No exceptions. And contrary to the popular notion that only unmarried women can make it to the top, the majority of the most successful female business leaders have partners. Of the twenty-eight women who have served as CEOs of Fortune 500 companies, twenty-six were married, one was divorced, and only one had never married.[10] Many of these CEOs said they "could not have succeeded without the support of their husbands, helping with the children, the household chores, and showing a willingness to move."[11]

Not surprisingly, a lack of spousal support can have the opposite effect on a career. In a 2007 study of well-educated professional women who had left the paid work-force, 60 percent cited their husbands as a critical factor in their decision.[12] These women specifically listed their husbands' lack of participation in child care and other domestic tasks and the expectation that wives should be the ones to cut back on employment as reasons for quitting. No wonder when asked at a conference what men could do to help advance women's leadership, Harvard Business School professor Rosabeth Moss Kanter answered, "The laundry."[13] Tasks like laundry, food shopping, cleaning, and cooking are mundane and mandatory. Typically, these tasks fall to women.

In January 2012, I received a letter from Ruth Chang, a doctor with two young children who had seen my TED Talk. She had been offered a new job overseeing seventy-five doctors in five medical clinics. Her first instinct was to say no out of concern that she could not handle the expanded responsibility in addition to taking care of her family. But then she wavered, and in that moment, Dr. Chang wrote me, "I heard your voice saying, 'Sit at the table' and I knew I had to accept the promotion. So that evening, I told my husband I was taking the job . . . and then handed him the grocery list." Sharing the burden of the mundane can make all the difference.

My career and marriage are inextricably intertwined. During that first year Dave and I were parents, it became clear that balancing two careers and two cities was not adding up to one happy family. We needed to make some changes. But what? I loved my job at Google and he felt enormously loyal to his team in L.A. We struggled through the commuting for another long year of marital less-than-bliss. By then, Dave was ready to leave Yahoo. He limited his job search to the San Francisco area, which was a sacrifice on his part, since more of his professional interests and contacts were in L.A. He eventually became CEO of SurveyMonkey and was able to move the company headquarters from Portland to the Bay Area.

Once we were in the same city, it still took us some time to figure out how to coordinate our work schedules. Even though Dave and I are extraordinarily fortunate and can afford exceptional child care, there are still difficult and painful decisions about how much time our jobs require us to be away from our family and who will pick up the slack. We sit down at the beginning of every week and figure out which one of us will drive our children to school each day. We both try to be home for dinner as many nights as we can. (At dinner, we go around the table and share the best and worst event from our day; I refrain from saying so, but my best is usually being home for dinner in the first place.) If one of us is scheduled to be away, the other almost always arranges to be home. On weekends, I try to focus completely on my kids (although I have been known to sneak off a few e-mails from the bathroom of the local soccer field).

Like all marriages, ours is a work in progress. Dave and I have had our share of bumps on our path to achieving a roughly fifty-fifty split. After a lot of effort and seemingly endless discussion, we are partners not just in what we do, but in who is in charge. Each of us makes sure that things that need to get done do indeed get done. Our division of household chores is actually pretty traditional. Dave pays bills, handles our finances, provides tech support. I schedule the kids' activities, make sure there is food in the fridge, plan the birthday parties. Sometimes I'm bothered by this classic gender division of labor. Am I perpetuating stereotypes by falling into these patterns? But I would rather plan a Dora the Explorer party than pay an insurance bill, and since Dave feels the exact opposite, this arrangement works for us. It takes continual communication, honesty, and a lot of forgiveness to maintain a rickety balance. We are never at fifty-fifty at any given moment—perfect equality is hard to define or sustain—but we allow the pendulum to swing back and forth between us.

In the coming years, our balancing act may get harder. Our children are still young and go to sleep early, which gives me plenty of time to work at night and even to watch what Dave considers to be truly bad TV. As the kids get older, we will have to adjust. Many of my friends have told me that teenage children require more time from their parents. Every stage of life has its challenges. Fortunately,

I have Dave to figure it out with me. He's the best partner I could imagine—even though he's wrong about my TV shows being bad.

Having a true partner like Dave is still far too rare. While we expect women to be nurturing, we don't have the same expectations of men. My brother, David, once told me about a colleague who bragged about playing soccer the afternoon that his first child was born. To David's credit, instead of nodding and smiling, he spoke up and explained that he didn't think that was either cool or impressive. This opinion needs to be voiced loudly and repeatedly on soccer fields, in workplaces, and in homes.

My brother had a wonderful role model in my father, who was an engaged and active parent. Like most men of his generation, my father did very little domestic work, but unlike most men of his generation, he was happy to change diapers and give baths. He was home for dinner every night, since his ophthalmology practice required no travel and involved few emergencies. He coached my brother's and sister's sports teams (and would have happily coached mine if I had been the slightest bit coordinated). He helped me with my homework regularly and was my most enthusiastic fan when I participated in oratory contests.

Studies from around the world have concluded that children benefit greatly from paternal involvement. Research over the last forty years has consistently found that in comparison to children with less-involved fathers, children with involved and loving fathers have higher levels of psychological well-being and better cognitive abilities.[14] When fathers provide even just routine child care, children have higher levels of educational and economic achievement and lower delinquency rates.[15] Their children even tend to be more empathetic and socially competent.[16] These findings hold true for children from all socioeconomic backgrounds, whether or not the mother is highly involved.

We all need to encourage men to lean in to their families. Unfortunately, traditional gender roles are reinforced not just by individuals, but also by employment policies. Most companies in the United States offer more time off for maternity than paternity leave, and men take far fewer extended breaks from work for family reasons.[17] Our laws support this double standard. In the United States, only five states provide any income replacement for the care of a new baby (which is a large problem in and of itself). In three of these states, this benefit is only offered to mothers and is characterized as a pregnancy disability benefit. Only two states offer a paid family leave benefit that fathers can use.[18] In general, fathers do not take much time off for a new child; a survey of fathers in the corporate sector found that the vast majority took off one week or less when their partners gave birth, hardly enough time to start out as an equal parent.[19] I'm proud that even before I arrived, Facebook offered equal time for maternity and paternity leave.

When family-friendly benefits like paternity leave or reduced work hours are offered, both male and female employees often worry that if they take advantage of these programs, they will be seen as uncommitted to their jobs.

And for good reason. Employees who use these benefits often face steep penalties ranging from substantial pay cuts to lost promotions to marginalization.[20] Both men and women can be penalized at work for prioritizing family, but men may pay an even higher price.[21] When male employees take a leave of absence or just leave work early to care for a sick child, they can face negative consequences that range from being teased to receiving lower performance ratings to reducing their chance for a raise or promotion.[22]

Fathers who want to drop out of the workforce entirely and devote themselves to child care can face extremely negative social pressure. Currently, fathers make up less than 4 percent of parents who work full-time inside the home, and many report that it can be very isolating.[23] My friend Peter Noone spent several years as a stay-at-home father and found that while people claimed to respect his choice, he did not feel welcomed into the social circles in his neighborhood. As a man at the playground or in the not-so-tactfully-named "Mommy and Me" classes, strangers viewed him with a certain amount of distrust. The friendly and easy connections that the women made were not extended to him.[24] Time and again, he was reminded that he was outside the norm.

Gender-specific expectations remain self-fulfilling. The belief that mothers are more committed to family than to work penalizes women because employers assume they won't live up to expectations of professional dedication. The reverse is true for men, who are expected to put their careers first. We judge men primarily by their professional success and send them a clear message that personal achievements are insufficient for them to be valued or feel fulfilled. This mind-set leads to a grown man bragging on the soccer field that he left his postpartum wife and newborn at the hospital to go kick a ball.

Making gender matters even worse, men's success is viewed not just in absolute terms, but often in comparison to their wives'. The image of a happy couple still includes a husband who is more professionally successful than the wife. If the reverse occurs, it's perceived as threatening to the marriage. People frequently pull me aside to ask sympathetically, "How *is* Dave? Is he okay with, you know, all your [*whispering*] *success*?" Dave is far more self-confident than I am, and given his own professional success, these comments are easy for him to brush off. More and more men will have to do the same, since almost 30 percent of U.S. working wives now outearn their husbands.[25] As that number continues to grow, I hope the whispering stops.

Dave and I can laugh off concerns about his supposedly fragile ego, but for many women, this is no laughing matter. Women face enough barriers to professional success. If they also have to worry that they will upset their husbands by succeeding, how can we hope to live in an equal world?

When looking for a life partner, my advice to women is date all of them: the bad boys, the cool boys, the commitment-phobic boys, the crazy boys. But do not marry them. The things that make the bad boys sexy do not make them good husbands. When it comes time to settle down, find someone who wants an equal partner. Someone who thinks women should be smart, opinionated, and ambitious. Someone who values fairness and expects or, even better, *wants* to do his share in the home. These men exist and, trust me, over time, nothing is sexier. (If you don't believe me, check out a fabulous little book called *Porn for Women*. One page shows a man cleaning a kitchen while insisting, "I like to get to these things before I have to be asked." Another man gets out of bed in the middle of the night, wondering, "Is that the baby? I'll get her.")[26]

Kristina Salen, the CFO of Etsy, told me that when she was dating, she wanted to see how much a boyfriend would support her career, so she devised a test. She would break a date at the last minute claiming there was a professional conflict and see how the guy would react. If he understood and simply rescheduled, she would go out with him again. When Kristina wanted to take a relationship to the next level, she gave him another test. While working in emerging markets in the late 1990s, she would invite the guy to visit her for the weekend . . . in São Paulo. It was a great way to find out if he was willing to fit his schedule around hers. The trials paid off. She found her Mr. Right and they have been happily married for fourteen years. Not only is her husband, Daniel, completely supportive of her career, he's also the primary caregiver for their two children.

Even after finding the right guy—or gal—no one comes fully formed. I learned from my mother to be careful about role definition in the beginning of a relationship. Even though my mother did most of the household work, my father always vacuumed the floor after dinner. She never had to persuade him to do this chore; it was simply his job from day one. At the start of a romance, it's tempting for a woman to show a more classic "girlfriendy" side by volunteering to cook meals and take care of errands. And, suddenly, we're back in 1955. If a relationship begins in an unequal place, it is likely to get more unbalanced when and if children are added to the equation. Instead, use the beginning of a relationship to establish the division of labor, just as Nora Ephron's dialogue in *When Harry Met Sally* reminds us:

> HARRY: You take someone to the airport, it's clearly the beginning of the relationship. That's why I have never taken anyone to the airport at the beginning of a relationship.
>
> SALLY: Why?
>
> HARRY: Because eventually things move on and you don't take someone to the airport and I never wanted anyone to say to me, "How come you never take me to the airport anymore?"

If you want a fifty-fifty partnership, establish that pattern at the outset. A few years ago, Mark Zuckerberg and his partner, now wife, Priscilla Chan, made a donation to improve the Newark, New Jersey, public school system and needed someone to run their foundation. I recommended Jen Holleran, who had deep knowledge and experience in school reform. She also had fourteen-month-old twins and had cut her hours by two-thirds since their birth. Her husband, Andy, is a child psychiatrist who was involved with raising the kids when he was home. But once Jen had reduced her workload, she ended up being responsible for all of the household work, including running errands, paying bills, cooking, and scheduling. When the offer came from Mark and Priscilla, Jen wasn't sure she was ready to upset the current order by committing to a full-time job with frequent travel. I urged her to set up the relationship dynamic she wanted sooner rather than later. Jen remembers my suggesting, "If you want an equal partnership, you should start now."

Jen and Andy discussed the opportunity and decided she should take the job because of the impact she could have. And who would pick up the slack? Andy would. He rearranged his work so he could be home with the boys each morning and night, and even more when Jen travels. He now pays all the bills and squeezes in grocery runs as much as she does. He cooks and cleans more, knows the details of the schedule, and is happy to be the number one, in-demand parent for half the week. A year and a half into this new arrangement, Andy told me that he loves his time alone with their boys and the increased role that he has in their lives. Jen loves her job and is glad that she and her husband now have a more equal marriage. "My time is now as valuable as his," she told me. "As a result, we are happier."

Research supports Jen's observation that equality between partners leads to happier relationships. When husbands do more housework, wives are less depressed, marital conflicts decrease, and satisfaction rises.[27] When women work outside the home and share breadwinning duties, couples are more likely to stay together. In fact, the risk of divorce reduces by about half when a wife earns half the income and a husband does half the housework.[28] For men, participating in child rearing fosters the development of patience, empathy, and adaptability, characteristics that benefit all of their relationships.[29] For women, earning money increases their decision-making ability in the home, protects them in case of divorce, and can be important security in later years, as women often outlive their husbands.[30] Also—and many might find this the most motivating factor—couples who share domestic responsibilities have more sex.[31] It may be counterintuitive, but the best way for a man to make a pass at his wife might be to do the dishes.

I also feel strongly that when a mother stays at home, her time during the day should still be considered real work—because it is. Raising children is at least as stressful and demanding as a paying job. It is unfair that mothers are frequently expected to work long into the night while fathers who work outside the home get the chance to relax from their day jobs. When the father is home, he should take on half the child care and housework. Also, most employed fathers interact with other grown-ups all day, while mothers at home are often starved for adult conversation by evening. I know a woman who gave up a career as a lawyer to be a stay-at-home mom and always insisted that when her husband, a TV writer, got home from work, he asked her, "How was your day?" before he launched into an account of his own.

True partnership in our homes does more than just benefit couples today; it also sets the stage for the next generation. The workplace has evolved more than the home in part because we enter it as adults, so each generation experiences a new dynamic. But the homes we create tend to be more rooted in our childhoods. My generation grew up watching our mothers do the child care and housework while our fathers earned the wages. It's too easy for us to get stuck in these patterns. It is no surprise that married and cohabitating men whose mothers were employed while they were growing up do more housework as adults than other men.[32] The sooner we break the cycle, the faster we will reach greater equality.

One of the reasons Dave is a true partner is because he grew up in a home where his father set an extraordinary example. Sadly, Dave's father, Mel, passed away before I had a chance to meet him, but he clearly was a man way ahead of his time. Mel's mother worked side by side with her husband running the family's small grocery store, so Mel grew up accepting women as equals, which was unusual in those days. As a single man, he became interested in the women's movement and read Betty Friedan's *The Feminine Mystique*. He was the one who introduced his wife (and Dave's mother), Paula, to this feminist wake-up call in the 1960s. He encouraged Paula to set up and lead PACER, a national nonprofit to help children with disabilities. A law professor,

Mel often taught classes at night. Since he wanted the family to have at least one meal together each day, he decided it would be breakfast and prepared the meal himself, complete with fresh-squeezed orange juice.

A more equal division of labor between parents will model better behavior for the next generation. I have heard so many women say that they wished their partners helped more with child care, but since it's only a few more years until their kids are off to school, it's not worth the battle to change the dynamic. In my opinion, it is always worth the battle to change an undesirable dynamic. I also worry that these women will face the same dynamic when it comes time to care for aging parents. Women provide more than twice as much care not only for their own parents, but for their in-laws as well.[33] This is an additional burden that needs to be shared. And children need to see it being shared so that their generation will follow that example.

In 2012, Gloria Steinem sat down in her home for an interview with Oprah Winfrey. Gloria reiterated that progress for women in the home has trailed progress in the workplace, explaining, "Now we know that women can do what men can do, but we don't know that men can do what women can do."[34] I believe they can and we should give them more chances to prove it.

This revolution will happen one family at a time. The good news is that men in younger generations appear more eager to be real partners than men in previous generations. A survey that asked participants to rate the importance of various job characteristics found that men in their forties most frequently selected "work which challenges me" as very important, while men in their twenties and thirties most frequently selected having a job with a schedule that "allows me to spend time with my family."[35] If these trends hold as this group ages, it could signal a promising shift.

Wonderful, sensitive men of all ages are out there. And the more women value kindness and support in their boyfriends, the more men will demonstrate it. Kristina Salen, my friend who devised the tests to screen her dates, told me that her son insists that when he grows up, he wants to take care of his children "like Daddy does." She and her husband were thrilled to hear this. More boys need that role model and that choice. As more women lean in to their careers, more men need to lean in to their families. We need to encourage men to be more ambitious in their homes.

We need more men to sit at the table . . . the kitchen table.

9

The Myth of Doing It All

HAVING IT ALL." Perhaps the greatest trap ever set for women was the coining of this phrase. Bandied about in speeches, headlines, and articles, these three little words are intended to be aspirational but instead make all of us feel like we have fallen short. I have never met a woman, or man, who has stated emphatically, "Yes, I have it all." Because no matter what any of us has—and how grateful we are for what we have—no one has it all.

Nor can we. The very concept of having it all flies in the face of the basic laws of economics and common sense. As Sharon Poczter, professor of economics at Cornell, explains, "The antiquated rhetoric of 'having it all' disregards the basis of every economic relationship: the idea of trade-offs. All of us are dealing with the constrained optimization that is life, attempting to maximize our utility based on parameters like career, kids, relationships, etc., doing our best to allocate the resource of time. Due to the scarcity of this resource, therefore, none of us can 'have it all,' and those who claim to are most likely lying."[1]

"Having it all" is best regarded as a myth. And like many myths, it can deliver a helpful cautionary message. Think of Icarus, who soared to great heights with his man-made wings. His father warned him not to fly too near the sun, but Icarus ignored the advice. He soared even higher, his wings melted, and he crashed to earth. Pursuing both a professional and personal life is a noble and attainable goal, up to a point. Women should learn from Icarus to aim for the sky, but keep in mind that we all have real limits.

Instead of pondering the question "Can we have it all?," we should be asking the more practical question "Can we do it all?" And again, the answer is no. Each of us makes choices constantly between work and family, exercising and relaxing, making time for others and taking time for ourselves. Being a parent means making adjustments, compromises, and sacrifices every day. For most people, sacrifices and hardships are not a choice, but a necessity. About 65 percent of married-couple families with children in the United States have two parents in the workforce, with almost all relying on both incomes to support their household.[2] Being a single working parent can be even more difficult. About 30 percent of families with children are led by a single parent, with 84 percent of those led by a woman.[3]

Mothers who work outside the home are constantly reminded of these challenges. Tina Fey noted that when she was promoting the movie *Date Night* with Steve Carell, a father of two and star of his own sitcom, reporters would grill Fey on how she balances her life, but never posed that question to her male costar. As she wrote in *Bossypants*, "What is the rudest question you can ask a woman? 'How old are you?' 'What do you weigh?' 'When you and your twin sister are alone with Mr. Hefner, do you have to pretend to be lesbians?' No, the worst question is 'How do you juggle it all?' . . . People constantly ask me, with an accusatory look in their eyes. 'You're fucking it *all* up, aren't you?' their eyes say."[4]

Fey nails it. Employed mothers and fathers both struggle with multiple responsibilities, but mothers also have to endure the rude questions and accusatory looks that remind us that we're shortchanging both our jobs *and* our children. As if we needed reminding. Like me, most of the women I know do a great job worrying that we don't measure up. We compare our efforts at work to those of our colleagues, usually men, who typically have far fewer responsibilities at home. Then we compare our efforts at home to those of mothers who dedicate themselves solely to their families. Outside observers reminding us that we must be struggling—and *failing*—is just bitter icing on an already soggy cake.

Trying to do it all and expecting that it all can be done exactly right is a recipe for disappointment. Perfection is the enemy. Gloria Steinem said it best: "You can't do it all. No one can have two full-time jobs, have perfect children and cook three meals and be multi-orgasmic 'til dawn. . . . Superwoman is the adversary of the women's movement."[5]

Dr. Laurie Glimcher, dean of Weill Cornell Medical College, said the key for her in pursuing her career while raising children was learning where to focus her attention. "I had to decide what mattered and what didn't and I learned to be a perfectionist in only the things that mattered." In her case, she concluded that scientific data had to be perfect, but reviews and other mundane administrative tasks could be considered good enough at 95 percent. Dr. Glimcher also said she made it a priority to get home at a reasonable hour, adding that when she got there, she refused to worry about whether "the linens were folded or the closets were tidy. You can't be obsessive about these things that don't matter."[6]

A few years before I became a mother, I spoke on a women's panel for a local business group in Palo Alto. One of the other panelists, an executive with two children, was asked the (inevitable) question about how she balances her work and her children. She started her response by saying, "I probably shouldn't admit this publicly . . . ," and then she confessed that she put her children to sleep in their school clothes to save fifteen precious minutes every morning. At the time, I thought to myself, *Yup, she should not have admitted that publicly.*

Now that I'm a parent, I think this woman was a genius. We all face limits of time and patience. I have not yet put my children to sleep in their school clothes, but there are mornings when I wish I had. I also know that all the planning in the world cannot prepare us for the constant challenges of parenting. In hindsight, I appreciate my fellow panelist's candor. And in the spirit of that candor, I probably shouldn't admit this publicly either . . .

Last year, I was traveling with my children to a business conference. Several other Silicon Valley folks were attending too, and John Donahoe, the CEO of eBay, kindly offered us a ride on the eBay plane. When the flight was delayed for several hours, my main concern was keeping my kids occupied so they would not disturb the other adult passengers. I made it through the delay by allowing them to watch endless TV and eat endless snacks. Then just as the flight finally took off, my daughter started scratching her head. "Mommy! My head itches!" she announced loudly, speaking over the headset she was wearing (as she watched even *more* TV). I didn't think anything of it until her itching grew frantic and her complaints grew louder. I urged her to lower her voice, then examined her head and noticed small white *things*. I was pretty sure I knew what they were. I was the only person bringing young children on this corporate plane—and now my daughter most likely had *lice*! I spent the rest of the flight in a complete panic, trying to keep her isolated, her voice down, and her hands out of her hair, while I furiously scanned the web for pictures of lice. When we landed, everyone piled into rental cars to caravan to the conference hotel, but I told them to go ahead without me; I just needed to "pick something up." I dashed to the nearest pharmacy, where they confirmed my diagnosis. Fortunately, we had avoided direct contact with anyone else on the plane, so there was no way for the lice to have spread, which saved me from the fatal embarrassment of having to tell the group to check their own heads. We grabbed the shampoo that I needed to treat her and, as it turned out, her brother—and spent the night in a marathon hair-washing session. I missed the opening-night dinner, and when asked why, I said my kids were tired. Frankly, I was too. And even though I managed to escape the lice, I could not stop scratching my head for several days.

It is impossible to control all the variables when it comes to parenting. For women who have achieved previous success by planning ahead and pushing themselves hard, this chaos can be difficult to accept. Psychologist Jennifer Stuart studied a group of Yale graduates and concluded that for such women, "the effort to combine career and motherhood may be particularly fraught. The stakes are high, as they may expect nothing less than perfection, both at home and in the workplace. When they fall short of lofty ideals, they may retreat altogether—from workplace to home or vice versa."[7]

Another one of my favorite posters at Facebook declares in big red letters, "Done is better than perfect." I have tried to embrace this motto and let go of unattainable standards. Aiming for perfection causes frustration at best and paralysis at worst. I agree completely with the advice offered by Nora Ephron in her 1996 Wellesley commencement speech when she addressed the issue of women having both a career and family. Ephron insisted, "It will be a little messy, but embrace the mess. It will be complicated, but rejoice in the complications. It will not be anything like what you think it will be like, but surprises are good for you. And don't be frightened: you can always change your mind. I know: I've had four careers and three husbands."[8]

I was extremely fortunate that early in my career I was warned about the perils of trying to do it all by someone I deeply admired. Larry Kanarek managed the Washington, D.C., office of McKinsey & Company where I interned in 1994. One day, Larry gathered everyone together for a talk. He explained that since he was running the office, employees came to him when they wanted to quit. Over time, he noticed that people quit for one reason only: they were burnt out, tired of working long hours and traveling. Larry said he could understand the complaint, but what he could not understand was that all the people who quit—every single one—had unused vacation time. Up until the day they left, they did everything McKinsey asked of them before deciding that it was too much.

Larry implored us to exert more control over our careers. He said McKinsey would never stop making demands on our time, so it was up to us to decide what we were willing to do. It was our responsibility to draw the line. We needed to determine how many hours we were willing to work in a day and how many nights we were willing to travel. If later on, the job did not work out, we would know that we had tried on our own terms. Counterintuitively, long-term success at work often depends on *not* trying to meet every demand placed on us. The best way to make room for both life and career is to make choices deliberately—to set limits and stick to them.

During my first four years at Google, I was in the office from 7:00 a.m. to 7:00 p.m. every day at a minimum. I ran the global operations teams and thought it was critical that I stay on top of as many details as possible. No one ever demanded that I work this schedule; typical of Silicon Valley, Google was not the type of place to set hours for anyone. Still, the culture in those early days promoted working around the clock. When my son arrived, I wanted to take the three months of maternity leave Google offered, but I worried that my job would not be there when I returned. Events leading up to his birth did not put my mind at ease. Google was growing quickly and reorganizing frequently. My team was one of the largest in the company, and coworkers often suggested ways to restructure, which usually meant that they would do more and I would do less. In the months before my leave, several colleagues, all men, ramped up these efforts, volunteering to "help run things" while I was gone. Some of them even mentioned to my boss that I might not return, so it made sense to start sharing my responsibilities immediately.

I tried to take Larry Kanarek's advice and draw my own line. I decided that I wanted to focus entirely on my new role as a mother. I was determined to truly unplug. I even made this decision public—a trick that can help a commitment stick by creating greater accountability. I announced that I was going to take the full three months off.

No one believed me. A group of my colleagues bet on how long I would be off e-mail after giving birth, with not a single person taking "more than one week" as his or her wager. I would have been offended, except they knew me better than I knew myself. I was back on e-mail from my hospital room the day after giving birth.

Over the next three months, I was unable to unplug much at all. I checked e-mail constantly. I organized meetings in my living room, during which I sometimes breast-fed and probably freaked several people out. (I tried to set these gatherings for times when my son would be sleeping, but babies make their own schedules.) I went into the office for key meetings, baby in tow. And while I had some nice moments with my son, I look back on that maternity leave as a pretty unhappy time. Being a new mother was exhausting, and when my son slept, I worked instead of resting. And the only thing worse than *everyone* knowing that I was not sticking to my original commitment was that *I* knew it too. I was letting myself down.

Three months later, my non-leave maternity leave ended. I was returning to a job I loved, but as I pulled the car out of the driveway to head to the office for my first full day back, I felt a tightness in my chest and tears started to flow down my cheeks. Even though I had worked throughout my "time off," I had done so almost entirely from home with my son right next to me. Going back to the office meant a dramatic change in the amount of time I would see him. If I returned to my typical twelve-hour days, I would leave the house before he woke up and return after he was asleep. In order to spend any time with him at all, I was going to have to make changes . . . and stick to them.

I started arriving at work around 9:00 a.m. and leaving at

5:30 p.m. This schedule allowed me to nurse my son before I left and get home in time to nurse again before putting him to sleep. I was scared that I would lose credibility, or even my entire job, if anyone knew that these were my new in-the-office hours. To compensate, I started checking e-mails around 5:00 a.m. Yup, I was awake *before* my newborn. Then once he was down at night, I would jump back on my computer and continue my workday. I went to great lengths to hide my new schedule from most people. Camille, my ingenious executive assistant, came up with the idea of holding my first and last meetings of the day in other buildings to make it less transparent when I was actually arriving or departing. When I did leave directly from my office, I would pause in the lobby and survey the parking lot to find a colleague-free moment to bolt to my car. (Given my awkwardness, we should all be relieved that I once worked for the Treasury Department and not the CIA.)

Looking back, I realize that my concern over my new hours stemmed from my own insecurity. Google was hard charging and hypercompetitive, but it also supported combining work and parenthood—an attitude that clearly started at the top. Larry and Sergey came to my baby shower and each gave me a certificate that entitled me to one hour of babysitting. (I never used the certificates, and if I could find them, I bet I could auction them off for charity, like lunch with Warren Buffett.) Susan Wojcicki, who blazed a trail by having four children while being one of Google's earliest and most valuable employees, brought her children to the office when her babysitter was sick. Both my boss, Omid, and David Fischer, the most senior leader on my team, were steadfast supporters and did not allow others to take over parts of my job.

Slowly, it began to dawn on me that my job did not really require that I spend twelve full hours a day in the office. I became much more efficient—more vigilant about only attending or setting up meetings that were truly necessary, more determined to maximize my output during every minute I spent away from home. I also started paying more attention to the working hours of those around me; cutting unnecessary meetings saved time for them as well. I tried to focus on what really mattered. Long before I saw the poster, I began to adopt the mantra "Done is better than perfect." Done, while still a challenge, turns out to be far more achievable and often a relief. By the time I took my second maternity leave, I not only unplugged (mostly), but really enjoyed the time with both my children.

My sister-in-law, Amy, a doctor, experienced almost the exact same evolution in attitude. "When I had my first child, I worked twelve-hour days while trying to pump at work," she told me. "I wanted to feel connected to my baby in the limited hours that I was home, so I made myself her sole caregiver many nights. I believed that others were demanding this of me—my bosses at work and my daughter at home. But in truth, I was torturing myself." With the birth of her second child, Amy adjusted her behavior. "I took three months off and handled my return to work in my own way, on my own terms. And despite what I had previously feared, my reputation and productivity weren't hurt a bit."

I deeply understand the fear of appearing to be putting our families above our careers. Mothers don't want to be perceived as less dedicated to their jobs than men or women without family responsibilities. We overwork to overcompensate. Even in workplaces that offer reduced or flextime arrangements, people fear that reducing their hours will jeopardize their career prospects.[9] And this is not just a perception problem. Employees who make use of flexible work policies are often penalized and seen as less committed than their peers.[10] And those penalties can be greater for mothers in professional jobs.[11] This all needs to change, especially since new evidence suggests working from home might actually be more productive in certain cases.[12]

It is difficult to distinguish between the aspects of a job that are truly necessary and those that are not. Sometimes the situation is hard to read and the lines are hard to draw. Amy told me about a conference dinner she attended with a group of fellow physicians, including one who had given birth to her first child several weeks earlier. About two hours into the meal, the new mom was looking uncomfortable, glancing repeatedly at her cell phone. As a mother herself, Amy was sensitive to the situation. "Do you need to leave and pump?" she whispered to her colleague. The new mom sheepishly admitted that she had brought her baby and her mother to the conference. She was looking at her cell phone because her mother was texting her that the baby needed to be fed. Amy encouraged the new mom to leave immediately. Once she left, the young mother's mentor, an older male physician, admitted that he had no idea that she had brought her baby. If he had known, he would have encouraged her to leave earlier. She was torturing herself unnecessarily. This is one instance where I would have recommended *not* to sit at the table.

Technology is also changing the emphasis on strict office hours since so much work can be conducted online. While few companies can provide as much flexibility as Google and Facebook, other industries are starting to move in a similar direction. Still, the traditional practice of judging employees by face time rather than results unfortunately persists. Because of this, many employees focus on hours clocked in the office rather than on achieving their goals as efficiently as possible. A shift to focusing more on results would benefit individuals and make companies more efficient and competitive.[13]

In his latest book, General Colin Powell explains that his vision of leadership rejects "busy bastards" who put in long hours at the office without realizing the impact they have on their staff. He explains that "in every senior job I've had I've tried to create an environment of professionalism and the very highest standards. When it was necessary to get a job done, I expected my subordinates to work around the clock. When that was not necessary, I wanted them to work normal hours, go home at a decent time, play with the kids, enjoy family and friends, read a novel, clear their heads, daydream, and refresh themselves. I wanted them to have a life outside the office. I am paying them for the quality of their work, not for the hours they work. That kind of environment has always produced the best results for me."[14] It is still far too rare to work for someone as wise as General Powell.

A related issue that affects many Americans is the extension of working hours.[15] In 2009, married middle-income parents worked about eight and a half hours more per week than in 1979.[16] This trend has been particularly pronounced among professionals and managers, especially men.[17] A survey of high-earning professionals in the corporate world found that 62 percent work more than fifty hours a week and 10 percent work more than eighty hours per week.[18] Technology, while liberating us at times from the physical office, has also extended the workday. A 2012 survey of employed adults showed that 80 percent of the respondents continued to work after leaving the office, 38 percent checked e-mail at the dinner table, and 69 percent can't go to bed without checking their in-box.[19]

My mother believes that my generation is suffering greatly from this endless work schedule. During her childhood and mine, a full-time job meant forty hours a week—Monday through Friday, 9:00 a.m. to 5:00 p.m. She tells me over and over, "There's too much pressure on you and your peers. It's not compatible with a normal life." But this is the new normal for many of us.

The new normal means that there are just not enough hours in the day. For years, I attempted to solve this problem by skimping on sleep, a common but often counterproductive approach. I realized my mistake partially from observing my children and seeing how a happy child can melt into a puddle of tears when he's shy a couple hours of sleep. It turns out that adults aren't much different. Sleeping four or five hours a night induces mental impairment equivalent to a blood alcohol level above the legal driving limit.[20] Sleep deprivation makes people anxious, irritable, and confused. (Just ask Dave.) If I could go back and change one thing about how I lived in those early years, I would force myself to get more sleep.

It's not only working parents who are looking for more hours in the day; people without children are also overworked, maybe to an even greater extent. When I was in business school, I attended a Women in Consulting panel with three speakers: two married women with children and one single woman without children. After the married women spoke about how hard it was to balance their lives, the single woman interjected that she was tired of people not taking her need to have a life seriously. She felt that her colleagues were always rushing off to be with their families, leaving her to pick up the slack. She argued, "My coworkers should understand that I need to go to a party tonight—and this is just as legitimate as their kids' soccer game—because going to a party is the only way I might actually meet someone and start a family so I can have a soccer game to go to one day!" I often quote this story to make sure single employees know that they, too, have every right to a full life.

My own concerns about combining my career and family rose to the forefront again when I was considering leav-

ing Google for Facebook. I had been at Google for six and
a half years and had strong leaders in place for each of my
teams. By then, Google had more than 20,000 employees
and business procedures that ran smoothly and allowed
me to make it home for dinner with my children almost
every night. Facebook, on the other hand, had only 550
employees and was much more of a start-up. Late-night
meetings and all-night hackathons were an accepted part of
the culture. I worried that taking a new job might under-
mine the balance I had worked hard to achieve. It helped
that Dave was working as an entrepreneur-in-residence at
a venture capital firm, so he had almost complete control of
his schedule. He assured me that he would take on more at
home to make this work for our family.

My first six months at Facebook were really hard. I know
I'm supposed to say "challenging," but "really hard" is
more like it. A lot of the company followed Mark's lead and
worked night-owl engineering hours. I would schedule a
meeting with someone for 9:00 a.m. and the person would
not show up, assuming that I meant 9:00 p.m. I needed
to be around when others were and I worried that leaving
too early would make me stand out like a sore—and old—
thumb. I missed dinner after dinner with my kids. Dave
told me that he was home with them and they were fine.
But I was not.

I thought about Larry Kanarek's speech back at McKinsey and realized that if I didn't take control of the situation, my new job would prove unsustainable. I would
resent not seeing my family and run the risk of becoming

the employee who quit with unused vacation time. I started forcing myself to leave the office at five thirty. Every competitive, type-A fiber of my being was screaming at me to stay, but unless I had a critical meeting, I walked out that door. And once I did it, I learned that I could. I am not claiming, nor have I ever claimed, that I work a forty-hour week. Facebook is available around the world 24/7, and for the most part, so am I. The days when I even think of unplugging for a weekend or vacation are long gone. And unlike my job at Google, which was based almost exclusively in California, my Facebook role requires a lot of travel. As a result, I have become even more vigilant about leaving the office to have dinner with my children when I'm not on the road.

I still struggle with the trade-offs between work and home on a daily basis. Every woman I know does, and I know that I'm far luckier than most. I have remarkable resources—a husband who is a real partner, the ability to hire great people to assist me both in the office and at home, and a good measure of control over my schedule. I also have a wonderful sister who lives close by and is always willing to take care of her niece and nephew, occasionally at a moment's notice. She's even a pediatrician, so my kids are not just in loving hands, they're in medically trained hands. (Not all people are close to their family, either geographically or emotionally. Fortunately, friends can be leaned on to provide this type of support for one another.)

If there is a new normal for the workplace, there is a new normal for the home too. Just as expectations for how many hours people will work have risen dramatically, so have expectations for how many hours mothers will spend focused on their children. In 1975, stay-at-home mothers spent an average of about eleven hours per week on primary child care (defined as routine caregiving and activities that foster a child's well-being, such as reading and fully focused play). Mothers employed outside the home in 1975 spent six hours doing these activities. Today, stay-at-home mothers spend about seventeen hours per week on primary child care, on average, while mothers who work outside the home spend about eleven hours. This means that an employed mother today spends about the same amount of time on primary child-care activities as a nonemployed mother did in 1975.[21]

My memory of being a kid is that my mother was available but rarely hovering or directing my activities. My siblings and I did not have organized playdates. We rode our bikes around the neighborhood without adult supervision. Our parents might have checked on our homework once in a while, but they rarely sat with us while we completed it. Today, a "good mother" is always around and always devoted to the needs of her children. Sociologists call this relatively new phenomenon "intensive mothering," and it has culturally elevated the importance of women spending large amounts of time with their children.[22] Being judged against the current all-consuming standard means mothers who work outside the home feel as if we are failing, even if we are spending the same number of hours with our kids as our mothers did.

When I drop my kids off at school and see the mothers who are staying to volunteer, I worry that my children are worse off because I'm not with them full-time. This is where my trust in hard data and research has helped me the most. Study after study suggests that the pressure society places on women to stay home and do "what's best for the child" is based on emotion, not evidence.

In 1991, the Early Child Care Research Network, under the auspices of the National Institute of Child Health and Human Development, initiated the most ambitious and comprehensive study to date on the relationship between child care and child development, and in particular on the effect of exclusive maternal care versus child care. The Research Network, which comprised more than thirty child development experts from leading universities across the country, spent eighteen months designing the study. They tracked more than one thousand children over the course of fifteen years, repeatedly assessing the children's cognitive skills, language abilities, and social behaviors. Dozens of papers have been published about what they found.[23] In 2006, the researchers released a report summarizing their findings, which concluded that "children who were cared for exclusively by their mothers did not develop differently than those who were also cared for by others."[24] They found no gap in cognitive skills, language competence, social competence, ability to build and maintain relationships, or in the quality of the mother-child bond.[25] Parental behavioral factors—including fathers who are responsive and positive, mothers who favor "self-directed child behavior," and parents with emotional intimacy in their marriages—influence a child's development two to three times more than any form of child care.[26] One of the findings is worth reading slowly, maybe even twice: "Exclusive maternal care was not related to better or worse outcomes for children. There is, thus, no reason for mothers to feel as though they are harming their children if they decide to work."[27]

Children absolutely need parental involvement, love, care, time, and attention. But parents who work outside the home are still capable of giving their children a loving and secure childhood. Some data even suggest that having two parents working outside the home can be advantageous to a child's development, particularly for girls.[28]

Although I know the data and understand intellectually that my career is not harming my children, there are times when I still feel anxious about my choices. A friend of mine felt the same way, so she discussed it with her therapist and, later, shared this insight: "My therapist told me that when I was worrying about how much I was leaving my girls, that separation anxiety is actually more about the mom than the kids. We talk about it as though it is a problem for children, but actually it can be more of an issue for the mom."

I always want to do more for my children. Because of work obligations, I've missed doctor's appointments and parent-teacher conferences and have had to travel when my kids were sick. I haven't missed a dance recital yet, but it probably will happen. I have also missed a level of detail about their lives. I once asked a mother at our school if she knew any of the other kids in the first-grade class, hoping for a familiar name or two. She spent twenty minutes reciting from memory the name of every child, detailing their parents, siblings, which class they had been in the year before, and their interests. How could she possibly know all this? Was I a bad mother for not knowing *any* of this? And why should it even bother me?

I knew the answer to that last question. It bothered me because like most people who have choices, I am not completely comfortable with mine. Later that same year, I dropped my son off at school on St. Patrick's Day. As he got out of the car wearing his favorite blue T-shirt, the same mother pointed out, "He's supposed to be wearing green today." I simultaneously thought, *Oh, who the hell can remember that it's St. Patrick's Day?* and *I'm a bad mom.*

Guilt management can be just as important as time management for mothers. When I went back to my job after giving birth, other working mothers told me to prepare for the day that my son would cry for his nanny. Sure enough, when he was about eleven months old, he was crawling on the floor of his room and put his knee down on a toy. He looked up for help, crying, and reached for her instead of me. It pierced my heart, but Dave thought it was a good sign. He reasoned that we were the central figures in our son's life, but forming an attachment to a caregiver was good for his development. I understood his logic, especially in retrospect, but at the time, it hurt like hell.

To this day, I count the hours away from my kids and feel sad when I miss a dinner or a night with them. Did I have to take this trip? Was this speech really critical for

Facebook? Was this meeting truly necessary? Far from worrying about nights he misses, Dave thinks we are heroes for getting home for dinner as often as we do. Our different viewpoints seem inextricably gender based. Compared to his peers, Dave is an exceptionally devoted dad. Compared to many of my peers, I spend a lot more time away from my children. A study that conducted in-depth interviews with mothers and fathers in dual-earner families uncovered similar reactions. The mothers were riddled with guilt about what their jobs were doing to their families. The fathers were not.[29] As Marie Wilson, founder of the White House Project, has noted, "Show me a woman without guilt and I'll show you a man."[30]

I know that I can easily spend time focusing on what I'm not doing; like many, I excel at self-flagellation. And even with my vast support system, there are times when I feel pulled in too many directions. But when I dwell less on the conflicts and compromises, and more on being fully engaged with the task at hand, the center holds and I feel content. I love my job and the brilliant and fascinating people I work with. I also love my time with my kids. A great day is when I rush home from the craziness of the office to have dinner with my family and then sit in the rocking chair in the corner of my daughter's room with both of my kids on my lap. We rock and read together, just a quiet (okay, not always quiet), joyful moment at the end of their day. They drift off to sleep and I drift (okay, run) back to my laptop.

It's also fun when my two worlds collide. For a period of time, Mark hosted Monday-night strategy sessions at his house. Because I wouldn't be making it home for dinner, my kids came into the office. Facebook is incredibly family friendly, and my children were in heaven, entranced by pizza, endless candy, and the huge pile of Legos that the engineers kindly share with young visitors. It made me happy that my kids got to know my colleagues and my colleagues got to know them. Mark had been teaching my son how to fence, so they would sometimes practice with pretend foils, which was adorable. Mark also taught both my kids various office pranks, which was slightly less adorable.

I would never claim to be able to find serenity or total focus in every moment. I am so far from that. But when I remember that no one can do it all and identify my real priorities at home and at work, I feel better, and I am more productive in the office and probably a better mother as well. Stanford professor Jennifer Aaker's work shows that setting obtainable goals is key to happiness.[31] Instead of perfection, we should aim for sustainable and fulfilling. The right question is not "Can I do it all?" but "Can I do what's most important for me and my family?" The aim is to have children who are happy and thriving. Wearing green T-shirts on St. Patrick's Day is purely optional.

If I had to embrace a definition of success, it would be that success is making the best choices we can . . . and accepting them. Journalist Mary Curtis suggested in *The Washington Post* that the best advice anyone can offer "is for women and men to drop the guilt trip, even as the minutes tick away. The secret is there is no secret—just doing the best you can with what you've got."[32]

In December 2010, I was standing with Pat Mitchell, waiting to go onstage to give my TED Talk. The day before, I had dropped my daughter off at preschool and told her I was flying to the East Coast so I wouldn't see her that night. She clung to my leg and begged me not to leave. I couldn't shake that image and, at the last minute, asked Pat if I should add it to my speech. "Absolutely tell that story," said Pat. "Other women go through this, and you'll help them by being honest that this is hard for you too."

I took a deep breath and stepped onstage. I tried to be authentic and shared my truth. I announced to the room—and basically everyone on the internet—that I fall very short of doing it all. And Pat was right. It felt really good not just to admit this to myself, but to share it with others.

Let's Start Talking About It

SOMETIMES I WONDER what it would be like to go through life without being labeled by my gender. I don't wake up thinking, *What am I going to do today as Facebook's female COO?*, but that's often how I'm referred to by others. When people talk about a female pilot, a female engineer, or a female race car driver, the word "female" implies a bit of surprise. Men in the professional world are rarely seen through this same gender lens. A Google search for "Facebook's male CEO" returns this message: "No results found."

As Gloria Steinem observed, "Whoever has power takes over the noun—and the norm—while the less powerful get an adjective."[1] Since no one wants to be perceived as less powerful, a lot of women reject the gender identification and insist, "I don't see myself as a woman; I see myself as a novelist/athlete/professional/fill-in-the-blank." They are right to do so. No one wants her achievements modified. We all just want to be the noun. Yet the world has a way of reminding women that they are women, and girls that they are girls.

In between my junior and senior years of high school, I worked as a page in Washington, D.C., for my home-town congressman, William Lehman. The Speaker of the House at the time was the legendary Massachusetts repre-sentative Tip O'Neill, and Congressman Lehman prom-ised to introduce me to him before the summer ended. But as the days ticked by, it didn't happen. And it didn't happen. Then, on the very last day of the session, he made good on his promise. In the hall outside the House floor, he pulled me over to meet Speaker O'Neill. I was nervous, but Con-gressman Lehman put me at ease by introducing me in the nicest way possible, telling the Speaker that I had worked hard all summer. The Speaker looked at me, then reached over and patted my head. He turned to the congressman and remarked, "She's pretty." Then he turned his attention back to me and asked just one question: "Are you a pom-pom girl?"

I was crushed. Looking back, I know his words were intended to flatter me, but in the moment, I felt belittled. I wanted to be recognized for the work I had done. I reacted defensively. "No," I replied. "I study too much for that." Then a wave of terror struck me for speaking up to the man who was third in line for the presidency. But no one seemed to register my curt and not-at-all-clever response. The Speaker just patted me on the head—again!—and moved along. My congressman beamed.

Even to my teenage self, this sexism seemed retro. The

Speaker was born in 1912, eight years before women were given the right to vote, but by the time I met him in the halls of Congress, society had (mostly) evolved. It was obvious that a woman could do anything a man could do. My childhood was filled with firsts—Golda Meir in Israel, Geraldine Ferraro on the Mondale ticket, Sandra Day O'Connor on the Supreme Court, Sally Ride in space.

Given all these strides, I headed into college believing that the feminists of the sixties and seventies had done the hard work of achieving equality for my generation. And yet, if anyone had called me a feminist, I would have quickly corrected that notion. This reaction is prevalent even today according to sociologist Marianne Cooper (who also contributed her extraordinary research assistance to this book). In her 2011 article, "The New F-Word," Marianne wrote about college English professor Michele Elam, who observed something strange in her Introduction to Feminist Studies course. Even though her students were interested enough in gender equality to take an entire class on the subject, very few "felt comfortable using the word 'feminism.' " And even "fewer identified themselves as feminists." As Professor Elam noted, it was as if "being called a feminist was to suspect that some foul epithet had been hurled your way."[2]

It sounds like a joke: Did you hear the one about the woman taking a feminist studies class who got angry when someone called her a feminist? But when I was in college, I embraced the same contradiction. On one hand, I started a group to encourage more women to major in economics and government. On the other hand, I would have denied being in any way, shape, or form a feminist. None of my college friends thought of themselves as feminists either. It saddens me to admit that we did not see the backlash against women around us.[3] We accepted the negative caricature of a bra-burning, humorless, man-hating feminist. She was not someone we wanted to emulate, in part because it seemed like she couldn't get a date. Horrible, I know— the sad irony of rejecting feminism to get male attention and approval. In our defense, my friends and I truly, if naïvely, believed that the world did not need feminists anymore. We mistakenly thought that there was nothing left to fight for.

I carried this attitude with me when I entered the workforce. I figured if sexism still existed, I would just prove it wrong. I would do my job and do it well. What I didn't know at the time was that ignoring the issue is a classic survival technique. Within traditional institutions, success has often been contingent upon a woman not speaking out but fitting in, or, more colloquially, being "one of the guys." The first women to enter corporate America dressed in manly suits with button-down shirts. One veteran banking executive told me that she wore her hair in a bun for ten years because she did not want anyone to notice she was a woman. While styles have relaxed, women still worry about sticking out too much. I know an engineer at a tech start-up who removes her earrings before going to work so coworkers won't be reminded that she is—*shhh!*—not a man.

Early in my career, my gender was rarely noted (except for the occasional client who wanted to fix me up with his son). Manly suits were no longer in fashion, and I neither hid nor emphasized femininity. I have never reported directly to a woman—not once in my entire career. There were higher-level women at the places I worked, but I wasn't close enough to see how they dealt with this issue on a daily basis. I was never invited to attend a single meeting that discussed gender, and there were no special programs for women that I can recall. That all seemed fine. We were fitting in, and there was no reason to call attention to ourselves.

But while gender was not openly acknowledged, it was still lurking below the surface. I started to see differences in attitudes toward women. I started noticing how often employees were judged not by their objective performance, but by the subjective standard of how well they fit in. Given that the summer outing at McKinsey was a deep-sea fishing trip and most company dinners ended with whiskey sipping and cigar smoking, I sometimes struggled to pass the "fitting in" test. One night, encouraged by the male partners, I puffed away on a cigar—just one of the guys. Except that the smoking nauseated me and I reeked of cigar smoke for days. If that was fitting in, I stuck out.

Others also seemed aware that I was not one of the guys. When I was named the Treasury Department's chief of staff in 1999, several people remarked to me, "It must have helped that you were a woman." It was infuriating. Their intent may not have been malicious, but the implication was clear: I had not gotten the job on merit. I also figured that for every person pointing out my "advantage" to my face, there were probably a dozen others saying it less politely behind my back. I considered my possible responses. I could explain that the last time I checked there was no affirmative action for women at Treasury. I could mention that my credentials lined up with those of the men who had previously held this position. If there was enough time, I could recount centuries of discrimination against women. Or I could just slap the person across the face. I tried all these options at least once. Okay, not the slap. But of the responses I did try, none of them worked.

It was a no-win situation. I couldn't deny being a woman; even if I tried, people would still figure it out. And defending myself just made me seem . . . defensive. My gut and the signals I received from others cautioned me that arguing the issue would make me sound like a strident feminist. And I still did not want that. I also worried that pointing out the disadvantages women face in the workforce might be misinterpreted as whining or asking for special treatment. So I ignored the comments. I put my head down and worked hard.

Then, as the years ticked by, I started seeing female friends and colleagues drop out of the workforce. Some left by choice. Others left out of frustration, pushed out the door by companies that did not allow flexibility and welcomed home by partners who weren't doing their share of the housework and child rearing. Others remained but scaled back their ambitions to meet outsized demands. I watched as the promise my generation had for female leadership dwindled. By the time I had been at Google for a few years, I realized that the problem wasn't going away. So even though the thought still scared me, I decided it was time to stop putting my head down and to start speaking out.

Fortunately, I had company. In 2005, my colleagues Susan Wojcicki and Marissa Mayer and I all noticed that the speakers who visited the Google campus were fascinating, notable, and almost always male. In response, we founded Women@Google and kicked off the new series with luminaries Gloria Steinem and Jane Fonda, who were launching the Women's Media Center. As a former aerobics instructor, I was excited to meet Jane Fonda—and sucked in my stomach the whole time. From what I knew about the women's rights movement, I expected Gloria Steinem to be formidable and brilliant, which she was. But she was also charming and funny and warm—the absolute opposite of my childish image of the humorless feminist.

After the Women@Google event, Gloria invited me to speak at the Women's Media Center in New York. I said yes without hesitating. The day before the talk, I headed to the airport with Kim Malone Scott, who ran the Google publishing teams. Kim is an experienced writer, so I figured she would help me craft a speech during the long flight. By the time I got through all of my backlogged e-mails, it was almost midnight. I turned to Kim for help and saw that she had fallen asleep. Long before Facebook made it popular, I thought about giving her a poke. But I couldn't bear to wake her up. Staring at the blank computer screen, I was at a complete loss. I had never spoken about being a woman in public before. Not once. I had no talking points or notes to turn to. Then I realized how striking this was . . . and that I actually had quite a lot to say.

I began my talk the next day by explaining that in business we are taught to fit in, but that I was starting to think this might not be the right approach. I said out loud that there are differences between men and women both in their behavior and in the way their behavior is perceived by others. I admitted that I could see these dynamics playing out in the workforce, and that, in order to fix the problems, we needed to be able to talk about gender without people thinking we were crying for help, asking for special treatment, or about to sue. A lot poured out of me that day. Then I returned to Northern California and put the conversation on hold.

In the following four years, I gave two talks on women in the workplace, both behind closed doors to professional women's groups at nearby Stanford. Then one day, Pat Mitchell called to tell me that she was launching TED-Women and invited me to speak on social media. I told her I had another subject in mind and started pulling together a talk on how women can succeed in the workforce (a talk that TED later named "Why We Have Too Few Women Leaders"). Very quickly, I became excited. And just as quickly, I learned that no one else shared my excitement. Friends and colleagues—both male and female—warned me that making this speech would harm my career by instantly typecasting me as a female COO and not a real business executive. In other words, I wouldn't be blending in.

I worried they might be right. Speaking at TED would be different from my previous keynotes. Although I would be addressing a sympathetic room, the talk would be posted on the web, where *anyone* could watch, and judge, and criticize.

Inside Facebook, few people noticed my TED Talk, and those who did responded positively. But outside of Facebook, the criticism started to roll in. One of my colleagues from Treasury called to say that "others"—not him, of course—were wondering why I gave more speeches on women's issues than on Facebook. I had been at the company for two and a half years and given countless speeches on rebuilding marketing around the social graph and exactly *one* speech on gender. Someone else asked me, "So is this your thing now?"

At the time, I didn't know how to respond. Now I would say yes. I made this my "thing" because we need to disrupt the status quo. Staying quiet and fitting in may have been all the first generations of women who entered corporate America could do; in some cases, it might still be the safest path. But this strategy is not paying off for women as a group. Instead, we need to speak out, identify the barriers that are holding women back, and find solutions.

The response to my TED Talk showed me that addressing these issues openly can make a difference. Women forwarded the video to their friends, colleagues, daughters, and sisters. I began receiving e-mails and letters from women all over the world who wanted to share their stories of how they gained the courage to reach for more opportunities, sit at more tables, and believe more in themselves.

One of my favorite letters came from Sabeen Virani Dhanani, a consultant based in Dubai and the only woman in an office of more than three hundred employees. She responded to my story about the executive who could not point me to the women's bathroom because, as she explained, the women's bathroom did not even exist when she was working for a client in Saudi Arabia. Sabeen described how during her first week on the project, the client took her team out to dinner, but she couldn't join because the restaurant didn't allow women. Talk about not sitting at the table—she couldn't even get into the restaurant! Some of the men were openly hostile to Sabeen. Others just ignored her. But rather than give up and go to work for a friendlier client, she decided that she could demonstrate to everyone that women are competent professionals. In the end, she won her coworkers over and the client converted a bathroom into a women's bathroom just for her. She sent me a photo of her standing in front of a door with a printed sign that read simply and powerfully "Toilets for women only."

It was also enormously gratifying that men reacted positively to the talk too. Dr. John Probasco of the Johns Hopkins University School of Medicine told me that my story about women being more reluctant than men to raise their hands rang true for him so he decided to do away with the old hand-raising system during rounds. Instead, he started calling on male and female students evenly. He quickly realized that the women knew the answers just as well—or even better—than the men. In one day he increased female participation. By making one small change to his behavior, he changed a much larger dynamic.

Major changes can result from these kinds of "nudge techniques," small interventions that encourage people to behave in slightly different ways at critical moments.[4] The simple act of talking openly about behavioral patterns makes the subconscious conscious. For example, Google has an unusual system where engineers nominate themselves for promotions, and the company found that men nominated themselves more quickly than women. The Google management team shared this data openly with the female employees, and women's self-nomination rates rose significantly, reaching roughly the same rates as men's.

All the feedback from TED convinced me that I should keep speaking up and encouraging others to do the same. It is essential to breaking the logjam. Talking can transform minds, which can transform behaviors, which can transform institutions.

I know it isn't easy. Anyone who brings up gender in the workplace is wading into deep and muddy waters. The subject itself presents a paradox, forcing us to acknowledge differences while trying to achieve the goal of being treated the same. Women, especially those at junior levels, worry that raising gender issues makes them appear unprofessional or as if they are blaming others. I have listened to women vent frustration over being undervalued and even demeaned on a daily basis at work. When I ask if they have aired any of these complaints to their superiors, they've responded, "Oh no! I couldn't." There is so much fear that speaking up will make the situation worse or even result in being penalized or fired. It seems safer to bear the injustice.

For men, raising this subject can be even harder. A male friend who runs a large organization once confided in me, "It's easier to talk about your sex life in public than to talk about gender." The fact that he wouldn't go on record with this quote shows he meant it. Vittorio Colao, CEO of Vodafone, told me that he showed my TED Talk to his senior management team because he shares my belief that women sometimes hold themselves back. He also believed this message was easier to hear from a woman than a man. His point is valid. If a man had delivered the same message or even gently pointed out that women might be taking actions that limited their options, he would have been pilloried.

Shutting down discussion is self-defeating and impedes progress. We need to talk and listen and debate and refute and instruct and learn and evolve. And since the majority of managers are men, we need them to feel comfortable addressing these issues directly with female employees. When a woman sits on the side of a room, a man needs to be able to wave her over to the table and explain why so she will know to sit at the table the next time.

Ken Chenault, CEO of American Express, is a leader on this front. Ken openly acknowledges that in meetings, both men and women are more likely to interrupt a woman and give credit to a man for an idea first proposed by a woman. When he witnesses either of these behaviors, he stops the meeting to point it out. Coming from the top, this really makes employees think twice. A more junior woman (or man) can also intervene in the situation when a female colleague has been interrupted. She can gently but firmly tell the group, "Before we move on, I'd like to hear what [senior woman] had to say." This action not only benefits the senior woman but can raise the stature of the junior woman as well, since speaking up for someone else displays both confidence and a communal spirit. The junior woman comes across as both competent and nice.

At Facebook, I teach managers to encourage women to talk about their plans to have children and help them continue to reach for opportunities. I give men the option of quoting me if the words don't feel right coming out of their mouths. Still, this approach is a bit of a crutch and it does not translate to other companies. It would be preferable if everyone had permission to talk about this subject both publicly and behind closed office doors.

One stumbling block is that many people believe that the workplace is largely a meritocracy, which means we look at individuals, not groups, and determine that differences in outcomes must be based on merit, not gender. Men at the top are often unaware of the benefits they enjoy simply because they're men, and this can make them blind to the disadvantages associated with being a woman. Women lower down also believe that men at the top are entitled to be there, so they try to play by the rules and work harder to advance rather than raise questions or voice concerns about the possibility of bias. As a result, everyone becomes complicit in perpetuating an unjust system.

At the same time, we must be careful not to inject gender into every discussion. I know a male CEO who is enormously dedicated to hiring and promoting women. When a female employee kicked off a negotiation by insisting that she should have a higher title and was underleveled because she was a woman, it immediately put him on the defense. She was speaking her truth, but in this case, her truth was an accusation with legal ramifications. As soon as she framed the issue in those terms, the CEO had no choice but to put their friendly talks on hold and call in HR. It might have served her better to explain how she was contributing to the company and ask for the promotion first.

Even today, mentioning gender in work situations often makes people visibly uncomfortable. To their credit, many institutions have worked hard to sensitize people to these issues, especially sexual harassment. But while human resources seminars can raise consciousness and help protect employees, they have also raised the specter of legal action, which can create real barriers to these conversations. The federal and state laws that are designed to protect employees against discrimination specify only that an employer cannot make decisions based on certain protected characteristics such as gender, pregnancy, and age. But companies usually take the policy a step further and teach managers not to ask anything related to these areas. Anyone making even a benign inquiry such as "Are you married?" or "Do you have kids?" can later be accused of basing a personnel decision on this information. As a result, a manager who is trying to help a female employee by pointing out a gender-driven style difference could be charged with discrimination for doing so.

The first time I asked a prospective employee if she was considering having children soon, I understood that doing so could expose me and my company to legal risk. Unlike many women, I was in a position to evaluate that risk and chose to take it. The laws that protect women and minorities and people with disabilities, among others, from discrimination are essential, and I am not suggesting they be circumvented. But I have also witnessed firsthand how they can have a chilling effect on discourse, sometimes even to the detriment of the people they are designed to defend. I don't have a solution to this dilemma and will leave it to public policy and legal experts to solve. I do think this is worth some serious attention so we can find a way to deal with these issues in a way that protects but doesn't suppress.

Most people would agree that gender bias exists . . . in others. *We*, however, would never be swayed by such superficial and unenlightened opinions. Except we are. Our preconceived notions about masculinity and femininity influence how we interact with and evaluate colleagues in the workplace. A 2012 study found that when evaluating identical résumés for a lab manager position from a male student and a female student, scientists of both sexes gave better marks to the male applicant. Even though the students had the same qualifications and experience, the scientists deemed the female student less competent and offered her a lower starting salary and less mentoring.[5] Other studies of job applicants, candidates for scholarships, and musicians auditioning for orchestras have come to the same conclusion: gender bias influences how we view performance and typically raises our assessment of men while lowering our assessment of women.[6] Even today, gender-blind evaluations still result in better outcomes for women.[7] Unfortunately, most jobs require face-to-face interviews.

All of us, myself included, are biased, whether we admit it or not. And thinking that we are objective can actually make this even worse, creating what social scientists call a "bias blind spot." This blind spot causes people to be too confident about their own powers of objectivity so that they fail to correct for bias.[8] When evaluating identically described male and female candidates for the job of police chief, respondents who claimed to be the most impartial actually exhibited *more* bias in favor of male candidates. This is not just counterproductive but deeply dangerous. Evaluators in that same study actually shifted hiring criteria to give men an advantage. When a male applicant possessed a strong educational record, that quality was considered critical to the success of a police chief. But when a male applicant possessed a weaker educational record, that quality was rated as less important. This favoritism was not shown to female applicants. If anything, the reverse happened. When a woman possessed a particular skill, ability, or background, that quality tended to carry less weight. The infuriating takeaway from this study is that "merit" can be manipulated to justify discrimination.[9]

Social scientists are uncovering new examples of bias all the time. In 2012, a series of studies compared men in more "modern" marriages (whose wives worked outside the home full-time) to men in more "traditional" marriages (whose wives worked at home). The researchers wanted to determine if a man's home arrangement affected his professional behavior. It did. Compared to men in modern marriages, men in more traditional marriages viewed the presence of women in the workforce less favorably. They also denied promotions to qualified female employees more often and were more likely to think that companies with a higher percentage of female employees ran less smoothly. The researchers speculated that men in traditional marriages are not overtly hostile toward women but instead are "benevolent sexists"—holding positive yet outdated views about women.[10] (Another term I have heard is "nice guy misogynists.") These men might even believe that women have superior strengths in certain areas like moral reasoning, which makes them better equipped to raise children—and perhaps less equipped to succeed in business.[11] In all likelihood, men who share this attitude are unaware of how their conscious and unconscious beliefs hurt their female colleagues.

Another bias arises from our tendency to want to work with people who are like us. Innovisor, a consulting firm, conducted research in twenty-nine countries and found that when men and women select a colleague to collaborate

with, both were significantly more likely to choose someone of the same gender.[12] Yet diverse groups often perform
better.[13] Armed with this information, managers should
take a more active role in mixing and matching when
assigning teams. Or, at the very least, managers should
point out this tendency to give employees the motivation
to shake things up.

My own attempts to point out gender bias have generated more than my fair share of eye rolling from others. At best, people are open to scrutinizing themselves
and considering their blind spots; at worst, they become
defensive and angry. One common instance of bias crops
up during job performance evaluations. When reviewing a
woman, the reviewer will often voice the concern, "While
she's really good at her job, she's just not as well liked by
her peers." When I hear language like that, I bring up
the Heidi/Howard study and how success and likeability
are negatively correlated for women. I ask the evaluator
to consider the possibility that this successful female may
be paying a gender-based penalty. Usually people find the
study credible, nodding their heads in agreement, but then
bristle at the suggestion that this might be influencing
the reaction of *their* management team. They will further
defend their position by arguing that it cannot be gender
related because—*aha!*—both men *and* women have problems with that particular female executive. But the success
and likeability penalty is imposed by both men and women.
Women perpetuate this bias as well.

Of course, not every woman deserves to be well liked.

Some women are disliked for behaviors that they would do well to change. In a perfect world, they would receive constructive feedback and the opportunity to make those changes. Still, calling attention to this bias forces people to think about whether there is a real problem or a perception problem. The goal is to give women something men tend to receive automatically—the benefit of the doubt.

In turn, women might also want to give their bosses the benefit of the doubt. Cynthia Hogan served as chief counsel for the Senate Judiciary Committee under then-senator Joe Biden before leaving in 1996 after her first child was born. Her plan was to return to the workforce a few years later. But when her second child was born prematurely, those plans changed. A full twelve years later, Vice President–Elect Biden called Cynthia to ask her to join his staff as chief legal counsel in the White House. "My first reaction was that I no longer owned any clothes other than yoga pants!" Cynthia said. But her larger concern was whether she could manage the long hours in the White House and still see her family. She put it beautifully: "I knew that whether this would work depended on two men. So first I asked my husband if he could step in and take on more of the responsibility for the kids. He said, 'Of course, it's your turn.' And then I told the Vice President–elect that I really wanted to have dinner with my kids most nights. And his response was, 'Well, you have a phone and I can call you when I need you after dinnertime.' "[14]

Cynthia believes that the lesson of her story is "Don't be afraid to ask," even if it seems like a long shot. Being offered a senior job, especially after being at home for so long, presented a great opportunity. Many women would have accepted it without even trying to carve out the time they needed for their families. Others would have turned it down, assuming that having dinner at home most nights was not negotiable. Being forthright led to opportunity.

Every job will demand some sacrifice. The key is to avoid *unnecessary* sacrifice. This is especially hard since our work culture values complete dedication. We worry that even mentioning other priorities makes us less valuable employees. I have faced this too. As I described, once I had children, I changed my working hours to be home for dinner. But only fairly recently did I start talking about this change. And while the impact of my actually leaving work early was negligible, *admitting* that I went home at five thirty turned out to be kind of a big deal.

I first openly discussed my office hours at the launch of Facebook Women, an in-house resource group. The initial meeting, run by Lori Goler and Facebook's head of engineering, Mike Schroepfer, was open to any Facebook employee, including men. During the Q&A, I was asked the (inevitable) question about how I balanced my job and family. I talked about leaving work to have dinner with my children and then getting back online after they went to bed. I said that I was sharing my schedule because I wanted to encourage others to personalize their schedules too. Even though I had planned in advance to discuss this, I felt nervous. Years of conditioning had taught me never to suggest that I was doing anything other than giving 100 percent to my job. It was scary to think that someone, even people working for me, might doubt my diligence or dedication. Fortunately, it didn't happen. A few people at Facebook thanked me for mentioning it, but that was it.

A few years later, producer Dyllan McGee interviewed me for her Makers video series. We spoke on a wide range of subjects, including my daily work schedule. The video was posted to the web and was instantly the subject of heated debate. Thanks to social media (*serves me right*), everyone had an opinion about my leaving the office at five thirty. I got flowers with an anonymous thank-you note. Mike Callahan, Yahoo's general counsel at the time, told me that several of the more senior women in his legal department said my admission struck a chord and they were going to follow my example. Author Ken Auletta said that I could not have gotten more headlines if I had murdered someone with an ax. While I was glad to jump-start the discussion, all the attention gave me this weird feeling that someone was going to object and fire me. I had to reassure myself that this was absurd. Still, the clamor made me realize how incredibly hard it would be for someone in a less-senior position to ask for or admit to this schedule. We have a long way to go before flextime is accepted in most workplaces. It will only happen if we keep raising the issue.

The discussions may be difficult, but the positives are many. We cannot change what we are unaware of, and once we are aware, we cannot help but change.

Even a well-established institution like Harvard Business School (HBS) can evolve rapidly when issues are addressed head-on. Historically at HBS, American male students have academically outperformed both female and international students. When Nitin Nohria was appointed dean in 2010, he made it his mission to close this gap. He began by appointing Youngme Moon as senior associate dean of the MBA program, the first woman to hold that position in the school's century-plus history. He also created a new position for Robin Ely, an expert on gender and diversity.

Associate Dean Moon, working with Professor Frances Frei, spent the first year rigorously examining the school's culture. They visited each classroom and discussed the challenges women and international students faced. Then they used that knowledge to create what Dean Nohria calls "a level of mindfulness." Without calling for major overhauls, they tackled the soft stuff—small adjustments students could make immediately, like paying more attention to the language they used in class. They laid out a new, communal definition of leadership: "Leadership is about making others better as a result of your presence and making sure that impact lasts in your absence." They held students responsible for the impact their behavior had on others. Those who violated that principle, or even hosted an event where that principle was violated, were held accountable. The second year, HBS introduced small group projects to encourage collaboration between classmates who would not naturally work together. They also added a year-long field course, which plays to the strengths of students who are less comfortable contributing in front of large classes.

By commencement, the performance gap had virtually disappeared. Men, women, and international students were represented proportionally in the honors awarded. There was another benefit too. In a result many considered surprising, overall student satisfaction went up, not just for the female and international students, but for American males as well. By creating a more equal environment, everyone was happier. And all of this was accomplished in just two short years.[15]

Social gains are never handed out. They must be seized. Leaders of the women's movement—from Susan B. Anthony to Jane Addams to Alice Paul to Bella Abzug to Flo Kennedy to so many others—spoke out loudly and bravely to demand the rights that we now have. Their courage changed our culture and our laws to the benefit of us all. Looking back, it made no sense for my college friends and me to distance ourselves from the hard-won achievements of earlier feminists. We should have cheered their efforts. Instead, we lowered our voices, thinking the battle was over, and with this reticence we hurt ourselves.

Now I proudly call myself a feminist. If Tip O'Neill were alive today, I might even tell him that I'm a pom-pom girl for feminism. I hope more women, and men, will join me in accepting this distinguished label. Currently, only 24 percent of women in the United States say that they consider themselves feminists. Yet when offered a more specific definition of feminism—"A feminist is someone who believes in social, political, and economic equality of the sexes"—the percentage of women who agree rises to 65 percent.[16] That's a big move in the right direction.

Semantics can be important, but I don't think progress turns on our willingness to apply a label to ourselves. I do think progress turns on our willingness to speak up about the impact gender has on us. We can no longer pretend that biases do not exist, nor can we talk around them. And as Harvard Business School has demonstrated, the result of creating a more equal environment will not just be better performance for our organizations, but quite likely greater happiness for all.

Working Together
Toward Equality

I BEGAN THIS BOOK by acknowledging that women in the developed world are better off than ever, but the goal of true equality still eludes us. So how do we move forward? First, we must decide that true equality is long overdue and will be achieved only when more women rise to the top of every government and every industry. Then we have to do the hard work of getting there. All of us—men and women alike—have to understand and acknowledge how stereotypes and biases cloud our beliefs and perpetuate the status quo. Instead of ignoring our differences, we need to accept and transcend them.

For decades, we have focused on giving women the choice to work inside or outside the home. We have celebrated the fact that women have the right to make this decision, and rightly so. But we have to ask ourselves if we have become so focused on supporting personal choices that we're failing to encourage women to aspire to leadership. It is time to cheer on girls and women who want to sit at the table, seek challenges, and lean in to their careers.

Today, despite all of the gains we have made, neither men nor women have real choice. Until women have supportive employers and colleagues as well as partners who share family responsibilities, they don't have real choice. And until men are fully respected for contributing inside the home, they don't have real choice either. Equal opportunity is not equal unless everyone receives the encouragement that makes seizing those opportunities possible. Only then can both men and women achieve their full potential.[1]

None of this is attainable unless we pursue these goals together. Men need to support women and, I wish it went without saying, women need to support women too. Stanford professor Deborah Gruenfeld makes the case: "We need to look out for one another, work together, and act more like a coalition. As individuals, we have relatively low levels of power. Working together, we are fifty percent of the population and therefore have real power."[2] As obvious as this sounds, women have not always worked together in the past. In fact, there are many discouraging examples where women have actually done the opposite.

We are a new generation and we need a new approach.

In the summer of 2012, my former Google colleague Marissa Mayer was named CEO of Yahoo. Like several of her friends and the Yahoo board, I knew that she was heading into her third trimester of pregnancy. Of course, many men take big jobs when their wives are weeks away from giving birth, and no one raises it as an issue, but Marissa's condition quickly became headline news. She was heralded as the first pregnant CEO of a Fortune 500 company. Feminists cheered. Then Marissa let it be known: "My maternity leave will be a few weeks long, and I'll work throughout it."[3] Many feminists stopped cheering. Since taking such a short leave is not feasible or desirable for everyone, they argued that Marissa was hurting the cause by setting up unreasonable expectations.

So was this one giant leap forward for womankind and one baby step back? Of course not. Marissa became the youngest CEO of a Fortune 500 company . . . while pregnant. She decided how she wanted to manage her career and family and never claimed that her choice should apply to anyone else. If she had cut Yahoo's maternity leave to two weeks for all employees, then concern would have been in order. She did not do this, but she was still roundly criticized. Even a European cabinet member weighed in.[4] Like any individual, Marissa knows best what she is capable of given her particular circumstances. And as journalist Kara Swisher also noted, Marissa "has a husband who can actually take care of the child, and no one seems to remember that."[5] Women who want to take two weeks off . . . or two days . . . or two years . . . or twenty years deserve everyone's full support.

As Marissa's experience demonstrates, women in powerful positions often receive greater scrutiny. Because the vast majority of leaders are men, it is not possible to generalize from any one example. But the dearth of female leaders causes one woman to be viewed as representative of her entire gender.[6] And because people often discount and dislike female leaders, these generalizations are often critical. This is not just unfair to the individuals but reinforces the stigma that successful women are unlikeable. A perfect and personal example occurred in May 2012, when a *Forbes* blogger posted an article entitled "Sheryl Sandberg Is the Valley's 'It' Girl—Just Like Kim Polese Once Was." He began his comparison by describing Kim, an early tech entrepreneur, as a "luminary" in the mid-1990s who never really earned her success, but was "in the right place at the right time [and was] young, pretty and a good speaker." The blogger then argued, "I think Polese is a good cautionary tale for . . . Sheryl Sandberg."[7] *Ouch.*

Kim and I had never met or spoken before this incident, but she defended both of us. In a published response, she described reading the blog post and how her "immediate thought was—*how sad.* How sad that as an industry and a society we haven't advanced over these past two decades when it comes to views on women and leadership. As with all the past lazy, stereotype-ridden articles like this one, it gets the facts wrong." After correcting the facts, she continued, "Views like these are all too commonplace, and part of a pervasive pattern that belittles, demeans and marginalizes women as leaders."[8] So many other readers joined her in calling the post sexist that the blogger posted an apology and retraction.[9]

I was grateful for Kim's vocal support. The more women can stick up for one another, the better. Sadly, this doesn't always happen. And it seems to happen even less when women voice a position that involves a gender-related issue. The attacks on Marissa for her maternity leave plans came almost entirely from other women. This has certainly been my experience too. Everyone loves a fight—and they *really* love a catfight. The media will report endlessly about women attacking other women, which distracts from the real issues. When arguments turn into "she said/she said," we all lose.

Every social movement struggles with dissension within its ranks, in part because advocates are passionate and unlikely to agree on every position and solution. Betty Friedan famously and foolishly refused to work with—or even to shake hands with—Gloria Steinem. They both did so much to further women's rights. But what if they had been able to work together? Couldn't they have furthered the cause even more?

There are so many of us who care deeply about these matters. We should strive to resolve our differences quickly, and when we disagree, stay focused on our shared goals. This is not a plea for less debate, but for more constructive debate. In Marissa's case, it would have been great to keep the focus on her breakthrough achievements. Thanks to her high-profile appointment, other companies might consider hiring pregnant women for big jobs, and expectant mothers might be more inclined to apply for them. By diminishing Marissa's accomplishment, the attacks diminished us all.

It is a painful truth that one of the obstacles to more

women gaining power has sometimes been women already in power. Women in the generations ahead of me believed, largely correctly, that only one woman would be allowed to ascend to the senior ranks in any particular company. In the days of tokenism, women looked around the room and instead of bonding against an unfair system, they often viewed one another as competition. Ambition fueled hostility, and women wound up being ignored, undermined, and in some cases even sabotaged by other women.

In the 1970s, this phenomenon was common enough that the term "queen bee" was used to describe a woman who flourished in a leadership role, especially in male-dominated industries, and who used her position to keep other female "worker bees" down. For some, it was simple self-preservation. For others, it reflected their coming-of-age in a society that believed men were superior to women. In this sense, queen bee behavior was not just a cause of gender discrimination but also a consequence of that discrimination. Queen bees internalized the low status of women and in order to feel worthy themselves wanted only to associate with men. Often, these queen bees were rewarded for maintaining the status quo and not promoting other women.[10]

Unfortunately, this "there can be only one" attitude still lingers today. It makes no sense for women to feel that we are competing against one another anymore, but some still do. In certain instances, women question their female colleagues' level of career commitment, aggressiveness, and leadership abilities.[11] One study found that female profes-

sors believed that male Ph.D. students were more committed to their careers than female Ph.D. students, even
though a survey of the students found no gender difference
in their reported levels of commitment.[12] Other research
suggests that once a woman achieves success, particularly
in a gender-biased context, her capacity to see gender discrimination is reduced.[13]

It's heartbreaking to think about one woman holding another back. As former secretary of state Madeleine
Albright once said, "There's a special place in hell for
women who don't help other women."[14] And the consequences extend beyond individual pain. Women's negative
views of female coworkers are often seen as an objective
assessment—more credible than the views of men.[15] When
women voice gender bias, they legitimize it. Obviously, a
negative attitude cannot be gender based if it comes from
another woman, right? *Wrong.* Often without realizing it,
women internalize disparaging cultural attitudes and then
echo them back. As a result, women are not just victims of
sexism, they can also be perpetrators.

There is hope that this attitude is changing. A recent
survey found that "high-potential women" working in business want to "pay it forward," and 73 percent have reached
out to other women to help them develop their talents.[16]
Almost all of the women I have encountered professionally have gone out of their way to be helpful. When I was
a lowly summer intern at McKinsey, I met Diana Farrell,
a star consultant, at a company-wide conference in Colo-
rado. Diana had just spoken at a panel that I attended and

we bumped into each other afterward—where else?—in the women's room. We ended up having a talk that continued beyond the sinks, and she became a close friend and trusted advisor. Years later, she was one of the few who encouraged me to join Google.

The more women help one another, the more we help ourselves. Acting like a coalition truly does produce results. In 2004, four female executives at Merrill Lynch started having lunch together once a month. They shared their accomplishments and frustrations. They brainstormed about business. After the lunches, they would all go back to their offices and tout one another's achievements. They couldn't brag about themselves, but they could easily do it for their colleagues. Their careers flourished and each rose up the ranks to reach managing director and executive officer levels.[17] The queen bee was banished, and the hive became stronger.

I know that not every woman encounters this kind of positive female support, and yet oddly, we often expect it. Most women don't assume that men will reach out and help, but with our own gender, we assume there will be a connection. We imagine women will act communally and maybe we do so out of our own bias. Once in my career, I felt that a senior woman treated me poorly. She would complain about me and my team behind my back but would not discuss any concerns she had with me, even when I asked directly. When I first met her, I had high hopes that she would be an ally. When she turned out to be not just unhelpful but actually spiteful, I was not just disappointed; I felt betrayed.

Sharon Meers explained to me that this feeling of betrayal was predictable. Both men and women do, in fact, demand more time and warmth from women in the workplace. We expect greater niceness from women and can become angry when they don't conform to that expectation. "I think that's a big part of the protest about executive women being 'mean' to other women," Sharon told me. "I think it's about a double standard we have when we look at female versus male superiors."

I now recognize that had this senior woman been a man and acted the same way, I still would have been frustrated, but I wouldn't have taken it so personally. It's time to drop the double standard. Gender should neither magnify nor excuse rude and dismissive treatment. We should expect professional behavior, and even kindness, from everyone.

Any coalition of support must also include men, many of whom care about gender inequality as much as women do. In 2012, Kunal Modi, a student at Harvard's Kennedy School, wrote an article imploring men to "Man Up on Family and Workplace Issues." He argued that "for the sake of American corporate performance and shareholder returns, men must play an *active* role in ensuring that the most talented young workers (often women . . .) are being encouraged to advocate for their career advancement. . . . So men, let's get involved now—and not in a patronizing manner that marginalizes this as some altruistic act on behalf of our mothers, wives, and daughters—but on behalf of ourselves, our companies, and the future of our country."[18]

I applaud Kunal's message, especially his focus on active engagement. Men of all ages must commit to changing the leadership ratios. They can start by actively seeking out qualified female candidates to hire and promote. And if qualified candidates cannot be found, then we need to invest in more recruiting, mentoring, and sponsoring so women can get the necessary experience.

An "us versus them" crusade will not move us toward true equality. Nor will an "us versus us" crusade, which U.C. Hastings law professor Joan Williams calls the "gender wars." These wars are being waged on many fronts, but the mommy wars, which pit mothers who work outside the home against mothers who work inside the home, attract the most attention. As Professor Williams explains, "These mommy wars are so bitter because both groups' identities are at stake because of another clash of social ideals: The ideal worker is defined as someone always available for work, and the 'good mother' is defined as always available to her children. So ideal-worker women need to prove that, although they weren't always there, their children are fine, fine, fine. . . . Women who have rejected the ideal-worker norm and settled for a slower career (or no career) need to prove that their compromise was necessary for the good of their families. So you have each group of women judging the other, because neither group of women has been able to live up to inconsistent ideals."[19]

Professor Williams is absolutely right. One of the conflicts inherent in having choice is that we all make different ones. There is always an opportunity cost, and I don't know any woman who feels comfortable with all her decisions. As a result, we inadvertently hold that discomfort against those who remind us of the path not taken. Guilt and insecurity make us second-guess ourselves and, in turn, resent one another.

In a letter to *The Atlantic* in June 2012, Barnard president Debora Spar wrote about this messy and complicated emotion, exploring why she and so many successful women feel so guilty. She decided that it's because women "have been subtly striving all our lives to prove that we have picked up the torch that feminism provided. That we haven't failed the mothers and grandmothers who made our ambitions possible. And yet, in a deep and profound way, we are failing. Because feminism wasn't supposed to make us feel guilty, or prod us into constant competitions over who is raising children better, organizing more cooperative marriages, or getting less sleep. It was supposed to make us free—to give us not only choices but the ability to make these choices without constantly feeling that we'd somehow gotten it wrong."[20]

Stay-at-home mothers can make me feel guilty and, at times, intimidate me. There are moments when I feel like they are judging me, and I imagine there are moments when they feel like I am judging them. But when I push past my own feelings of guilt and insecurity, I feel grateful. These parents—mostly mothers—constitute a large amount of the talent that helps sustain our schools, nonprofits, and communities. Remember that mom who pointed out that my son should be wearing a green T-shirt on St. Patrick's Day? She is a tireless volunteer in the classroom and our community. So many people benefit from her hard work.

Society has long undervalued the contributions of those who work without a salary. My mother felt this slight keenly. For seventeen years, she worked more than full-time as a mother and on behalf of Soviet Jewry. She understood that the compensation for her efforts was making a difference in the lives of persecuted people halfway across the world, but many people in her own neighborhood did not consider her work to be as important as a "real job." She was still regarded as "just a housewife"—undercutting the very real but unpaid work of raising children and advocating for human rights.

We all want the same thing: to feel comfortable with our choices and to feel validated by those around us. So let's start by validating one another. Mothers who work outside the home should regard mothers who work inside the home as real workers. And mothers who work inside the home should be equally respectful of those choosing another option.

A few years ago on a visit to the U.S. Naval Academy, I met an extraordinary woman who was about to join the U.S. Submarine Force as one of its first female officers. She was nervous about her new role and aware that there were risks in being an officer and *not* a gentleman. I asked her to let me know how it went. A year later, she followed up with a heartfelt e-mail. "Truthfully I was prepared for opposition and the possibility of being discounted," she wrote. "But it did not happen. I was respected the moment I stepped on board and I can truly say that I am a valued part of the crew." Unfortunately, she told me that she encountered resentment from another source—the navy wives. At an onshore "welcome" dinner, the wives of her colleagues pounced and accused her of being a "bra-burning feminist out to prove a point." They forced her to defend her career choice, reputation, and personal life. "I was shocked! Talk about uncomfortable!" she wrote. "I did my best to answer their questions and stand my ground. Eventually they backed off and started in on my husband!"

We must work harder to rise above this. The gender wars need an immediate and lasting peace. True equality will be achieved only when we *all* fight the stereotypes that hold us back. Feeling threatened by others' choices pulls us all down. Instead, we should funnel our energy into breaking this cycle.

Sharon Meers tells a story about a school parents' night she attended in which the children introduced their parents. Sharon's daughter Sammy pointed at her father and said, "This is Steve, he makes buildings, kind of like an architect, and he loves to sing." Then Sammy pointed at Sharon and said, "This is Sharon, she wrote a book, she works full-time, and she never picks me up from school." To Sharon's credit, hearing this account did not make her feel guilty. Instead, she said, "I felt mad at the social norms that make my daughter feel odd because her mother doesn't conform to those norms."

The goal is to work toward a world where those social norms no longer exist. If more children see fathers at school pickups and mothers who are busy at jobs, both girls and boys will envision more options for themselves. Expectations will not be set by gender but by personal passion, talents, and interests.

I am fully aware that most women are not focused on changing social norms for the next generation but simply trying to get through each day. Forty percent of employed mothers lack sick days and vacation leave, and about 50 percent of employed mothers are unable to take time off to care for a sick child.[21] Only about half of women receive any pay during maternity leave.[22] These policies can have severe consequences; families with no access to paid family leave often go into debt and can fall into poverty.[23] Part-time jobs with fluctuating schedules offer little chance to plan and often stop short of the forty-hour week that provides basic benefits.[24]

Too many work standards remain inflexible and unfair, often penalizing women with children. Too many talented women try their hardest to reach the top and bump up against systemic barriers. So many others pull back because they do not think they have a choice. All of this brings me back to Leymah Gbowee's insistence that we need more women in power. When leadership insists that these policies change, they will. Google put in pregnancy parking when I asked for it and it remains there long after I left. We must raise both the ceiling and the floor.

———

MY MOTHER HAD fewer choices than I did, but with my father's support, she has always worked hard. During my childhood, she chose to be a devoted mother and volunteer. When I left for college, she went back to school to study teaching English as a second language. She taught full-time for fifteen years and felt that teaching was her calling. "At one point, I was asked to become the administrator for the entire school," my mother told me. "I said no, preferring to stay in the classroom and work with my students. I was exactly where I wanted to be."

In 2003, my mother left the workforce to take care of her ailing parents. She was sorry to leave her teaching career, but family has always been her top priority. After my grandparents passed away, she reentered the workforce. She founded Ear Peace: Save Your Hearing, a nonprofit to prevent noise-induced hearing loss in young people. At the age of sixty-five, she has returned to her love of teaching, running workshops and speaking to students from elementary to high school.

My mother has leaned in her entire life. She raised her children, helped her parents spend their final years in dignity and comfort, and continues to be a dedicated and loving wife, mother, and grandmother. She has always contributed to her community and the world. She is my inspiration.

My mother wants to see society achieve true equality. She sees the barriers that women still face, but she also sees new opportunities. She believes that what I have achieved, and much more, is possible for many others. I agree. And more important, so many women that I have encountered agree. Filled with energy, optimism, and self-confidence, they are scrambling along that jungle gym and moving toward their long-term dream.

It's up to us to end the self-fulfilling belief that "women can't do this, women can't do that." Throwing up our hands and saying "It can't be done" ensures that it will *never* be done.

I have written this book to encourage women to dream big, forge a path through the obstacles, and achieve their full potential. I am hoping that each woman will set her own goals and reach for them with gusto. And I am hoping that each man will do his part to support women in the workplace and in the home, also with gusto. As we start using the talents of the entire population, our institutions will be more productive, our homes will be happier, and the children growing up in those homes will no longer be held back by narrow stereotypes.

I know that for many women, getting to the top of their organization is far from their primary focus. My intention is not to exclude them or ignore their valid concerns. I believe that if more women lean in, we can change the power structure of our world and expand opportunities for all. More female leadership will lead to fairer treatment for *all* women. Shared experience forms the basis of empathy and, in turn, can spark the institutional changes we need.

Critics have scoffed at me for trusting that once women are in power, they will help one another, since that has not always been the case.[25] I'm willing to take that bet. The first wave of women who ascended to leadership positions were few and far between, and to survive, many focused more on fitting in than on helping others. The current wave of female leadership is increasingly willing to speak up. The more women attain positions of power, the less pressure there will be to conform, and the more they will do for other women. Research already suggests that companies with more women in leadership roles have better work-life policies, smaller gender gaps in executive compensation, and more women in midlevel management.[26]

The hard work of generations before us means that equality is within our reach. We can close the leadership gap *now*. Each individual's success can make success a little easier for the next. We can do this—for ourselves, for one another, for our daughters, and for our sons. If we push hard now, this next wave can be the last wave. In the future, there will be no female leaders. There will just be leaders.

When Gloria Steinem marched in the streets to fight for the opportunities that so many of us now take for granted, she quoted Susan B. Anthony, who marched in the streets before her and concluded, "Our job is not to make young women grateful. It is to make them ungrateful so they keep going."[27] The sentiment remains true today. We need to be grateful for what we have but dissatisfied with the status quo. This dissatisfaction spurs the charge for change. We must keep going.

The march toward true equality continues. It continues down the halls of governments, corporations, academia, hospitals, law firms, nonprofits, research labs, and every organization, large and small. We owe it to the generations that came before us and the generations that will come after to keep fighting. I believe women can lead more in the workplace. I believe men can contribute more in the home. And I believe that this will create a better world, one where half our institutions are run by women and half our homes are run by men.

I look toward the world I want for all children—and my own. My greatest hope is that my son and my daughter will be able to choose what to do with their lives without external or internal obstacles slowing them down or making them question their choices. If my son wants to do the important work of raising children full-time, I hope he is respected and supported. And if my daughter wants to work full-time outside her home, I hope she is not just respected and supported, but also liked for her achievements.

I hope they both end up exactly where they want to be. And when they find where their true passions lie, I hope they both lean in—all the way.

Sara's Story: I Overcame My Fear and Ran for Mayor of My Town

I CAN STILL REMEMBER how the phone conversation went.

"Sara, the mayor is not running for reelection. You should consider running."

I responded with, "No, I'm not qualified."

Now, in reality, I was as qualified as the mayor who was stepping down. I have a master's degree in public administration. I work for a public agency that connects me to all of our local cities and community leaders. I sit on the Polk County Conservation Board. I am a member of the Planning and Zoning Commission and have served on other boards and committees in my city. So why did I so quickly insist that I wasn't qualified?

My next rationale for why I should not run for mayor was even better than the first: "I can't. I have two young children."

Later that night, before going to bed, I began reading chapter 7 of *Lean In* ("Don't Leave Before You Leave"). I finished the chapter and had a realization: I was holding myself back by believing that I couldn't be both a good mayor and a good mother. In general, I am a strong, independent woman who is used to challenging the world around me, but in that moment, I was shutting myself out of an opportunity. No man would say, "No, I can't run for office because I have two young children at home. I can't be a good dad *and* a good mayor." So the next day I made it known that I would be running for mayor of Pleasant Hill, Iowa. I had officially leaned in.

While I was campaigning, most of the conversations went as follows:

> MAN: Wow, you could be the first female mayor of our city. That's great. So tell me, what did your husband say? Is he okay with you running?

> MAN: It would be great to have you as our mayor; you have excellent credentials. But is your skin thick enough for this?

My guess is that those questions are not asked nearly as frequently of male candidates, if asked at all. Even as I became more and more aware of stereotypes I had to overcome, I found myself once again making a blunder. Right before a fund-raising event, I coached my husband on how to answer a question. "If anyone asks us if we have kids, just say, 'Yes, two boys,' " I told him. "Don't tell them their ages unless they ask."

Our sons were eleven months and two and a half years old at the time, and I was petrified that someone would think that only a heartless mother would run for office when her kids were so young. In reality, that is not the case at all. I am a mother and a passionate public servant. Who is to say that I am not capable of being both?

I was elected mayor of my town on November 5, 2013, with 78 percent of the vote. At the age of twenty-nine, I made history as the youngest and first female mayor of my city.

Even now that I'm in office, there are some who still ask, "How can you do this when you have two young children at home?" My very calm response is always the same: "Why are men allowed to do that and women are not?"

Sara Kurovski is the mayor of Pleasant Hill, Iowa.

Allison's Story: We Are Not Leftover. We Are Leaning In.

"You have a boyfriend, right? When are you getting married?" asked my middle-aged manager. "Remember," he advised, "sooner is always better than later at your age."

I am twenty-seven. I have a boyfriend, and we've been dating for more than two years. We are happy the way things are, yet this is the kind of comment I hear often. Of the eighty people in my department at work, I am one of three women age twenty-seven or older who are not married. I am under constant scrutiny.

In China, where I work for a state-owned bank, I am considered *"shengnu,"* or "leftover." The idea of the Leftover Woman is simple: no matter how many accomplishments, advanced degrees, or professional and personal accolades a woman acquires, if she is past her midtwenties and still single, she is a failure. In the eyes of mainstream society, we are unwanted—decreasing in value day by day.

On the surface, there are a lot of things about the state of women in China that are ahead of much of the world. Most companies here provide three to six months of paid maternity leave. Compared to our neighbors like Japan and South Korea, the proportion of working Chinese women is much larger. And yet the warnings about becoming "leftover" come from all directions, pressuring young women to prioritize family over career.

When I first read *Lean In*, I couldn't help but think that women in China need to hear this! I started talking with a friend, and we decided to form a Lean In Circle to discuss these issues. We now have twelve women, all in our twenties and thirties—from Mainland China, Hong Kong, the United States, and Singapore—who meet twice each month. We work in law, philanthropy, finance, media, and telecommunications. Two of us are married. One of us is taking time off to focus on her young child. Most of us are "leftover."

It can be hard to apply some of the lessons of *Lean In* to the Chinese workplace. At my company, for example, there's no such thing as going to your boss and asking for a raise: salaries are nonnegotiable. The culture in Chinese state-owned companies does not reward taking initiative or risks. Women who are aggressive, outspoken, and "stand out" are marginalized.

There are no easy solutions to these problems, but we're trying to work through them as a group. Our team has helped create more Lean In Circles throughout Beijing. We are working to connect with successful female business leaders to provide positive role models. Of course, we are still dating and getting married. We share stories about romance. But we also are working together to understand that our identities and worth should not be determined by our marital status. We have realized that creating a community makes us stronger.

We are not leftover women. We are women leaning in—China style.

Allison Ye is a twenty-seven-year-old communications professional in Beijing, China.

Own Who You Are

Mellody Hobson

RECENTLY, A WOMAN stopped me at a conference and said, "I heard you speak about ten years ago and you said something that completely blew me away." Obviously, I was intrigued. She continued, "You were on a panel and proclaimed, 'I feel bad for white women.' Everyone in the room stiffened. Then you explained, 'As black women, we know from early childhood that we are going to be discriminated against. It is a fact that runs through most of our lives. So when we get to corporate America, there are no surprises for us. White women, however, are in shock.' "

In this book, Sheryl writes that she graduated from college believing that equality would be achieved in our generation. I was raised to know we still had a long way to go. Once, I came home from a birthday party where I was the only black kid invited and the first question my mother asked was, "How did they treat you?" I responded, "Why would they treat me differently?" And she said, "They're not always going to treat you well." I was seven. My mother was ruthlessly realistic.

The Third Rail

I understand why the white women at the conference stiffened when I pointed out this difference. Gender in the workplace is a difficult topic by itself. Complicating it further with race makes it that much more challenging. Despite the breakthrough election of President Obama, race in America remains a controversial and historically shameful issue. Any mention of it seems taboo. It's the conversational equivalent of touching the third rail—the effect is shock followed by a *long* silence.

Many of Sheryl's friends advised her not to speak out about gender, insisting it would kill her career. Many of my friends shared a similar concern when I decided to write this chapter. One practically grabbed me by the lapels and implored me not to get sucked into "the race thing." She worried that I'd come across as one-dimensional, where all roads lead back to prejudice. And yet I feel compelled to speak out because my mother's question still hangs in the air: *How did they treat you?*

While a black president clearly represents progress, racism is far from dead and sexism isn't either. Over my twenty-two years in the workplace, I have faced repeated and stubborn bias. Of course, I do not pretend to speak for all women of color. No one person can speak for all. We are each unique ... which is why it is so wrong to be lumped together by stereotypes or viewed with narrowed expectations based on skin color or chromosomes. The irony is that dealing with this prejudice *becomes* our shared experience.

Closing the Achievement Gap

All women struggle, but women of color must overcome "double jeopardy," the one-two punch of sexism and racism.[1] The achievement gap between women and men is wider in the African-American and Latino communities than it is in the white community. The educational gap between men and women is more pronounced among African Americans and Latinos, with women earning even more degrees relative to men.[2] Yet this educational achievement is not translating into higher pay or greater leadership roles.

For every dollar a white man earns in the United States, white women earn 78 cents, African-American women earn 64.5 cents, and Latina women earn just 54 cents.[3] Of the Fortune 500 companies, only six have a black CEO and only one is a woman.[4] About 70 percent of corporate board seats are held by white men, and 30 percent of Fortune 250 companies don't have a single black board member.[5] This matters because there is a direct correlation between board diversity and diversity in the executive ranks.[6] Only two publicly traded companies are chaired by a black woman. Ursula Burns, CEO of Xerox, is one. I am the other.

I have always been ambitious—and I say that with pride. I am the youngest of six kids raised by a single mother who married at nineteen and had four children by the age of twenty-four. I was not planned; my oldest sister is more than two decades older than I am, and my closest sibling is nine years older. Although I have my father's name, I never really knew him and my parents never married.

I adored my mother for the unconditional love and encouragement she offered along with her realism. When I was five, I wondered out loud about what presents Santa might bring me and was informed point-blank, "Mommy is Santa." Years later, when I asked my mother why she didn't attend PTA meetings like the other moms, she responded, "Your mom doesn't have that luxury." She said it without apologies or guilt. "It is what it is" has been a mantra throughout my life.

Still, my mother remained optimistic. As often as she told me that "life isn't fair," she also told me, "You can do anything." She was extraordinarily industrious and would always wake up before sunrise. She would then rouse me, saying, "If you sleep past six a.m., life will pass you by." (To this day, I am my mother's daughter, often rising by four in the morning during the week.) Her own options were limited by both her circumstances and her choices. She went into the real estate business, converting old buildings into condominiums, but her work ethic and gut instincts were not enough to drive success. For most of my life, she was a study in contrasts, working extremely hard but consistently unable to make ends meet. In her aspirations for me to have the best, she sometimes overextended herself, buying Easter dresses instead of paying the phone bill.

Sometimes we lived in apartments in downtown Chicago close to one of the country's best public grade schools, which I was fortunate to attend. We were frequently evicted, and when things got really rough, we would move to the South Side, living in partially completed apartments, isolated to a room or two and at times heating water for baths on hot plates. While my childhood was often unsettling, it was not as difficult as some.

School provided tremendous stability for me. I was good at it too. Even in the hardest classes up against the top students, I excelled. I had to. One thing I have learned is that there is little tolerance for error if you're a woman . . . and zero tolerance if you're a woman of color.[7] That's why when one of us achieves, we crush it.

After high school, I headed to Princeton. When this comes up with older folks in professional settings, they sometimes look at me in a way that almost makes me feel like I need to add, "No, I did not take your kid's spot." It amazes me how often some make disheartening insinuations that race got me into the Ivy League. The not-at-all-subtle implication is that my achievements aren't real. This suspicious attitude follows most black people in the workforce, including a chief resident at a top New York City hospital, where patients constantly ask her, "Where did you go to medical school?" She asked fellow residents if they received the same grilling. All the white males said no. Her one black male colleague said yes.

Minorities so often get the worst of both worlds: the assumption of affirmative action without the help of actual diversity programs. I am an unabashed advocate for affirmative action to help offset centuries of slavery and institutionalized racism. There is still much to be done to ensure fairness, equality, and inclusion. Some people of color share my views and others believe these programs hold us back by implying that we are not as good. I respect differences of opinion on this issue. In the end, we all want the same thing.

When we are hired, we don't want any standards to be lowered; we just want those standards to be applied consistently. And we should not pit minorities and women against each other. I have heard so many executives point to white female advancement as a clear signal of progress. When pressed about advancements among people of color, they immediately refer back to white women. This is dangerous, because it suggests diversity and inclusion are a zero-sum game where some win at others' expense.

I was desperate to understand money as a child, so it is no accident that I went into the investment field. After graduating from Princeton with a degree in international relations and public policy, I joined Chicago-based Ariel Investments in client services and marketing. Within a few years, I had worked my way up to be an informal chief of staff to John Rogers, Ariel's founder and my mentor. Soon after I turned thirty-one, I was named president and remain in that position today.

Even though I will never be evicted again, I am haunted

by those times and still work relentlessly. When I think of my career and why I leaned in, it comes down to basic survival. A din of anxiety born out of the dissonance of my childhood stayed with me. Drove me. I leaned in—all in— because I felt I had no other choice.

Go All In

It would be lovely to think that my success was a result of being extraordinary, but the answer is far more boring. I worked hard. Really hard. And that is the key. I was competing with people who were more knowledgeable and better connected. The one thing I knew I could do is outwork everybody.

I also learned early how to study others. I am in some ways the quintessential "inside outsider." All through my life, I've kept an eye out for people who were doing cool things, and I took notes. I still do. When I meet interesting people, I ask them how they spend their day and whom they admire. Some have even remarked that meeting me is like being interviewed. It is not always a compliment, but I can take it. It's worth it to me to keep learning.

Like everyone who succeeds, I had help from others. My first day at Ariel, John gave me an important piece of advice. He explained that I was going to be in a room with people who made a lot of money and had huge titles, but he advised, "Don't assume that just because you are new and young that you don't have great ideas. I want them."

John instilled in me the value of speaking up. He also

instilled in me the value of listening. For the first two years, he took me to all of his meetings, and I heard him pitch Ariel over and over. After the first few months, I started to play a game in my head. Someone would ask John a question and I would try to answer it silently before he did. When I could match his answer, I knew I was getting it. Then I took the game a step further. I started pressing myself, *Do I have an even better answer?* When I thought I did, I would tell him. The first time, John was taken aback; I mean, Ariel was his firm. But when my answer was an improvement, he acknowledged it, thanked me, and offered me even more responsibility.

John's belief in my abilities gave me a seat at the table and a voice early on. Even if you don't have that support from the top, I urge you to participate fully, not in a smug or cocky way, but with humility combined with confidence. If you have an idea, don't hesitate to tell a colleague. Be willing to speak up and stand out. I've seen so many young women hang back, adopting the attitude "Tell me what you expect me to be and I'll be it." A far better approach is to say, "This is who I am and I have value. I hope you will accept it, but if you don't, I'm still good with who I am."

Battling Stereotypes

In my twenties, I crossed paths with a high-ranking woman at a major communications company and asked her for advice. "Smile a lot!" she replied. This struck me as a superficial comment until she dove into its deeper importance. "We all want to work with people who are happy and optimistic," she explained. "We want to work with 'energy givers,' not 'energy takers.'" She was right. I decided that in addition to being considered smart and conscientious, I also wanted to be someone who projected happiness.

This is especially important for black women, who must deal with the stereotype that we are angry. (The parallel for Latinas is that they are overly emotional hotheads; just watch the character Gloria Delgado-Pritchett on *Modern Family*.) I am still amazed by the number of people who meet me for the first time and say, "You are so much nicer than I thought you would be." After some years, I realized the perceptions had very little to do with me or any behavior I had exhibited. It was all about expectations. The assumption is that black women *must* be angry because we are downtrodden or we had to be brutal to survive and make it to where we are. But even if we have every right to be angry, it's better not to give in to that emotion. As Yoda says in *Star Wars:* "Fear leads to anger. Anger leads to hate. Hate leads to suffering." (These words were written by George Lucas, whom I married in 2013.)

Getting labeled "too aggressive" is another red flag. Recently, I was on the phone being my normal hard-driving self with a prospective client. When I sensed he wasn't responding, I knew what I had to do. *The Art of War* advises that sometimes you have to "crouch to conquer." I have seen this tactic work and will consciously make myself small in order to win the bigger prize. In this instance, I decided to pull back. Instead of selling hard, I softened my tone. I inquired about the client's holiday plans. I crouched to conquer.

It may seem odd that I would advise crouching, but in some circumstances I choose to modulate myself. I always try to understand motivations, and I recognize that fear is a deal killer. I don't feel this modulation lessens my sense of self. I actually feel empowered because I know I am in control. Also, I've watched enough men sell, and the best ones modulate too. The trick is to remain authentic while understanding that pounding the table at every meeting will not necessarily advance your larger goals.

Being aware of your culture, including its fears and biases, is hard but essential. Years ago, before traveling to Japan, I was warned that business cards must be accepted with both hands and you must take a moment to read the card and then look up and acknowledge the person who handed it to you. Just as we recognize cultural sensitivities in a foreign country, we must recognize them in our own work environments.

In the investment field, I know that we can't control the stock market, so I try to control everything else within my power. I use the same approach to deal with bias. We can't control other people (unfortunately), but we can control our reactions to them. We can also control how we focus our time and energy and manage our priorities.

Even now in meetings, I'll pitch an idea that is ignored until a white guy says the same thing and everyone loves it. I sit there wondering, *Did they not hear me say that already?*

But I shake off the frustration quickly. Most of the time, there's no gain in calling attention to the last idea. It only keeps you from thinking up the next.

Of course, there are times when it is important and necessary to put a stake in the ground. A while back, I traveled to Texas with two black male colleagues to meet a potential client, who greeted us at the door of his huge office. He ushered us in, then walked over to his desk and told my colleagues to take the two chairs and gestured to the sofa far off by the door for me. I gauged the situation and envisioned myself sitting literally outside the conversation. I immediately responded, "None of us will sit here." Without another word, we all moved to the soft seating area and had our meeting.

Stop Admiring the Problem

At Ariel, when we have hashed and rehashed some injustice or wrong, we are known to say, "We have admired this problem long enough. What are we going to do about it?" When it comes to race and gender, I believe we have admired the problem long enough. What do we do now?

Researchers have coined the term "color blindness" to describe a learned behavior where some pretend they don't even notice race. But instead of exhibiting a lack of prejudice, these people are simply ignoring the problem. This is not helpful. As a recent study concludes, "Rather than avoiding race, smart companies deal with it head-on—and they recognize that 'embracing diversity' means recognizing all races, including the majority one, to avoid showing preference or creating a backlash."[8]

I was driving to a meeting at the Rainbow PUSH offices in Chicago with one of my twentysomething colleagues, who innocently asked, "Am I going to be the only white person there?" I smiled and said, "Have you ever wondered how I feel being the only black person in the room, which is most of the time?" She considered this and said, "I've never thought about that before." Instead of skirting the issue, we need to focus on race, look at it from different angles, and let awareness lead to action.

My mother—and many in her generation—harbored a deep distrust of white people. I don't share this. I am aware that I won't necessarily be treated equally, but that's not something I carry around with me. When possible, I try to use standing out to my advantage, figuring that it's easier for me to be memorable as a black woman in the corporate world. *It is what it is.* I also try to remind myself that so many people grow up surrounded by people who look just like them and do not have the benefit of a diverse environment. Even today when I struggle with feelings of unfairness, John will remind me, "This person has never, ever in his life met someone like you." He is not excusing the person's behavior but trying to view it in context.

I try to remember John's words when I watch grown men struggling to meet my gaze even as they look my white male colleagues squarely in the eye. I try to remember them when I'm at a black-tie event and someone asks me if

I'm with the band. I try to laugh when I'm in first class on an airplane and a white man assumes I'm a flight attendant or when a former board member chastises me, the president, during a meeting because we're out of Diet Coke. Moving to greater equality will change these assumptions and behaviors.

Beware of First and Only

There's a concept in the black community called "first and only." We like being first and only. There are a lot of bios that get written where the person is the first and only of this, that, or the other. And there's a little bit of pride that some people take in that. I think it's dangerous. In 2002, Ariel launched the Black Corporate Directors Conference to bring together board members from Fortune 500 companies and highlight issues of race. We believe those with a seat at the table have a responsibility to push for more representation. Appointing diverse candidates to a board of directors should be the beginning, not the end, of a discussion about diversity. "First and only" is a start. "Fifteen of many" will signal true progress.

I know this is asking a lot of people who are already under enormous pressure. I spoke recently to José Santiago, the first Latino commissioner of the Chicago Fire Department. Historically, fire departments in major cities have been mostly white, so it's very hard for others to break in and especially hard for them to lead. He explained his success to me: "I was serving in places like Iraq, where you always have to be on guard. You're always looking around you. You have a heightened sense of reality. When you are a person of color, you have that heightened sense all the time." I agreed with him and added, "It's very tiring." He agreed with that too.

Of course, we can still use all the help we can get from others, especially those in power. Someone at the top who truly cares about diversity can make a difference. John Skipper, president of ESPN, has been an amazing advocate for diversity and inclusion. He was mentored by longtime ESPN president George Bodenheimer, who made it his mission to hire and promote women and people of color so that he might capture the attention of diverse audiences. Today, ESPN is the most valuable cable franchise in the world. John talks openly about how a heavy hand was needed at times to effect change. He would demand that every open job have a diverse slate of candidates for consideration. He talks about how senior leaders who bristled at the direction would often come to him when they had a minority or female candidate and say, "Do you want me to hire the minority and/or woman *or* the person who is most qualified for the job?" John's answer was always the same, a simple yes.

Own Who You Are

I love swimming (there, another stereotype busted), and one day my coach assigned a drill that required swimming to the end of the pool without taking a breath. It was really hard, and each time I failed, he made me start over. I thought it was a breath-holding exercise, but at the end, he explained it wasn't. I was stumped. Then what was it? "The point of the drill," he said, "was to make you feel comfortable feeling uncomfortable, because that's how most of us spend our day. It teaches you to relax into it and get through it."

It's uncomfortable to talk about race and gender. But we must do it. And when we start to feel comfortable feeling uncomfortable that will be a step in the right direction. If we can relax into it, we can all get through this together.

In 2005, I had an epiphany while sitting in the pews of the magnificent Rockefeller Chapel at the University of Chicago. Legendary disc jockey Tom Joyner was delivering a eulogy at the funeral of *Ebony* magazine founder John H. Johnson, whom he praised for being "unapologetically black." Although the idea had never before occurred to me, the concept landed with me powerfully. I immediately thought of all the times that I tiptoed around my race and gender. I flashed on the image of a church usher who murmurs, "Excuse me," while holding one finger in the air and quietly tiptoeing when seating people after church has started. Although the usher's goal is not to be noticed, he is hard to miss.

I was thirty-six years old and forever changed. Why was I subconsciously apologizing and what did I want to be excused for? I decided I would own who I am. From that day forward, I knew what I would be—unapologetically black and unapologetically a woman.

Mellody Hobson is president of Ariel Investments. She is chair of the board for DreamWorks Animation as well as a director of the Estée Lauder Companies, Groupon, and Starbucks. Mellody also serves on the board of the Chicago Public Education Fund and as chair of After School Matters, a nonprofit that provides Chicago teens with high-quality out-of-school programs. She lives in Chicago and San Francisco with her husband and young daughter.

Nola's Story: To Understand My Future, I Had to Understand My Past

IN HARLEM, where my family lives, the streets are named after storied icons of its past: Frederick Douglass Boulevard, Adam Clayton Powell Jr. Boulevard, W. E. B. DuBois Avenue. Not a single street is named after a woman. Walking through my neighborhood, I didn't doubt for a moment that these civil rights legends deserved to have streets named after them. But I also thought, *Couldn't they find one woman (or maybe two) who deserved a street named after her?*

People often say that New York is America's greatest man-made city, and they might mean this literally. The Empire State Building, Central Park, and the Statue of Liberty were all designed and built by men. At the Metropolitan Museum of Art, 97 percent of the artists in the contemporary section are male (but 83 percent of its nudes are, you guessed it, female). George Washington was inaugurated here. Edgar Allan Poe wrote "The Raven" here. On New York's streets I often feel like I'm walking in the shadow of greatness—of men.

Growing up, I attended a Quaker school in the city. I remember the time my English teacher stood up and recited Gloria Steinem's mantra: "The truth will set you free. But first it will piss you off."

When I look around the streets of Harlem, I remember that yes, this is where Langston Hughes wrote his finest verses, but it is also where Zora Neale Hurston wrote hers. Ella Fitzgerald took the stage for the very first time here. Construction of the Brooklyn Bridge may have been started by a man, but it was finished by a woman. After the chief engineer fell ill and became permanently bedridden, his wife, Emily Roebling, led the project through to its completion. She became the first person ever to cross the Brooklyn Bridge.

By the time I left for college, I understood that New York's history was also shaped by women. But could I ever be one of them? In a city this big, it's easy to feel small, and I still did.

I found inspiration not only in Harlem's past, but in its present. I was recently at a local McDonald's observing a dispute between a female cashier and her male supervisor. He was yelling at her in front of all the rush-hour customers, but she wouldn't back down. He asked her, in coarse and degrading language, why she was causing such a scene. She shot back: "I'm leaning in, motherf**ker!"

The truth set her free. It also pissed her off.

I knew what that felt like. I had been angry not to recognize myself in my own city's history. So when I returned to New York after college, I worked to bring attention to the story of the women of Harlem. I convinced tour guides to include more women's landmarks, such as Billie Holiday's first apartment, on their routes. I urged groups of graffiti artists to accept and highlight women street artists, and I was happy to see one young artist adopt the name Sojourner Truth.

My mother and I also successfully petitioned the city to plant more trees to make Harlem a greener place. Harlem has so much history, and those trees make us feel, in our own little way, like our family has a part in its future. New York's women have never been afraid to lean in. I am proud to join them.

Nola Barackman is a recent graduate of Tufts University and a new team member at LeanIn.Org.

Matthew's Story: I Learned to Sit at the Table

I STILL GET heart palpitations when I think about walking into that first meeting. It was a few years after college, and I'd been hired at a public affairs agency in Washington, D.C. I was fresh off my first job as a field organizer, rallying voters on a local level, and D.C. felt like the big leagues.

I was assigned to an important project, managing campaign organizers in fifteen states. It meant I was expected to attend the Monday-morning meetings with the senior team, dressed in a suit and tie.

I showed up in the only suit I owned (a tattered relic of bar mitzvah season 1998), feeling like a kid at the grown-ups' table. The room was large with a long, menacing conference table and half a dozen phones in a line down the middle. Around it sat lobbyists, former politicians, and political henchmen, all of whom had been at it for decades. I recognized their faces from the news.

As soon as I walked through the door, I was sure everyone quickly pegged me as an impostor. They could probably see my athletic socks underneath my slacks. This impostor feeling was so overwhelming that I made a conscious decision not to sit at the table and opted instead for a folding chair in the corner. I wish I could say this happened only at the first meeting, but it became routine. Week after week,

I plopped into a chair in a corner, avoiding eye contact in case someone tried to engage me in conversation.

The fact is I had unique expertise: I'd spent much of the past two years learning how best to rally people as a field organizer for a presidential campaign. On the subject of how to play the "ground game," I was the most knowledgeable person in the room. But I was paralyzed by fear. These were conversations about how to influence the top lawmakers in Washington. In a discussion about an influential senator, it wasn't uncommon for one of the seasoned lobbyists to stand up and proclaim, "Let me just call his cell." So I sat mute, terrified they might realize I didn't belong.

Then a funny thing happened. After hearing these experts in fancy suits talk week after week, I started to notice something that's stayed with me ever since. No matter how old, experienced, and confident they were, there was a sense of theater to it all. They used lots of buzzwords. They were steadfast in their belief about how a given situation should be handled. Even when their arguments lacked substance, they didn't waver. I started to realize that, to some degree, all of them were making it up as they went along. We all are.

A week came when the meeting topic was grassroots organizing, and I knew I had to weigh in. I decided it was time to take my seat at the table and earn the respect of the others in the room. I walked to an open seat. Not only did the silver-haired lobbyists on either side greet me, but after the meeting began I actually summoned the courage to offer my opinion.

Those meetings continued every week for almost a year. I still wore the same baggy suit, but I did buy a six-pack of black dress socks to my mother's delight. From that day forward, I made sure to arrive early and take my seat at the table—and came to believe I actually deserved to be there.

Matthew Slutsky is the managing director of partnerships at Change.org.

Man Up and Lean In

Kunal Modi

UNTIL A FEW YEARS AGO, I never thought much about gender. I was raised in a traditional home. My dad went to the office each day. My mom took care of my brother and me. I grew up loving math and football and combined the two when I started a fantasy football league at business school in 2011. I was never a total bro, but I've definitely had my fair share of frat-boy moments.

Then, early in my career as a consultant, I stood with my team making a presentation to a senior client. These meetings usually went smoothly, but this one was a train wreck. The client, a woman, expressed concerns about the work and suggested that we reconsider our analysis. When our mostly male team regrouped, we had plenty to discuss. But instead of talking about the project, my colleagues started in on the client.

"Sometimes she can be overly emotional; let's not over-react."

"Yeah, she can be moody, and I think she's under a lot of stress."

"We just have to calm her down."

I had never heard the words "moody" or "emotional" used to describe a male client. Weren't we just reducing our client to a stereotype? Why were we even discussing her mood? Wasn't the issue our work, not her reaction? All these questions raced through my head, but I sat through the debriefing in silence.

Looking back, I wish I'd spoken up and defended her. Still, I understand why I didn't. I was afraid of being that guy—the one who's overly sensitive. You know, *the wuss.*

But at the risk of being the wuss . . . or that preachy guy who no one likes . . . or a total tool, I am speaking up now. Because what happened that day happens all the time. And it will keep happening until men stop perpetuating the biases that hold women—and all of us—back.

Gender issues are men's issues too. Undervaluing half our population limits the performance of our economies and companies. Expecting men to focus primarily on their jobs often prevents us from being full partners at home, which harms our families and children. It's time to man up and lean in.

I have heard the skeptics. Some men are quick to point out, "Women are doing fine—our valedictorian was a woman and so is my boss." While much progress has been made in the past fifty years, women are still grossly under-represented in the top ranks of our society, from board-rooms to governments. Pointing out that women now hold 20 percent of the U.S. Senate seats ignores the fact that men still hold the other 80 percent.[1]

I've even heard some men insist, "Women actually have a leg up. They've got all these women-only conferences and networking events. I just recommended a friend for a job and they turned him down because they're looking for a woman." But stories like this just prove we are not living in a gender-neutral world. As we work toward gender equality, there will be uncomfortable moments and some decisions may seem unfair. But women have been dealing with discomfort and unfairness for a long time. The ultimate goal is greater fairness and real choice for all of us, both at work and in our homes.

Can we get there? We can try.

Admit We're All Biased

Like many, I was raised to believe that women and men are equals. But looking back, I can now see some of my own blind spots. When I set up that fantasy football league for my classmates in business school, I figured it would be a fun way to build relationships. I didn't invite any women, assuming that fantasy football was a guy thing. And maybe it was. But I should've opened up the invitation to class-mates of both genders and let them make that call. And if enough women weren't interested, maybe I should have thought of a more inclusive way to bond.

Other forms of sexism are more blatant. Just a few years ago, a prominent venture capitalist did a Q&A at my business school. Venture capital has long been an old boys' club, so it made sense when one of my female classmates asked him to give advice to women who wanted to go into his field. He bluntly replied that women should not pursue investing as a career because they would not fit into the work culture. As proof, he mentioned his firm's all-male investment team. This statement was surprisingly frank and sadly honest. An audible gasp was heard in the lecture hall. After the initial shock wore off, several women *and men* left the room and crossed that company's name off their job-hunting list.

Subtle or blatant, let's acknowledge that sexism exists. Biases are deeply ingrained from our earliest experiences. Toy planes for boys; toy ovens for girls. Computers for bro-grammers; dresses for princesses. As we grow older, these biases persist. Football and math for boys; cheerleading and poetry for girls. We're party animals; women are hot messes. We're players; women are sluts. And the biases continue when we enter the workforce. We're leaders; women are bossy. We're demanding; women are dramatic.

Because these biases run so deep, they won't go away overnight. But we can start calling out double standards when we see them. In the past, men in my generation have hesitated to do this. Half of millennial men agree that women are scrutinized more harshly in the workplace than their male colleagues, but I don't see men express that opinion to one another very often.[2] Instead, we remain silent—just as I did with the "emotional" client.

Let's drop the silence. Let's speak up when we hear women called "moody" or "stressed" or dismissed with the catchall put-down "she's crazy." Maybe she's not crazy after all. Maybe she's right.

Another subtle example of bias is to point out that a woman is "not that well liked" by her peers. I've witnessed this throughout my career. If I voice a provocative opinion, people think I'm taking charge and showing initiative. When a woman does the same, she's a bitch. So when you hear a woman described by a colleague—male or female—as too aggressive or not that well liked, ask the person to be more specific about what happened. You'll be surprised how often the answer is either vague—"She's just annoying"— or something we might all do in the course of our jobs. In either of these cases, you might raise the possibility that this negative view is the result of gender bias. Not everyone will see it that way, or be willing to admit it, but those who do can adjust their attitudes.

Don't cast women in supporting roles. During one project at work, my team affectionately referred to a female colleague as our "team mom." She was high energy, kept our team on track, and pitched in to help those struggling with their work. We thought of the nickname as a compliment but, in retrospect, the label likely boxed her into a narrow role and stopped her from getting the respect she deserved. Even though she was senior to me, I felt free to break the rules she set for timelines and due dates. Who always listens to his mom?

A female friend once pointed out that women frequently take notes in meetings, not necessarily because they are asked, but often because they volunteer. But whoever takes notes can't participate to the same degree. The person who has the good ideas in the meeting gets the promotion over the diligent note taker every time.

Jump in when women get interrupted. At the next meeting you attend, pay attention to who gets interrupted. If it happens a lot to women in your group, you can help. Be the one who says, "I'd like to hear where she was going with that idea." Or circle back with, "Was that all you had to say, or did you have more?" If it feels awkward to call out a serial interrupter in public, maybe pull him or her aside after the meeting and raise the issue. There's a good chance the person is not aware of this pattern.

Make sure women receive fair credit. Women have been socialized to downplay their success, while men are allowed to parade their accomplishments openly: *High five, bro!* And all of us tend to celebrate men more than women at work. So a man might have "a brilliant idea" while a woman with the same idea just "helped the team." Let's make sure our female colleagues are acknowledged and high-fived too.

Improve Your Company

Beyond influencing our immediate coworkers, we can also have a larger impact in the workplace even as entry-level employees.

Help set up mentorship programs. In almost every industry, there are not enough women in senior management to mentor all of the junior women. Senior men need to jump in and do their part. If your company doesn't have a formal mentorship program, suggest one. It's proven that they make a difference.[3]

Ask human resources to provide bias training. Bias is everywhere, and if you don't think you're affected by it, then you *really* need this training.

Evaluate company social events. Social activities at school or work aim to help people bond but can actually do the opposite. A friend of mine told me about her first company offsite: paintballing, her personal idea of hell. But she didn't want to seem like a bad sport, so she went along. When the man who planned the event—her boss—asked her if she'd had fun, she said she loved it. I bet some guys have lied about loving paintball too.

It's even tougher to monitor casual get-togethers. Assuming that women are not interested in sporting events or poker nights is exclusionary. Assuming that men are not interested in book clubs or cooking groups is exclusionary too. I'm not saying everyone has to invite everyone to everything. Just be mindful.

Talk about families at work. When I was interviewing for jobs, nobody asked me if or when I plan to have children. My female classmates fielded those questions regularly, reinforcing the idea that women have to choose between raising a family and having a career.

When a well-known female executive spoke at my business school, my classmates grilled her about the challenges of balancing a senior role and motherhood. When a well-known male executive spoke on campus, he was asked only about his career. It is just as important to ask our male role models about domestic responsibility as it is to ask senior women to share lessons on career advancement.

Male mentorship also overly focuses on work. But this may be changing. A group of fathers in my office recently started a new dads' initiative. The group created a forum for men in the office to share stories and tips about navigating early fatherhood while transitioning back into the rhythm of the workplace.

Do Your Job at Home

Compared to the homes we grew up in, millennial families are more likely to depend on both parents as breadwinners.[4] What hasn't changed as much is that women continue to do the majority of child care and household chores.[5] I believe this will shift in the next decade as fathers realize that being an involved parent is critical to their children's development.

My fiancée and I don't have children yet, but we are trying to establish an equal split right off the bat. Our weeks get hectic, so we spend fifteen minutes every Sunday planning who will do which chores and cook dinner during the upcoming week. Setting aside time to discuss how we'll share the load has helped us avoid arguments and miscommunication. Plus, we take on each responsibility willingly. I'm not helping my fiancée by making dinner. I'm simply making dinner.

Man Up and Do Your Part

My grandmother was pulled out of school at fifteen to be married off by her parents. She had different dreams and insisted that all of her children, including my mother, pursue an education. My mother became the first woman in our family to graduate from college and get a professional job. But after a bright start to her accounting career, she decided to stay home and raise her sons. My fiancée is the first woman in her family to earn an MBA and is a product manager at a health-tech company. What will be our family's story?

Will my wife's male colleagues help her overcome the biases and barriers in the workplace that could keep her from reaching the top? Will I be the kind of husband who fully shares responsibilities at home? Will our future children live in a world where everyone can achieve his or her full potential? Will I someday not be considered a wuss for thinking about this stuff?

I hope we can move forward together. I hope we can push beyond outdated, knee-jerk reactions about how men and women are supposed to act. Let's work toward gender equality—and not in a patronizing manner that cloaks this as a selfless endeavor on behalf of our mothers, wives, and daughters. We need to take action for ourselves and our future.

Kunal Modi is a consultant at McKinsey & Company, where he focuses on consumer and enterprise technology. A former strategy manager at Teach for America, he also served in the AmeriCorps program in Washington, D.C., with LIFT, a nonprofit combating poverty. Kunal lives in San Francisco with his fiancée.

Ursula's Story: Where I Was Didn't Define Who I Was

I WAS RAISED by a wonderful mother in the rough-and-tumble public housing projects on the Lower East Side of Manhattan. Many people told me I had three strikes against me: I was black. I was a girl. And I was poor.

Mom didn't see it that way. She constantly reminded me that where I was didn't define who I was. She knew that education was my way up and out. On a modest salary, Mom somehow managed to send me to good Catholic schools. Back then I was prepared for one of three career options: nun, teacher, or nurse.

None of those paths felt quite right for me, and I began to dream of becoming an engineer. Brooklyn Polytechnic Institute offered me a spot in the freshman class and I panicked—a classic case of being careful what you wish for. I didn't have the right preparation. The school was in a different borough of New York City that seemed foreign and distant. I feared the students would surely be smarter than me.

It was my first "lean back, lean in" crossroads. It would have been so simple to let go of my dreams and set out on a more predictable journey. However, the courage and confidence that my mother and Cathedral High School had given me enabled me to lean in. It wasn't easy. I had a lot of catch-up courses to master. I was an oddity in a sea of predominantly white males. I doubted myself big-time.

I started out in chemical engineering, which I hated, and switched to mechanical engineering, which I loved. And, ever so slowly, I regained my footing.

My life since then has been a series of lean in moments: taking an internship with Xerox in upstate New York, going to an Ivy League school for a graduate degree, signing on with Xerox, and climbing the ladder to the top. As CEO, I pulled the trigger on a major acquisition, which has transformed Xerox from a copy and printing company into a technology and services enterprise.

Dreams do come true, but not without the help of others, a good education, a strong work ethic, and the courage to lean in. That's why I spend so much time with organizations that help minorities and women gain the education and self-respect they need to take risks, to dream big, and, I hope, to someday pay it forward.

Ursula Burns is the CEO of Xerox.

Marie's Story: I Testified Against My Rapist

IN EARLY FEBRUARY 2012, my husband, Kyle, and I moved into a new home to accommodate our growing family. I had earned my master's degree in psychology and was working as a counselor and supervisor at an addiction treatment center. Our daughter was nineteen months old and the love of our lives. We planned on having a second child when Kyle was finished with his graduate studies. Life was rich with gratitude and joy.

Shortly after the move, our lives changed forever. On March 14, a man entered our home, tied me up, placed duct tape over my eyes, and raped me at gunpoint. I pleaded with him: "Please don't do this." He coldly commanded me to shut up. He threatened my life and the life of my child. He left me bound, blinded, and naked in a house that could never again be called my home.

The words "shut up" and threats to harm my daughter haunted me in the moments after he left. I managed to get myself up and open the door. My two dogs rushed in and began licking my wounds, pulling at the duct tape over my eyes. A corner loosened, and I could see.

I knew that I faced an agonizing choice countless women have had to make: Do I speak out or remain silent? There were grave risks and unspeakable losses associated with either decision.

Then a deep conviction came over me. Silence meant spiritual and emotional death, as if forever bound and sightless, unable to be a mother, a wife, a therapist, and a human being with the capacity to thrive. With my hands tied behind my back, I found my phone and dialed 911.

The perpetrator was apprehended. My husband and I have spent the last year engaged in court proceedings; my attacker attempted to deny or minimize the assault throughout. Just before trial, he pled guilty; the evidence was overwhelming and we would not be silenced.

On the day of the sentencing, my husband and I addressed the court and the perpetrator directly. I thought of the countless female survivors still bound by terror, believing that their voices do not matter. I ached to invite each of them into the courtroom to stand beside me.

As I began my statement, my voice trembled, but with the vision and unsung strength of my sisters beside me, the reality of loved ones behind me, and the support of our community surrounding me, my voice steeled. My eyes met the eyes of the perpetrator, and I numbered his crimes. Hope replaced fear. I inhabited my body for the first time since my rape. Following our statements, the judge sentenced him to thirty-one and a half years in prison without parole.

I refused to shut up. Instead, I have added my voice to a growing culture of advocacy that is transforming silence into a chorus of human empowerment and reclaimed hope.

Marie Tueller is a mental health counselor in Prescott, Arizona.

Listen to Your Inner Voice

Rachel Simmons

COMING OUT of college, I believed life was a test I could ace. I just had to work hard, excel, and impress everyone I ever met. I moved to a dingy hole-in-the-wall in New York City's East Village and focused—okay, *obsessed*—about my future. I wrote out a list of goals. I even tacked it to the back of my bathroom door, so that every time I peed I was staring at all I was going to accomplish.

A year later, I won a Rhodes Scholarship to study at the University of Oxford. I was working for Mayor Rudy Giuliani at the time, and he hosted a press conference to announce my award, inviting my family and college president to sit proudly in the front row. The next day, the New York *Daily News* ran a headline: "Finally, a Genius in City Hall." My college plastered me all over their admissions materials, and I flew off to England to study politics.

Pretty impressive, right? Except the story doesn't end

there. In England, I was unhappy in my classes and failed to make good friends. After a year, I dropped out. I moved back in with my bewildered and sometimes angry parents. No one could understand how I would bail on the Rhodes Scholarship. My college president said I had embarrassed our school. I was ashamed and rarely left my childhood bedroom. I sat on the carpeted floor, crying and looking at sports trophies collecting dust. I felt like I was collecting dust too.

I soon realized that doing my homework and working late nights had allowed me to achieve my goals while ignoring my desires. My self-esteem had become so intertwined with racking up accomplishments and earning praise that when I stopped succeeding, my sense of self shattered. "I don't know who I am anymore," I kept saying to my friends.

In this book, Sheryl asks a powerful question: "What would you do if you weren't afraid?" Looking back at those days sitting on the floor of my bedroom, I realize I was scared. And that feeling lasted a long time.

My story is not unique. Many of the students I teach today feel paralyzed and overwhelmed. More of them need to understand that it's okay to freak out, worry, and wonder as they make the transition into the real world. Through my work as a co-founder of the Girls Leadership Institute, I encourage them to accept uncertainty and pursue leadership on their own terms.

What Should I Do Now?

I get a lot of panicked questions from recent grads, but most of them boil down to the same thing: "What should I do now?" I explain that it's normal to be confused, that the path through your twenties is messy and often painful. They wait for me to say more, and when I don't, they react with disappointment. They press again. *Just tell me what to do,* they say.

That question is a big part of the problem. As we shift from being students to being workers, we need to listen less to other people and more to ourselves. The truth is that there is no "perfect" next step waiting for you like the mythical love of your life. So why are we looking for it? And why would we expect someone else to tell us how to find it?

Unfortunately, many young women are not trained to listen to themselves. Instead, they are told that they have to excel at all costs and there is one "right path" that will lead to success. And while these routes result in a lot of pats on the back, they also deliver a sucker punch to our *inner* voice. We need to listen to the inner voice that helps us know and express how we feel, face failure gracefully, and deal with conflict directly. Your inner voice is your compass. It will help you figure out the answer to "What should I do now?"

I can now admit that I never wanted to study political theory in England. I wanted to be a Rhodes Scholar—to win an award and be told I was special. I could have saved myself a lot of unhappiness if I had honestly answered the question "Do I really want to move to England to read essays written by dead white guys?" Had I listened to my inner voice, I would have made different decisions.

Breaking the Rules

So many students are plagued by stress as they strive for perfection—the overachieving girl's ruthless trifecta of being academically successful, well rounded, and attractive.[1] But even as they pursue perfection, they hold themselves back, avoiding opportunities and challenges that may sully their shiny image. They don't speak up unless they have the right answer . . . or take a class that might be hard but interesting . . . or pursue any goal that is not a sure thing. They trade the experience of learning and growing for the appearance of flawlessness. This pursuit of a "right path" may be exacerbated by professors, parents, and career development officers who warn that veering off may result in an unfulfilled, unhappy life, possibly involving multiple cats.

These messages, combined with normal confusion, send some new graduates into a tailspin. My friend and former intern Jahleese calls it the "senior year slap in the face." It's that moment when you realize that you alone have to make your own decisions and you alone will have to face the consequences: *What if the job doesn't lead to where I want to go? What if I can't get a job in the first place? What if I hate grad school? What if I make the wrong choice?* These questions arise not because there is no path but because we expect there to be a *single* one. Uncertainty should invite curiosity and reflection, but instead it generates fear.

Learn to accept uncertainty as an important first step to true self-discovery. To start finding *your* path, begin listening to that inner voice. Tap into what *you* think and feel, what *you* truly care about. Don't worry about finding your passion and life's calling immediately. Those usually take time. But do avoid becoming a passenger in your own life.

Internalized gender norms are a big reason why women struggle with taking risks and speaking out. We're socialized to please others before ourselves, which further disconnects us from that inner voice. Leaning in to your true feelings isn't something you're born knowing how to do. It requires practice. The great news is that these skills are like muscles: the more you use them, the stronger they get.

Take direct eye contact. That's not something that comes naturally to everyone, especially to those of us who come from cultures where it's considered disrespectful. Many of us have to make an effort to do it, and keep doing it, every day. Sometimes we have good days and make what I call FLEC—fierce lady eye contact. Sometimes we lose our nerve and look down. But the only way we get better is with practice.

What Are You Thinking Right Now?

As you read this sentence, you might be hearing a voice in your head. Perhaps it's saying, *I'm hungry.* Or, *I want to check my Instagram.* These are the sounds of the authentic thoughts that flit around your brain. Tuning in to that voice doesn't mean you're crazy; it means you are connected with what's going on inside.

For many years, every time I met someone new, I instantly tried to be his or her friend. I smiled a lot, asked questions, cracked self-deprecating jokes. Then one day, it hit me: I never stopped to ask myself if I actually liked the person I had just met. I simply assumed it was my job to make him or her like *me*. Once I started paying attention to my feelings, my behavior changed. I became more deliberate about making friends, which paid off in better boundaries and less drama.

What does your inner voice say? Does it edit your ideas before you speak up? Does it say, *I am tired of putting up with my friend being late to meet me?* Does it say, *Please stop interrupting me?* Does it say, *You're not really into that guy you've been seeing. You're actually into the girl sitting next to him . . . which means, I believe, that you're gay?* (Okay, that last one was definitely mine.) Our thoughts fuel our actions. If you don't tune in, you may be letting someone else take the wheel.

And, trust me, the more you listen, the louder that voice will get. Recently, on my way to work, I picked up coffee at my usual place. I get a discount because I'm a frequent patron, but that day the barista forgot and overcharged me. My first instinct was to let it go, be nice, and do the "good girl" thing. I didn't want the guy to think I was demanding or harsh. But I heard the voice in my head saying, *Isn't it supposed to be a dollar twenty?* So I repeated it out loud . . . and got forty cents back, with an apology.

Does that seem like a tiny and ordinary example? That's part of my point. You can practice listening to and sharing that voice in the most mundane moments. Maybe it's when you change your order at a restaurant. Or maybe it's when you sit down with your roommates and ask them to start doing the chores they've been neglecting. (Texting or leaving a note on the fridge doesn't count. You have to say it.)

Each time you listen to your inner voice and then act, you flex the muscle and build the habit, so that when your boss offers you $35,000 but you want to ask for $40,000, you'll be ready to speak up. As you build to moments like this, you get closer to leading the life you truly want.

Make the First Down, Not the Touchdown

As your dreams take shape, keep in mind that having robust ambition is a great thing, but placing unreasonable pressure on yourself isn't.

You know that famous saying "Do one thing every day that scares you"? Well, I can't stand it. It's a misleading statement that can hold you back. Who wants to be scared every day? How about "Do one thing every day that makes you slightly nervous"? Not as catchy, I know, but that's actually the way real, meaningful change happens.

Now twenty-five, Jahleese dreams of having her own

bakery, but she can't afford to start her own business, nor does she want the burden of financing culinary school on the weekends. So she works a day job to pay the bills and interns two nights a week at a New York City bakery. Little by little, night by night, Jahleese is moving the ball forward.

What's a goal you have right now? If pursuing the whole goal is too much, try breaking it down into smaller steps. Because small goals are more manageable, they eliminate the toxic mix of anxiety, perfectionism, and shame that often hinders our progress. So if you're scared to speak up at work but know it's necessary for success, here are some possible first steps to take:

- Make a list of all the benefits of speaking up.
- Spend time getting to know colleagues so you feel less anxious about speaking up.
- Talk with your supervisor about your goal to speak up.
- Write down what you want to say before you have to say it.
- Practice speaking up with someone you're more comfortable with, like a parent or friend or coworker you trust.

Once you decide on your small goal, make a date and time to go for it. As you take these smaller steps, you'll become more confident and comfortable. When it's time to raise your hand and speak, you'll be able to do it.

And lean on your peers, even if their goals are different from yours. These people don't need to be mentors or even know what their next life step is. They just need to be trying, like you are, and be able to offer the feedback and encouragement that will help you take your next step forward.

What's the Worst That Can Happen?

When you're scared to take a risk, it also helps to ask two questions: "What's the worst that can happen?" and "Can I live with that?" For most people, imagining a worst-case scenario takes some of the mystery out of the risk. In the case of speaking up, the worst that can happen probably includes: "I'll have the wrong answer," "I'll say it the wrong way," "People will judge me."

All of those things are possible. Maybe even probable, since they happen to everyone. But focusing exclusively on the negative only allows the fear to grow. Being wrong doesn't mean you're stupid, it means you're trying. And isn't that something you can—and maybe even should— live with? Also take a moment to consider the best thing that can happen. You get the right answer, express yourself clearly, and solve a problem or help your team.

Anxiety, like cheap takeout, is a staple of life after graduation—even for your peers who seem to have it all figured out. Feeling afraid doesn't have to lead to feeling paralyzed. You don't need to know what you want to do with the rest of your life, or even the rest of the evening, to start listening to your inner voice.

Some experiences are hard, but sticking them out is worth it. Others are just wrong for who you are. If you feel miserable and tortured, drop out. Leave. But don't go sit on your bedroom floor for weeks as I did. Don't punish yourself because you took a wrong turn. As Oprah Winfrey said in a recent commencement address, "There is no such thing as failure. Failure is just life trying to move us in another direction."[2]

Lick your wounds, cry your eyes out, but then get back out there. When we invest ourselves in worrying about what other people think, we lose touch with what we stand for. By seeking others' approval and trying to be perfect at everything we do, we disconnect from our internal compass. We value how we appear to others over who we really are. Keep listening to that inner voice and taking those small steps forward along your own path.

I was speaking at a high school in South Africa when I told my Rhodes dropout story for the first time. (Yes, I was so afraid to share my story publicly that I had to do it in another hemisphere.) After I finished, there was a pause. Then the students and their parents stood up and cheered. I finally understood that my experience was not a mistake that needed to be hidden. It was the beginning of leaning in to my more authentic self.

Rachel Simmons is co-founder of the Girls Leadership Institute, a national nonprofit that empowers girls. She is the author of two best-selling books, Odd Girl Out *and* The Curse of the Good Girl, *and develops programs for the Wurtele Center for Work and Life at Smith College. She lives in Northampton, Massachusetts, with her daughter.*

Ty-Licia's Story: I Learned to Be Myself

LIKE MANY STUDENTS in urban communities across America, I grew up surrounded by violence, poverty, and failing schools. The messages I received told me I was set up for teenage pregnancy, prison, and an early death. I was born to a young mother. My teenage father was murdered down the street from my home. I have more cousins in prison than have graduated from high school. By age ten, I was very conscious of who I was *supposed* to become.

I was also blessed with a mother and grandmother who believed I could be more. My mother worked three jobs to support our family. When I was in third grade, she asked me if I'd learned anything in school. I told her I hadn't and that it had been that way since kindergarten. She sprang into action, and a year later, I was attending a charter school that my mother and other members of our community had rallied to open.

It was there that I fell in love with learning. It was also there that I realized what I was up against as a young black woman in East Oakland, California. I remember vividly the day my sixth-grade class was lined up for P.E. and a car rolled by and the people inside opened fire. Instantly I began to question, *Why did they shoot at us? What did we do?*

My family moved to Stockton to try to get away. Stockton remains one of the poorest communities in America, yet it was far enough from Oakland that I felt I could be myself. Most days, I spent my lunch period reading. I asked my teachers for extra assignments and got good grades. By sophomore year, I was involved in the poetry club, the debate club, and the mayor's youth advisory committee. I was even elected president of my class—three times!

Malcolm X once stated that "education is the passport to the future." My senior year, I remember getting a call from a friend asking what colleges I would apply to. I had a high GPA and had done lots of community service, but my guidance counselor encouraged me to attend community college. It was her doubt that pushed me to apply to a four-year university. I wanted to prove her wrong. I decided that I would be the first in my family to attend college.

In 2008, I entered the University of the Pacific, a private school in Stockton, and majored in political science. Four years later, as I made my way across the floor of the gym to receive my diploma, my family stood and cheered, waving homemade signs. There were thirty of them, ranging in age from seventy to one. Looking at their faces, I could see the tears streaming down my mother's cheeks. And it hit me: my college graduation was more than a celebration of academic achievement; it was a celebration of my mother's hard work, my grandmother's prayers, and my family's protection.

During college, I focused my studies on the role that education plays in building communities and creating leaders. I wanted to understand who gets what in this country and why. Through my courses and my engagement with the broader Stockton community, I began to see the complexities of a system that creates a glass ceiling for women, minorities, and the poor. I realized the difference between agency and structure: that there are some situations people can control and others created by the system. I began to see academia as a great connector between theory and practice. At the same time, I became so frustrated by the constant listing of problems—and the lack of action—that I knew I had to do something.

Today I am the proud co-founder of a program that empowers teens to become agents of change. Our students are not those you might consider traditional "leaders." Some are at risk of dropping out of high school and have had disciplinary problems. Like me, many of them had been told that they would never amount to much. Our goal is to prove those voices wrong. Through skills training, organizing, and mentoring, we try to reach the students who wouldn't ordinarily have the chance to experience life on a university campus. We're taking children who've been labeled "problems" and training them to be thinkers and leaders.

My life did not begin under perfect circumstances, but I had a family who believed I could persevere. I am blessed to know I can be that positive voice and source of support for others.

Ty-Licia Hooker is the co-founder of the Summer Success and Leadership Academy at the University of the Pacific.

Mana's Story: I Spoke Out About
My Eating Disorder and Recovery

S EVEN YEARS AGO, I wrote my first "coming out" story.

As a freshman in college, I had disappeared for a few months. Without telling anyone at school except my therapist, I checked myself into an eating disorder treatment facility and fought my way through the most painful four months of my life.

The roots of my eating disorder were deeply complex. I had been diagnosed with anorexia nervosa as a senior in high school, and despite months of therapy, my disorder worsened during my first semester of college. I was constantly exhausted, disappointed with myself, and officially done with being sick. I flew home across the country and told my parents that I couldn't go back to school. I was ready to get some serious help.

Checking myself into rehab saved my life. But equally important, it profoundly changed my perspective, my priorities, and my definition of happiness. I came out of treatment feeling empowered and prepared to overcome anything. But I still wasn't ready to tell others. I feared that I would be labeled the "rehab girl," an identity I thought I couldn't handle. All I wanted was a fresh start.

When I returned to school, I chose a new major, found new housing, and made new friends. I also got healthier, developed new ambitions, and began to love college. But something was always missing. I began to realize that I was incredibly proud of the challenges I had overcome, and I wanted my close friends to know that I was who I was *because* of rehab, not despite it. Without sharing my story, I felt as if I was hiding my true identity.

Very slowly, I began opening up to friends about where I had been and what I had experienced. Once I started sharing, people shared back. Almost everyone had a story about herself, her friends, or her family, and they all pointed to a similar theme: getting help for a mental health issue was seen as a weakness. I realized that this was the same mindset that had kept me sick for so long. I wanted to help fight this stigma around mental health issues. I wanted others to know that getting help was an empowering process and not one to be ashamed of. But how could I do that if I was still afraid to share my own story?

I knew it was time to come out of hiding. As I began writing about my journey and the power I gained through treatment, my fears transformed into passion. When our college paper published my story as an op-ed, I received e-mails from individuals all over campus, sharing their hopes for improved mental health at our university.

After the article, I teamed up with diverse student leaders to tackle the stigma surrounding mental illness. We fought for increased funding for our counseling center and launched campaigns to destigmatize seeking out mental health services.

Being open about my experience taught me that sometimes the things I'm most scared to pursue are the most important ones to act on. After overcoming my fear to write that article, anything seems possible.

Mana Nakagawa is a doctoral student at Stanford University.

Find Your First Job

Mindy Levy

A FEW YEARS AGO, when interviewing applicants for a job at my company, I met a candidate who had all the right skills. At the end of the interview, he thanked me and told me it was his dream to work for one of the top accounting firms. That would have been the perfect way to end the interview—if I worked for an accounting firm. Needless to say, he didn't get the job.

I've seen my share of rookie mistakes. We all make them. But we make fewer when we prepare and practice. As an industrial psychologist, I've spent much of my career working with organizations to help employees reach their full potential. As a leadership coach, I help individuals listen to their internal voices and guide them into fulfilling jobs.

Taking the first step onto your career path takes tremendous courage. It's humbling to go from being at the top of the college pyramid to the base of the workforce in a matter of weeks. So start by getting yourself into the right frame of mind.

In this book, Sheryl describes how the Facebook office walls are lined with posters, including one that reads, "Proceed and be bold." Adopt this as your job search mantra. Getting a job in this tough economy will require a variety of skills, a lot of energy, and the ability to endure ups and downs. Being bold is especially important for women because we often fear putting ourselves out there. Men will apply for jobs if they think they meet just 60 percent of the job requirements, while women will apply only if they think they meet all of the job requirements.[1] Now who's got a better chance of getting that job—the man who applies for it or the woman who doesn't? Exactly.

If you see a listing that appeals to you, go for it. Many skills can be picked up on the job. If asked directly, be honest about your experience and then explain that you have the capacity to learn. This is not cheating; it's competing.

Proceed and . . . Get Organized

A job search has a lot of moving parts. You need a calendar, a computer file or actual folder for your research, and a spreadsheet to track your contacts, résumés sent, and interviews. And yes, there are apps for this.

Look at your online presence. In a recent survey, 75 percent of recruiters said their company's formal hiring process includes researching candidates online.[2] You would do the same before a date, right? Google yourself to see what's out there. Check your social media photos and, if possible, hide or delete any embarrassing ones . . . even if your hair looks *really* good. Annoyed tweets about your stupid professor and photos of you dancing on tables will throw up red flags. Make sure your e-mail address and voice mail message are short and professional. Your friends may laugh every time they're greeted with "Hi, Taylor Swift can't come to the phone right now because she's busy breaking up with someone," but most employers won't.

Create a LinkedIn profile with a strong professional headline. A recent graduate who studied marketing and wants to work in technology might use "Up-and-coming marketer with a passion for consumer tech." Include your jobs, internships, and skills. Ask former employers and professors to add recommendations. Comment on posts and join school and industry groups. And don't hesitate to send link requests to the people you meet during your job search. It may feel forward, but consider yourself "an enthusiastic network builder with a passion to find a job."

Résumé

Unless your plan is to become a rock star, you'll need a résumé, so make it a good one.

Keep it clear and succinct. Recent graduates should be able to fit everything on a single page. Standard format for new grads is to list your education first, then your jobs and internships in reverse chronological order, and close with relevant interests and skills. Bullet points are better than prose.

Focus on success. Many women underplay their accomplishments. A résumé is no place to be modest. Be proud of your achievements, but always be accurate. When possible, use action verbs and metrics, such as "Set up company's Tumblr presence and grew it to 7,500 followers in three months." Don't hesitate to list an impressive GPA or campus leadership position. It's not bragging; it's you.

Incorporate your soft skills. Employers look for critical soft skills: leadership, problem solving, communication, teamwork, and work ethic.[3] Call these out whenever possible. It's always better to show than to tell. For example, Snow White could claim that she "exhibited strong leadership skills by managing a team of seven dwarves to thwart an evil queen while collaborating with woodland creatures on housekeeping and other activities."

Use keywords. Many recruiters use keyword searches to find candidates on LinkedIn and other career sites and in their internal applicant tracking systems. If you don't use the right keywords, they may not find you. Keywords can point to function (marketing, sales, engineering), skills and expertise (financial modeling, PowerPoint, speaks French), degrees or qualifications (B.A., CPA). While you can't predict exactly which words an employer will search for, you can comb through the job posting and weave the most commonly used terms into your résumé.

Proofread. Many years ago, LeanIn.Org president Rachel Thomas founded a staffing agency that placed recent college graduates. Her team found that 98 percent of the résumés they received contained at least one grammatical or typographical error—98 percent! So proofread your résumé and cover letter as if your job depends on it . . . because it might. Ask a friend or family member to double-check your work. Read it out loud to yourself. Then read it backward to trick your eye into seeing the words for the first time. Then read it upside down while in a headstand. (Okay, not that last one.)

Customize. Your résumé should present your skills and experiences in a way that's tailored to a particular job or employer. Be prepared to create multiple résumés that emphasize different strengths. For example, Harry Potter would want to highlight his defeat of Lord Voldemort when applying to become an Auror at the Ministry of Magic. But if Harry was applying for a job at the Three Broomsticks, he would stress his knowledge of butterbeer. Again, proofread each version carefully.

Show that you are a real person. A common résumé mistake is to adopt "office-speak." Write simply and clearly and don't sound overly formal. Mention your hobbies. Tasteful humor or creativity can also go a long way, like the person who wrote "Spicy sense of humor for an accountant" on his résumé, or my sister-in-law Dori who was applying to be a dietitian at a zoo and hand delivered her résumé in an animal cracker box.

Put it online. Depending on your field, think about creating a website to showcase your skills and material. Are you looking for a design job? Display pieces from your portfolio. Are you a developer? Post your favorite app. Are you a writer? Share your best blogs and stories. Are you applying for a video editing job? Make a video résumé.

Elevator Pitch

Develop your "elevator pitch," a thirty-second rundown of your most relevant experience, skills, and interests. My elevator pitch is: "I'm Mindy Levy. In my day job, I work in performance management at Booz Allen Hamilton, a strategy and technology consulting company. I also moonlight as an executive coach, helping people get 'unstuck' so they can pursue their ambitions without fear. Oops, here's our floor." The idea is to be able to impress quickly if the opportunity arises at a party, a sporting event, or even in an actual elevator.

E-mail/Cover Letter

Always introduce yourself. Whether you use a short e-mail or a formal cover letter, the goal is to make yourself stand out in two or three paragraphs.

Address it to someone specific. Find the appropriate person so you can avoid "To whom it may concern." If you're unsure, identify someone who might be the right person and ask him or her to point you to the correct contact.

Make it personal. Highlight your most relevant qualifications and look for opportunities to connect. If you were referred by someone at the company, include his or her name. If you can mention a small detail that shows you're familiar with the organization, do it. One job applicant got my attention by noting that he grew up in my hometown. And, of course, always explain why you're well suited for the position. For example, if you're applying for a teaching position, mention your experience volunteering as a Big Sister.

Do your research. And make it known that you've done it. Weave in a surprising fact or figure, cite a recent news article, or refer to an executive's quote. Without something relevant to the reader, your e-mail can read like a generic form letter you're sending to every firm under the sun.

And again, proofread. I realize mentioning this again may seem like beating a dead horse, but some metaphorical horses need extra beating. I once received a cover letter that said, "I would like to be considered for an organizational development or a leadership development position ass appropriate." Yes, that was the spelling of "as."

Formatting. Unless given specific instructions on how to submit your résumé and cover letter, paste them into the body of your e-mail *and* attach both documents. It is best to save as PDFs to avoid formatting issues.

Proceed and . . . Begin Your Search

To use a football analogy, your job search should be part ground game and part air game. Most winning teams rely on both. A good ground game means covering all the basics. Apply to jobs posted on career sites such as Monster, CareerBuilder, and Craigslist. But don't stop there—only a fraction of people get their jobs this way.[4] Watch the career pages of the companies and professional organizations in your industry. Follow the companies that interest you and their human resources departments on social media. Get to know the advisors in your school's career center on a first-name basis. Participate in campus career fairs and other recruiting events.

The air game is where you get more creative. Andrew, a college senior, was determined to land a job with a popular consumer research company. He'd identified the opportunity through on-campus recruiting and was aware that lots of other students were applying. So he started talking about the job to *everyone* in hopes of uncovering a remote connection to the company. That's how Andrew found Andrea, the sister of a friend of a friend of his college roommate's father. Even though she was in a different department, Andrea was able to contact the hiring manager and give Andrew a recommendation.

How does something like that happen? Start by mining your own connections. Talk to your family, teachers, and friends . . . and their friends and colleagues. Identify the people in your extended network who work for organizations that appeal to you. See who is connected to you on Facebook and LinkedIn. Are you three degrees of separation from the recruiter for your dream job? Follow the trail. Reach out to as many people as possible. Ask people to meet for coffee, but keep it short and to the point. You might even work backward and create a list of people you'd most like to get connected to and see if anyone in your extended network knows them.

Once you line up your contacts, target specific goals for each one: Do you want to learn the best way to apply to her company? Does he know someone you'd like to be introduced to? People generally want to help, but remember that they're busy. The more up-front thinking you do, the more productive your exchange will be. If you're lucky enough to have a contact who could hire you, don't waste your one shot asking basic questions. Make it clear you want the job.

If you're drawn to an industry that's outside your circle,

you'll have to reach out to people you don't know, both directly and through industry groups, your school's alumni network, and social media. Many companies tweet links to job openings, while others advertise jobs on social media exclusively. Many even have Twitter handles that are just for jobs: @googlejobs at Google, @BofA_Careers at Bank of America. Maintaining a strong online presence can help potential employers find you; in creative fields, writers have been asked to submit material to TV shows based on their amusing blogs and feeds.

When you apply to a job posting, send a second e-mail directly to the hiring manager or the best contact you can find. For example, if you're responding to a post for a marketing coordinator, reach out to the person who heads up marketing directly. Don't know his or her e-mail? Try to figure it out. Research the e-mail configuration the company uses and replicate it. It's fine to send a few résumés to the same company, but don't overdo it. And if there's a specific job at a specific company that you want, get your résumé to the best contact any way you can: e-mail, post, or even personal delivery. You may get the jump on a job before it's even advertised. It's a Hail Mary pass, but it just might work.

And through all of this, think outside the box. Want a position that doesn't exist yet? Don't be afraid to pitch it. Not sure how to get in contact with a recruiter? Tweet at them. This isn't your mother and father's job market—employers like creativity. I recently read about an advertising copywriter who bought Google ad space under the names of the executives he hoped to work for. He was relying on them to google themselves, and when they did, his résumé popped up. One of them called him for an interview and he got the job.

Fresh out of college, Ella met a woman at a party, and by the end of their conversation, Ella was desperate to work for her. Ella invited the woman to lunch, but she replied that her schedule was too packed for her to go out. So a week later, Ella showed up at her office with lunch—and got hired. Of course, you have to be realistic. These tactics won't work for everyone. But don't be afraid to try something creative and bold to get your foot in the door.

Proceed and . . . Prepare for Your Interview

Do your homework. Make sure you understand what the company does, who its primary customers and competitors are, and the latest industry trends and news coverage. Use the products of the company you are applying to join. For example, if you are interviewing at Procter & Gamble, you should know all the brands in their portfolio and be prepared to talk about your personal experience with some of them. If you know in advance who you're meeting, read up on them.

Do a mock interview. List the core skills and strengths you want to emphasize. Think of a story to illustrate each point. If you want to underscore your writing skills, tell a story about contributing to your school paper; if you also want to showcase your leadership skills, talk about how you worked your way up and became an editor. Then get a friend to mock interview you. Practice talking about yourself out loud. It will make you sound more natural. Then practice again.

Be ready for the standard questions. *Can you tell me about yourself? What are your strengths and weaknesses? Why do you want this job?* Make sure you are ready to answer these questions authentically. Don't say that your weakness is that you are a perfectionist. Remember that anything on your résumé is fair game, so be ready to discuss every point. If you included your summer as a camp counselor, be prepared to talk about what you learned. Be real . . . but professional. Jeff, a D.C. law partner, once asked a candidate what his friends would say about him, and the guy replied, "They would say that I know how to leave work at the office and have a blast." Jeff thought, *If I were looking for a friend, you'd be high on my list, but I am hiring an associate.*

Look the part. Like it or not, appearance matters. Consider the job you're applying for and pay attention to the signals you're sending. An outfit that looks great for a night out may send the wrong message to a future employer. In some companies wearing a suit is a must, but in others it screams out "I'm here to sell a copier." And this applies once you are hired as well. Years ago, I had a summer intern who came to work every day in short skirts and high-heeled flip-flops. Nobody took her seriously. After I explained what was going on, she made some easy changes, and people started paying attention to her work.

Proceed and . . . Convince

Actions speak louder than words. When preparing for interviews, most people spend the majority of their time focused on what they will say. Yet when people meet you, what you say accounts for only 7 percent of the impression they form.[5] When you greet your interviewer, hold your head up, smile, make eye contact, and offer a firm handshake. You may be a nervous wreck on the inside, but you can do this. Take deep breaths before you walk in; even a few long, deep breaths can slow a racing heart. Speak slowly to project confidence. If you cross your arms, you may be perceived as angry or closed minded. If you slump in your chair, you may be viewed as bored. If you lean in (literally!) and nod and smile, you'll look more engaged. (Watch "Power & Influence" at leanin.org/education to learn how to use body language to make the right impression.)

Focus on the needs of the organization and your interviewer. Ask not what the company can do for you but what you can do for the company. Recent graduates often focus on what they want rather than on what they can offer. It's refreshing when a candidate stresses how she can add the most value to an organization. Years ago, my friend Michael was applying for a sous chef position at a Caesars casino. When asked where he saw himself in a few years, he told the casino's vice president that he wanted to be sitting in his office with his job . . . and help the VP move to an even higher-level position. He got the job a few days later.

Have a positive attitude. Employers look for enthusiasm. Not everyone is naturally upbeat, so don't force it if it feels phony. But don't go into an interview complaining—even if you've been kept waiting for forty-five minutes. It may help to make a list of everything you like about the job and the company and then convey that excitement to your interviewer.

Ask insightful questions. Make sure you ask thoughtful questions. Avoid any that can be answered easily or by the company's website. Wait until you are offered the job to ask about benefits, vacation time, and more personal concerns. My colleague Amy was interviewing a recent grad and asked if she had any questions. After a long pause, the woman replied, "Oh, I do have a question. I understand I'll be sitting in an inside office without natural light. Can I get an office with windows instead?" She did not get any office at all.

Choose your words wisely. Much like body language, word choice sends a message. Avoid using verbal crutches such as "like" and "you know," and don't preface your statements with "I think" or end them with upspeak as if you're asking a question. Highlight your accomplishments, and also remember that women are often expected to use communal language that focuses on "we," not "I." So instead of saying, "I wrote a successful grant application," consider emphasizing your team's accomplishments and then mentioning your individual contribution: "In the end, my team was awarded a five-hundred-thousand-dollar grant. My role was writing the application."

Look for opportunities to stand out. Almost any hiring manager will say it's easier to remember candidates who do something out of the ordinary. Offer a useful product insight. Audit a company's social media and share ideas for making it better. Poll your friends for a millennial perspective on their brand. A friend of mine read a firm's promotional materials while sitting in the lobby between interviews. She discovered several errors and gave marked-up versions to the second interviewer, explaining, "I couldn't help but edit them. I hope my notes are helpful." She got the job and later discovered that she'd been the least-experienced candidate.

Address issues head-on. When I was in college, I applied for a summer internship in Florida. I was nervous, and my interview landed on what had to be the hottest day of the decade. When I sat down with my interviewer, sweat was pouring off me. Buckets of sweat. This made me even more anxious, which caused even more sweat. Then I figured I might as well address it. I smiled and said, "I hope you're not put off by the fact that I'm sweating all over your office. It's a hot day—and I really want this job. I promise in my normal life I do not sweat like this!" My interviewer laughed and we both were able to relax. Well, a little.

If you think you made a mistake during an interview, don't shy away from acknowledging it. Miranda, for example, was trying to make the leap from consulting to a high-tech firm. During her interview, she used the word "synergy," and she could tell from the look on her interviewer's face that she'd lost him. So she paused and said, "I think I just messed up by using the word 'synergy.' I know technologists often worry about hiring business types like me, and words like this can rub people the wrong way. I want to switch industries precisely to get away from these terms . . . and if you hire me, you will never have to hear that word again." He nodded, and from that point on, he seemed more engaged.

Sell yourself. Don't be afraid to sell yourself using anything you can. Sheryl's sister-in-law Leslye worked for years in an L.A. litigation consulting firm and then decided she wanted to become a recruiter. After applying for what felt like every recruiting job in the city and getting no interviews, she cold-called the senior people at all the major firms. Only one woman took her call. And while the woman insisted she could not hire someone with no experience, Leslye talked the woman into granting her a meeting. When they met, Leslye said, "I know I have no experience recruiting, but I think you should hire me anyway." The woman asked why, and Leslye said, "Because I was able to talk you into giving me this meeting. I will do the same to talk my way into prospective recruits' offices." The woman was convinced.

Proceed and . . . Follow Up

Nothing feels better than peeling off stockings and putting on sweats after an interview. But before you do that—or immediately after—jot down the names of everyone you met and what you discussed. I can't tell you how many candidates don't remember the names of their previous interviewers. You don't want to have to say, "I met with the guy . . . you know, the one with blue eyes who's kind of balding?"

Within twenty-four hours, send individual thank-you e-mails that don't just claim that you're interested in the job but explain *why*. It's a bonus if you can reinforce something that you discussed or point to an article, organization, or website that will be of interest. If you don't hear right back (and you often won't), wait a week and try again. Remain upbeat and persistent without becoming a pest.

With so much at stake, it can be hard to remain positive. Companies drag out interviews, send mixed messages, or flat-out ignore candidates. This can be especially hard for women. Studies show that when men and women receive negative feedback, women's self-esteem and self-confidence drop more than men's.[6] Additionally, men tend to attribute failure to external factors while women blame themselves, making it doubly hard for women to recover.[7]

When you are not selected for a position, try to find out why. One method is to ask your interviewer to provide suggestions for you on future interviews. Any feedback can help you make adjustments. And even once you are hired, continue asking for feedback on a regular basis. A study recently reported that openness to feedback and grit/resilience are two of the most common traits found in successful female executives.[8]

Proceed and . . . Good Luck

Finding your first job is a challenge, but it's one you can meet with preparation, perseverance, and optimism. Stay focused on your search. If you can, fill any extra time—even a few hours a week—with project or volunteer work that both energizes you and gives you a chance to keep building skills.

And don't beat yourself up for making mistakes. We all do. Learn from your mistakes and move on. Remaining positive in the face of rejection has many long-term benefits both in work and in life.

As of 2010, the average American had eleven jobs between the ages of eighteen and forty-six.[9] Even if your search is hard or you can't get the job you really want, remember that your first job is just . . . your first job. If you have to settle for something different from what you wanted, you can still use the opportunity to gain skills and experience. Making the most out of an imperfect situation is one of the keys to life. I say this not only as a trained psychologist, but also from the bottom of my heart.

Proceed and be bold.

Mindy Levy leads performance management and talent planning at Booz Allen Hamilton and is an executive coach. She writes and lectures on subjects ranging from networks and leadership development to how to manage difficult conversations. Mindy has a business degree from the Wharton School and a Ph.D. in industrial/organizational psychology from the George Washington University. She lives in Reston, Virginia, with her husband and three sons.

Regina's Story: Don't Deny Your Dream

I GREW UP in Ghana, and after graduating from college in 2005, I landed a job at a prestigious international bank in Accra. I was the first and only female in the IT department. I was very excited and worked twice as hard as my male colleagues to prove myself. Soon I was receiving acclaim for the software I developed. But even though my work was good, I kept getting passed over for promotions and found myself growing more and more frustrated.

When I confronted my supervisor with my feelings, I was told I was too young and the men in the department would not take kindly to me being promoted ahead of them. I then spoke to the human resources department and told them I would resign unless I was treated fairly. They listened to my concerns, and I was surprised when I was offered a double promotion to right the wrong. I was happy for a time, but soon I realized I wanted something more out of my career.

I had the secret desire to start my own company but was not bold enough to take the first step. Banking provided security and comfort; entrepreneurship felt too risky. So I ignored what I truly wanted and went to work for a smaller local bank instead. I tried to convince myself that my problem was the boredom associated with working for a larger institution and that developing software for a local bank would be better.

I was wrong. It took me four years and a lot of sleepless nights to realize that when you have a dream and a desire, it is like an alarm clock going off inside you. Hitting the snooze button doesn't work; the alarm will just go off again. Eventually, you have to wake up.

I finally gathered all my courage and quit. My supervisor cautioned me that entrepreneurship would be difficult and I would end up back in the banking sector. Others said I was too young and should wait until I was fifty to start my own company. I was given a day to reconsider my decision but returned an hour later with my signed resignation.

Now I am a social entrepreneur using technology to change lives in West Africa. I am very fulfilled and love what I am doing. Listening to my true desires was the best decision I've ever made. Each morning when I wake up, I am thankful for a new day and look forward to a bright future in which my technology solutions and success stories will be replicated in other developing countries.

Regina Agyare is the CEO of Soronko Solutions, which seeks to use technology to empower rural Ghanaian youth.

Jessica's Story: I Negotiated for a Raise

SINCE I WAS eleven years old, I knew I wanted to be a journalist. But by the time I graduated from college, the industry was crumbling around me.

I took a series of part-time jobs. The first, an internship at my hometown newspaper in Seattle, narrowly preceded the paper's collapse. The second, a fellowship at *The Boston Globe*, made me an awkward observer to tearful layoffs and shuttered bureaus. I moved to New York to work as a researcher for an investigative reporter at *The Village Voice*. A few months in, the once storied alt-weekly was sold, and a mass exodus began. By the time I was hired at *Newsweek*—as a six-month writing temp—I felt so relieved to be at a publication still in print that I almost hugged the HR rep.

I spent the next few years working my way up the ranks at *Newsweek*, from temp to part-timer to senior staff writer and editor. I happily worked odd jobs to supplement my paycheck: a weekend bartending gig; cocktail waitressing late-night events where, more than once, I spotted a *Newsweek* colleague and quickly ducked into the crowd. Still, I felt incredibly lucky—an outlier among my journalism school friends. I was the one with an actual writing job.

And then that "lucky" feeling started to fade. I was sick of waitressing. I was tired of being broke. I heard whispers of my (mostly male) colleagues' salaries. Many were making more than I was, and I learned that many of them had negotiated for it.

It was clear what I had to do: I had to stop feeling lucky. I had to ask for a raise. But the prospect terrified me. *What should I say? Would they think I was greedy? Why didn't they teach us this in school?*

Proving your worth in a field like magazine writing, where success is often subjective, is hard but not impossible. So I started making lists. I tracked traffic figures, awards, TV appearances, the number of stories I published, any data I could get my hands on. I asked editors to vouch for me.

And then I stalled.

I spent hours updating and perfecting my list. Then I'd edit again. I was paralyzed by the possibility of rejection.

Days became weeks, and finally I told myself I had to buck up. I copied my list into an e-mail, typed the name of the editor in charge, and forced myself to press send. I spent the next twelve hours obsessively refreshing my inbox, convinced I didn't deserve the raise at all.

The editor scheduled a meeting with me for the next week, and I headed to his office with a printout of my notes. I'd practiced my speech a dozen times . . . then forgot every word of it. I choked over my sentences. I felt ridiculous, like I was boasting. But I followed up with an e-mail, thanking him for taking the time to meet with me. I recapped what I'd tried to stammer, laid out neatly in bullet points.

A few days later, he e-mailed with news. I got the raise—and a title promotion along with it. He was delighted with my work.

I've negotiated for at least three salary increases since

then, and with every attempt, it gets a little bit easier. Nobody has yet said no, although in each case I am somehow convinced they will. But with every doubt, I try to remember the alternative: you're sure to get nothing if you don't ask at all.

Jessica Bennett is a writer and editor in New York City.

Negotiate Your Salary

Kim Keating

NEGOTIATION SKILLS ARE critical in every aspect of our lives. *What do you want for dinner tonight? Who gets the aisle seat? Dog or cat?* At home or at work, learning how to negotiate can mean the difference between accepting what comes your way and getting what you want out of life.

Some people are born negotiators. I was not. My strict and traditional African-American parents raised me with rules like "Respect your elders" and "Speak when spoken to." I was taught that "nice" girls looked pretty, smiled through thick and thin, and, once they got married, stood by their man. Few of my friends graduated from college. Virtually none left the state. Most of them expected that their futures would mirror their parents'—living paycheck to paycheck and struggling to keep their families safe in dangerous neighborhoods.

But I wanted a different life, and this hunger for more

intensified when my father passed away when I was sixteen. Even though I excelled in high school, my family was shocked when I announced that I was leaving North Little Rock, Arkansas, to study business more than three hundred miles away at Southern Methodist University in Dallas, Texas.

Throughout college, I often felt out of place. I was black at a nearly all white school and a woman in a male-dominated finance department. But I knew that if I did not make it, I would wind up back home, and that was not an option. So I learned to raise my hand in class, asked to join study groups that didn't invite me, and got extra help when I needed it.

After graduation, I had to focus—and I mean *focus*—on paying my rent, my bills, and my student loans. I fixed my gaze on Wall Street, where my degree in finance would, miraculously it seemed to me at the time, pay enough to meet my obligations and help my family as well.

If I had felt out of place in college, Wall Street took it to a whole new level. Most of my fellow analysts were savvy Ivy League graduates. With my southern twang and hand-me-down clothes, I stood out like a sore thumb. I was intimidated by my colleagues and terrified of my managers. I don't think anyone knew just how scared I felt, not because I hid it that well, but because no one was paying much attention to me. And that was a big problem, because in order to succeed, I needed to attract attention, not hide from it. My choice was simple: adapt or fail.

Slowly I began to find my voice and the courage to stick

my neck out. I got noticed. I learned how to deal with aggressive colleagues and clients, sometimes by ignoring them and sometimes by standing my ground with grace (I was still the southern girl my mother raised). I saw that as a woman of color, I had to work even harder than everyone else around me. So I did. I began negotiating projects for my company and, eventually, promotions and raises for myself. There were plenty of stumbles along the way, but my negotiation skills improved with each new job I took.

Over the years, I saw how the ability to negotiate affected every aspect of people's careers. This is why fourteen years after I left SMU for Wall Street, I started Keating Advisors, a human resources consulting firm. My goal is to help all people, especially women, get paid what they deserve.

My life's lesson proves that we women can train ourselves to be our own advocates. We can . . . and we must.

Why Women Don't Negotiate

Women have struggled to be paid fairly since jobs were invented, and that struggle is far from over. The wage gap between men and women in the United States has not improved in the last decade.[1] The average woman has to work almost twelve years longer to earn the same amount as her male peer.[2] This is not just unfair; it's unacceptable.

The inequality starts right out of the gate. A recent study found that women in their first year out of college were paid eighty-two cents for every dollar paid to their male peers.[3] This pay gap is caused by a number of factors:

outright discrimination, gender differences in college majors and occupations, the number of hours men and women work, and women negotiating less often than men, from their first salary forward.[4]

There are many reasons why women negotiate less frequently than men. We often underestimate our abilities. Many women are trained to listen, not to talk. We focus too much on pleasing others, settling for what other people think we're worth instead of what we deserve. Too much of the time, we are grateful for anything we get.

Cultural norms hold that men should be assertive and look out for number one. Women, however, are supposed to be nurturers. So men can ask for higher salaries, raises, or better assignments, but women are supposed to be "nice" girls, just as I was taught to be. Negotiating for what we deserve while still being agreeable and nonthreatening is like balancing on a tightrope: with one wrong step, we know we might fall. No wonder we are more likely to say "Thank you for this offer" than "Excuse me, I deserve more."

Becoming aware of the special challenges women face in negotiations is the first step to overcoming them. As I learned on Wall Street, sweet and upbeat can coexist with assertive. I didn't change who I was; I *added* to who I was.

How to Negotiate

With focus and practice, anyone can become a good negotiator. Here are four simple steps that can help you reach your compensation goals in your first job and beyond.

1. Do Your Homework—on Them and on You

For a successful salary negotiation, you need information about both parties—your potential employer and yourself. The time you invest can pay off in a big way. And I mean that literally.

There's more salary data available than most first-time job seekers think. Salary.com, GetRaised, and other sites offer free information on jobs and compensation, benefits and bonuses. Always take into account the industry, revenue size, number of employees, and location, as well as your experience and skills. It's especially helpful if you can get information from someone who works in the same field or, even better, at your target company. Supplement the facts with anecdotal evidence. Reach out to friends, parents of your friends, friends of your parents, family, neighbors, coworkers, and social media. Without a grasp of the market, you might name a figure that is well above what the employer had in mind and knock yourself out of the running. Or you could ask for a salary that is far too low and not just get paid under the market but possibly lose the job by seeming less qualified.

It also helps to have a sense of how much the company needs you. If the interviewer sees you as no more qualified than other candidates, you have less bargaining power. If the hiring manager believes you are the ideal candidate, her willingness to pay you more can increase dramatically.

That leads to the second party you must assess—you. How much would you like to make and how much would be enough? Define your ideal offer in terms of your financial goals for the next twelve to eighteen months: What do you need to support yourself, pay off your student loans, help your family, or even take a vacation? Identifying your goals will motivate you.

The flip side of your ideal offer is what we call your BATNA, business school talk for "best alternative to a negotiated agreement." Your BATNA is the lowest offer you'd consider accepting—your walk-away number. If you are going on your first interview in months and you have rent to pay, any offer may hit your BATNA. If you have multiple job offers or sufficient financial resources, then the offer on the table may fall short of your BATNA.

And remember, when looking for a job, no serial monogamy. You need to play the field. Every job you pursue is a chance to practice your interviewing and negotiating skills. Don't stop developing alternatives even if you think you are close to getting your dream job. Knowing that you have other options will give you the confidence to ask for what you deserve.

2. Don't Discuss Compensation Until You Have an Offer
Ironically, speaking up for yourself starts by holding your tongue. Your goal is to avoid discussing salary until after you have an offer. A future employer is more likely to give you what you want once she believes you are the ideal person for the job. If your interviewer raises the issue of salary early on, try to redirect the conversation to the position itself. Say things like:

- "Actually, I'd like to know more about the position before we discuss compensation. Can you tell me who this position reports to?"
- "I am confident that you've considered what the job involves and will offer a competitive salary. I'd love to hear more about the position's responsibilities."

Or deflect the issue entirely with:

- "My requirements are flexible. I am focusing on finding the right career path at this time."

If your interviewer still wants to discuss salary, remember that it is always better if she provides a range or number first. Say things like:

- "I need to consider a number of factors, including the job responsibilities, career development opportunities, and the working environment. Can you tell me what *you* think is a fair market value for this position?"
- "It is difficult to answer that question, because it depends on the internal salary range as well as the external market value. Can you tell me what the average salary range is for comparable positions in the company?"

If your interviewer insists you throw out a number first, your goal is to give a range with a low end that is just above the company's high end. For example, if the company's range is $35,000 to $40,000, you would ideally say your range is $41,000 to $45,000. That way, you are close enough to keep yourself in the game, but you've laid the groundwork to get to the top of their range or above. Of course, you almost never know the actual internal salary range, but doing your homework can get you as close as possible.

Just as you don't want to offer a salary figure first, don't volunteer your compensation history. If this information is required as part of the application process, give accurate and comprehensive information. Include all the components of your package—not only your base salary but also bonuses, vacation pay, health benefits, insurance, tuition reimbursement, and employee discounts.

3. Now That You've Got an Offer, It's Time to Negotiate

If just the thought of negotiating makes you anxious, don't worry. You are not alone. Even when you are nervous, you can guide the conversation and get your points across.

To prepare, I recommend you write a script. Sit down in front of a computer or even use an actual pen and paper and write out how you would like the conversation to go. Then get a friend or family member to role-play with you. You may feel self-conscious, but having the conversation out loud will force you to think through your strategy. When you come up with a good line, write it down and then practice saying it again. Get used to the sound of your own voice negotiating.

Even though it isn't fair, women achieve better outcomes when they communicate concern for organizational relationships during negotiations.[5] The more you can show concern for others, the better. In this book, Sheryl offers the following advice: "When negotiating, 'Think personally, act communally.'" There are several ways to do this. For example, you could say something like:

- "I am excited about this opportunity. If I come on board, I will do my best to make a contribution to the team's success. It is important to me to negotiate a salary that recognizes the education and the skills that enable me to do so."

- "I know that one of the reasons you want to hire me is that my negotiation skills will be of benefit to the company once I'm on board. This conversation about my compensation is a chance for me to show you these skills."

Another way to demonstrate connection to others is to ground the negotiation in gender pay issues:

- "Given that across the board women are paid less than men, we would both be disappointed if I didn't negotiate for myself."

And as much as I resent having to give this advice to women, it's important to use "we" as much as possible, not "I." And smile. A lot.

Don't accept the first offer! Once you get an offer, respond with enthusiasm. Even if you are not thrilled with the opening number, get the negotiation off to a positive start by demonstrating that you are truly excited about the opportunity. You will be more persuasive when negotiating if your interviewer believes you really want the job.

Even if the offer is wildly lower or even higher than your expectations, your first move is to get more information. Companies generally take into account three things when making an offer: the market value of the position, internal equity, and what you made at your last job.[6] Your goal is to figure out what they based the offer on so you can respond as effectively as possible.

To get more information, say, "I'd love to understand more." Next, ask one or two job-related questions. You are demonstrating that the job is what you are most focused on, while kicking off the back-and-forth conversation. You can say things like:

- "How does this position fit into the overall organization?"
- "What training and development opportunities are available?"
- "What is the career path for someone in this role?"
- "How much support is there for career advancement?"
- "Tell me about the company culture and the working environment."

Once the conversation is flowing, you can add in questions about the compensation:

- "What are the driving factors in determining the compensation for this position?"
- "How does this salary compare to other positions at a similar level within the organization?"
- If there is a bonus, ask, "What determines the bonus award amounts?"

Learning what the company based their offer on gives you the information you need to counter.

Make a counteroffer. Think of this as another opportunity to convince your prospective employers why they should hire you. Discuss the strong leadership skills you developed through coursework, clubs, or sports. Highlight your successes as a student, employee, volunteer, or intern. You can minimize the double bind women face by talking about how your unique skill set can help the company meet its goals.

Don't forget, your counteroffer can include more than just base pay. The most common forms of additional compensation are cash bonuses, equity, commissions, signing bonuses, moving allowances, training, telecommuting, and tuition reimbursement. Know which items are most important to you so that you can negotiate a package that best meets your needs. Don't bargain one item at a time; instead, focus the negotiation on the overall package. Say something like, "I'm interested in a market value of forty thousand dollars, but I'm flexible on how we get there."

During the discussion, explain why you want what you want. Unlike men, women often have to justify their requests.[7] If the position requires a lot of driving, you could say that to purchase and maintain a suitable car and meet your other obligations, you need a salary of $40,000. Articulating your underlying interest may open the conversation to exploring alternative options. If the company can't pay $40,000, there might be other ways to reduce your transportation costs. Remember to always tie your request back to why it will help you do a better job for the company.

If the salary offer does not reflect your view of what the market is paying for this position, you can counter as follows:

- "I believe this position is a great fit for me, but the compensation data I've researched suggests a higher range than you are offering."
- "This is a great opportunity and I'm really excited about this role. I was expecting the salary would be higher given the responsibilities of the job."

If the hiring manager tries to drive down your new salary by comparing it to what you earned in a previous job, counter by saying:

- "In my previous role, I accepted a low salary to gain skills and get experience. I now have those skills."

- "I am looking to earn what the market is paying for a position like this."

If you feel the salary is within the market range, here are some ways you can try to maximize the offer:

- "While the offer is competitive, based on my research it falls at about the midpoint of the salary range for comparable positions. I hope you would agree that my skills, experience, and education should put me at the top of the range."
- "I am excited about the job, although the salary is lower than I was expecting. I understand that your offer needs to be in line with what you are currently paying employees in similar jobs. Is there flexibility regarding a bonus, as this would offset the lower salary?"

This negotiation may very well be the beginning of a long-term working relationship, so set the expectation from the very beginning that you are comfortable speaking up for yourself. A candidate who handles herself well in a negotiation will impress a smart manager.

4. Make a Decision: Do You Accept or Walk?

Once you have a final offer, you have a choice: accept or walk away.

Accepting the offer. If you decide to accept, do so with enthusiasm. Get the offer in writing and make sure that it states your title, responsibilities, start date, benefits, salary, and any other forms of compensation. Let your new manager and colleagues know that you are looking forward to joining the team. Then it's time to do the happy dance.

Walking away. If you decide to reject the offer, do so graciously. Call the person you negotiated with directly. E-mail other individuals you met to thank them as well. Life is long. Assume that your paths will cross again, so leave the door open for future opportunities.

Beyond Your First Salary: How to Ask for a Raise or Promotion

Victoria Pynchon, co-founder of She Negotiates, asks every woman she meets, "When's the last time you asked for a raise?" All too frequently, Pynchon says, the answer is never.[8]

And while I would not recommend that you start negotiating for a raise on day one, salary negotiations are an ongoing part of building a career. Or at least they should be.

Keep doing your homework. Try to find out when budget and salary decisions are made and have a preliminary conversation with your manager about three months before. Understand your company's financial state; if there are wage freezes, this is not your moment. Some organizations publish their internal salary ranges; most do not, which makes getting compensation information difficult.

Approaching coworkers in the cafeteria and asking how much they are being paid is unlikely to go well. Gathering up-to-date market data is important. If you discover that you are being paid below market rates or less than your peers, talk with your manager about how you deserve a "salary adjustment" rather than a raise.

Understand evolving BATNAs. Your employer's BATNA will evolve as market conditions and your performance change. The best thing you can do to increase your compensation is to excel; your job performance will matter a lot more than even the best negotiation techniques. Making yourself irreplaceable is your best leverage when it's time to discuss a raise.

Your BATNA will also change over time as you gain more experience and skills. While constantly looking for new roles inside or outside your company can backfire, over time you should be willing to look for a new job if you don't get the raises you deserve. Don't be hasty in threatening to walk away, but don't stay in a position if you are undervalued.

Establish an ongoing dialogue with your manager. Talk with your manager periodically about how you hope to grow within the organization. Let it be known you're interested in stretch assignments and added responsibilities. Keep track of your accomplishments and be prepared to share the highlights. It is also important to be comfortable with constructive feedback, aware of any areas that need development, and willing to work on improving. Remember to communicate how you support your colleagues and contribute to your department's performance.

Now ask. When you sit down with your manager, say you want to understand your compensation better and, like all savvy professionals, you've been keeping on top of the market. Base your request for a raise on your performance and value to the company. You could start out by saying something like:

- "Thank you for taking the time to meet with me. I wanted to talk with you about my career and compensation opportunities. As you know, I've been working here for two years and have received consistently high performance evaluations. Over the next one to three years, I'd really like to achieve a level within the company with significant responsibilities and a salary in the range of X dollars. I was hoping we could talk about what steps I can take to make that possible."

If your manager is not willing to increase your compensation, try to find out why and then ask how to address his concerns. Tell your manager that you understand the current situation. Then get an agreement to discuss your compensation and career goals again within a certain period of time, say six months. If your manager responds that it will be a couple of years before your salary is reviewed or demands that you not bring up compensation again, it might be time to update your résumé.

Win or Lose, You Win

My mom still lives in the neighborhood where I grew up in North Little Rock, where "nice" girls still hear the same refrains I heard in my childhood. What I know now is that all of us need to be taught to speak, not just to listen. And I know now that no matter where anyone comes from, we all deserve to be paid fairly—and that means equally to men.

When I started my career, I didn't know how to stand up for myself, let alone negotiate. But I practiced and I learned. I did not win every negotiation. None of us do.

But, win or lose, you learn something every time you advocate for yourself. You learn which tactics work and which fall flat. You learn how to convince others that treating you fairly is not just in your interest, but in theirs. You learn how to articulate your skills and strengths. And you learn to ask for what you want in life, which is the only way to get it.

Kim Keating is the founder and managing director of Keating Advisors, a human resources consulting firm. A former financial analyst at Morgan Stanley and the chief financial officer for Teach for America, Kim helps individuals negotiate more effectively and speaks regularly about women and the pay gap. She lives in Washington, D.C., with her son and twin daughters.

Jana's Story: A Group to Boost My Confidence

IMMEDIATELY OUT of college, I was selected to be part of a new graduate training program at the largest health insurer in the country. There were sixteen of us, and at the end of our six-month intensive training course, it was time to decide if we'd go into sales, a job with more money and prestige, or account management, a behind-the-scenes role with lower but guaranteed income. Traditionally, women chose account management, while men chose sales roles where they could find big money and fast career advancement.

There were lots of reasons for me to go into sales. I'm gregarious, driven, and a good listener. I won the top spot in our consultative selling skills course and also had the top scores in the training course overall. But I bought into the stereotype. When it came time to choose, I asked to become an account manager.

I told myself I would move into sales later, when I knew everything about our products and felt ready. I didn't want to be the bumbling salesperson who is all show and no substance. I couldn't get past the fear of doing something I hadn't proven to be successful at yet, even though my scores and mentor reviews said I was qualified. I counted myself out before I even gave myself a chance. It didn't occur to me that I could have had both show *and* substance. I could have learned on the job. I could have done it!

Ultimately, I have made a very good career for myself. I was an account manager for six years, and my drive helped me get promoted faster than anyone expected. My strengths and skills were very useful in developing relationships and building strong customer loyalty. I worked hard and had amazing opportunities. But I will always wonder how successful I could have been if I had used those skills in a sales role. I'll never forget that I let my self-doubt change the trajectory of my life.

Ideally, we'd all have a true sense of our own value and capabilities, but sometimes we need others to remind us that the voice in our head that says we're not ready is simply wrong. And so, in June 2013, after I read *Lean In*, I reached out to twelve other women—friends and classmates—and started a Lean In Circle. Each week, we meet at a member's home in Seattle and share challenges and push one another to be brave. The Circle was so successful, we've started three other groups that now include fifty women.

If I'd had a circle of supporters when I was deciding which career path to take after college, I think I would have made a very different decision. My Lean In Circle does for me what I couldn't do for myself in my first job. We give one another the boost of confidence that we need to take our careers further than we'd thought possible.

Jana Morrelli is a health care entrepreneur and an MBA student at the University of Washington.

Sindhura's Story: I Took a Risk and Stepped on the Gas

I DON'T REMEMBER the flight to India. I do remember, however, the car ride to the new college I would be attending. For twenty-eight minutes, I sat in the passenger seat as the hired driver wove between cars, large trucks, tiny bicycles, scooters with six people on them, and herds of indifferent cows. My eyes widened in an attempt to take it all in, and it wasn't until we had stopped moving that I realized I'd barely been breathing.

"Why do I need a driver?" I asked my mom. I was nineteen and had grown up in America, where we all itched to get our driver's licenses as soon as possible. A driver's license was independence, the only freedom we could claim as teenagers living under our parents' roofs and rules. I was not ready to give that up, along with all the other things I had set aside to start medical school in India.

The driver chimed in before my mom could: "Girls don't drive around here. It's not safe."

"Here" was a tiny town in southern India where men drove themselves but women and children were chauffeured by drivers or husbands or used public transportation. Many women don't drive in parts of India because of the seldom-occurring but oft-feared dangers of being pulled over by a rogue police officer or being roadblocked and violated by men who halt cars that drive through the narrow village roads. Other women won't drive because of the social convention that links affluence to the ability to hire a driver. To make matters worse, public transportation at night was not (and still isn't) safe for females, so women became immobilized when their drivers went home at 5:00 p.m. each day.

A 5:00 p.m. curfew? That was all my teenage ears needed to hear.

Within a few weeks of settling in, I started secret lessons with my driver to learn how to drive a stick shift, got my Indian driver's license, and slowly began easing into the high-speed madness of India's morning rush hour. Within a few months, I was driving myself to school. I was the only female student to do so. It was 2005, a year that seems too recent for me to have been the first.

Then the most curious thing happened, almost imperceptibly at the start. One day, I noticed more and more of my female classmates driving themselves to school. I smiled at the women who pulled their cars up next to mine on the way to a late-night movie. I listened as my aunts made appointments without wondering if their husbands would be available to drive them. Over the course of the six years I was there, I witnessed the women in this small town realize they had given up more than the ability to drive. They had forsaken their freedom and independence for affluent customs and paternal protection, unknowingly contributing to the patriarchal culture that exists in India. They had willingly taken a backseat. But not anymore.

When I set out to drive myself around town, it wasn't with the intent to trigger a revolution. It was for my own selfish desire to preserve the independence I had grown up with. But that, I realized, is how change begins. It's one person recognizing he or she deserves a certain right and going after it. Then this person unknowingly becomes the face of opportunity, allowing others to see that something they deserve is within their reach as well.

Maybe I had nothing to do with the transformation that occurred in that small town. Maybe the female liberation that took place was bound to happen all along. I'll never be sure. All I know is that I leaned in and stepped on the gas, and everyone else who wanted to come along for the ride did too.

Sindhura Kolli is a recently graduated M.D. and writer living in Los Angeles.

Let's Lean In Together

Rachel Thomas

IT CAN BE SCARY to ask for a raise. That's why journalist Katherine Goldstein didn't even bring up salary during her 2012 end-of-year performance review. But after reading *Lean In* the following spring, she started to regret not speaking up. She knew she was valued at work and realized that she needed to be bolder. She also knew she needed some help. "My husband and my parents are great to talk to, but they don't have the same perspective as professional women my age," she explained.

To get the support she craved, Katherine formed a Lean In Circle with a mixture of old friends—one from fourth grade, one from college—and newer acquaintances. The six women in their twenties and thirties came from different fields but shared a dedication to their jobs. They started meeting once a month for about two hours, rotating apartments. They followed the recommended format of watching a video (their favorite was "Negotiation") and then completing exercises to build their skills. The results were immediate. "We all started becoming aware of the unconscious ways we were holding ourselves back," Katherine said. "I wasn't the only one who hadn't spoken up for herself."

The six discovered that they all downplay their achievements, and each agreed she would make a concerted effort to catch—and correct—that behavior. Then one by one, as opportunities arose at work, the Circle members started asking for what they deserved. In a short time, three got raises. "It was really motivating to see their success," said Katherine. The next year, she went into her performance review with a number in mind rather than waiting to see what she was offered. She was happy with the result.

When we launched LeanIn.Org, we dreamed of hearing stories like this. The community was founded to empower all women to achieve their ambitions. We believe in challenging the stereotypes that hold back women so we can create more opportunity for everyone. We believe true equality is within our reach and will bring big payoffs for all: happier families, more productive companies, and a stronger economy.

We offer three programs to provide women with ongoing inspiration and support: Lean In Circles, Lean In Education, and the Lean In Community. These programs are available online and are free to everyone.

Lean In Circles
leanin.org/circles

Graduation can be a time of great uncertainty in both your personal and your professional life. As you sort through decisions, it's important to seek out advice. For young women, finding a mentor may be difficult, but peers can be just as effective at offering guidance. This is the power of Lean In Circles. These small, self-organizing groups meet regularly to harness the experience and creativity of all their members. Research shows that people are more confident and are able to learn and accomplish more in groups.[1]

While we can't guarantee that everyone will get a raise, we can guarantee that a Circle will help you gain awareness and skills. Already more than fourteen thousand Circles have been created, spanning every U.S. state and more than fifty countries, including China, Brazil, India, Pakistan, and Tanzania. Circles are also rolling out at more than two hundred universities. Seven women in the graduate engineering department at the University of Tennessee started a Circle with the awesome name Systers. The Circle quickly tripled in size, and the university's provost is now helping to encourage Circles across the entire campus. At Harvard Business School, a group of Asian men started a Circle that focuses on battling their own cultural challenges. And a student at Howard University told us that she started her Circle to have a supportive space to talk about issues of both gender and race.

Last year, we visited an air force base in Minneapolis and met a group of courageous women who formed a Circle because, as they explained, being a woman in the U.S. military can be a very isolating experience. They are subtly—and not so subtly—undermined even as they stand side by side with men wearing the same uniform. After discovering how helpful their Circle was on their base, they expanded online to reach other women in the military. As one of them told us, "Now no one has to feel like the only woman in her unit."

We've seen how the influence of Circles can extend beyond the classroom or workplace. After a discussion about the importance of making your partner a real partner, a D.C. Circle member realized she needed "a partner who's a feminist." When it became clear that her boyfriend didn't support her aspirations, she moved on. A California woman was inspired by her Circle to ask her family to stop calling her bossy and recommended they call her successful instead.

It's thrilling to know that people are changing their attitudes and lives while connecting in ways they never imagined. For those who aren't able to join a Circle, our online community can provide another source of encouragement and education.

Lean In Education
leanin.org/education

In the past year, more than 35,000 people have watched a video on our website called "Power & Influence" by Deborah Gruenfeld, a professor of leadership and organizational behavior at the Stanford Graduate School of Business. Professor Gruenfeld's research shows that your tone of voice and body language matter much more than what you say in determining how others assess you. I urged my sister Corin to watch the talk before an upcoming meeting with her boss. A single mom, Corin needed more flextime at her job but was nervous about asking for it. The video taught her that if she kept her voice low and spoke slowly, she would come across as more comfortable and confident. After the meeting, she texted me, "Got the flextime!"

I picked up a confidence booster from the same video. According to Professor Gruenfeld, research shows that if you stand in a Wonder Woman pose—legs apart and hands on your hips—for three to five minutes, your cortisone level goes down and your testosterone level rises.[2] You physically feel more confident. It seems silly when you first try it, but I have done it many times . . . and it works. (Indestructible Wonder Woman bracelets are optional.)

Our online videos by world-renowned experts help you take action. Topics include playing to your strengths, understanding team dynamics, rethinking time, and managing difficult conversations—like that awkward situation when a coworker has let you down and you need to make sure it doesn't happen again. Each video comes with a discussion guide and exercises so that you can learn a skill one day and put it into practice the next.

Companies and nonprofits are also using these tools to trigger discussions. At TaskRabbit, a San Francisco tech start-up, fifty employees watched "Creating a Level Playing Field," a video focused on overcoming stereotypes. It opened the eyes of people of both genders. One man on the marketing team said it had never occurred to him that the statement "I have no idea how she does it" is rooted in stereotypes. That day, he realized he would never look at a male executive who has kids and wonder, *How does he juggle it all?*

Lean In Community
leanin.org or facebook.com/leaninorg

Our online community has grown to almost 400,000 members who come to our Facebook page and website for a daily dose of inspiration, ideas, and information. We post articles on gender issues, conduct live Q&A's, and celebrate milestones in women's achievements. On New Year's Eve, we asked the community to share their resolutions, and members responded with comments from the moving— "Be the real me at work and not the timid yes girl"—to the practical—"To be on time if not early"—to the emphatic— "Stop apologizing for myself! (Sorry to yell)."

You'll find inspirational quotes from Alicia Keys, Tina Fey, Maya Angelou, and Hillary Clinton. You'll also learn about lesser-known role models in our weekly feature "Trailblazing Women You May Not Know (But Should)," such as Mabel Fairbanks, the first African American inducted into the U.S. Figure Skating Hall of Fame, and Ellen Ochoa, the first Latina astronaut.

The site also offers a remarkable collection of Lean In Stories (leanin.org/stories) written by hundreds of women and men from all corners of the world who have found inspiring ways to lean in to their lives. Brenda Berkman writes about the challenge and eventual triumph of becoming the first female firefighter in New York City. Stephen Latham, a bioethicist, writes about taking on more childcare responsibility so his wife could accept her dream job in Washington, D.C. And Oscar-winning actress Reese Witherspoon talks about overcoming stage fright and a shaky voice when she had to speak up as herself. We promise you will find a story that inspires you, and we hope you will share your own story and inspire others.

Leaning In Together

A few months ago, we produced a video of a dozen recent graduates opening up about their fears. "I'm afraid of being judged," says one. "I'm afraid of feeling stupid," says another. Then the young women were asked an important question: "What would you do if you weren't afraid?" One answered, "If all fear was stripped away, I'd walk into the meeting and speak up."

In response to the video, thousands of women of all ages, and some men, started posting photos of themselves holding up signs of what they would do if they weren't afraid: "I would find a partner who supports me." "I would perform my music for someone other than my dog." "I would stop letting others control the direction of my life."

Sharing our struggles makes those struggles less daunting. Sharing our dreams makes those dreams more real.

We hope you join us—create or jump into a Circle, watch a video to learn a new skill, participate in our conversation and community. Together we can overcome the obstacles and stereotypes that hold women back. We will get to an equal world if we all lean in . . . together.

Rachel Thomas is co-founder and president of LeanIn.Org, a nonprofit committed to empowering all women to achieve their ambitions. Previously, she co-founded and served as president and CMO of Subtext, developer of the first collaborative reading platform for K–12 classrooms, and was vice president of marketing for Playdom, a leading social gaming company. Rachel lives in Palo Alto, California, with her husband, Scott, and their son and daughter.

The Beginning, Not the End . . .

What would you do if you weren't afraid?

We invite you to join us at LeanIn.Org, a community that encourages you to push past your fears and achieve your goals. We offer support, guidance, and expert education that will help you build your confidence and skills. You'll find everything you need to start or join a Lean In Circle, a small group that meets regularly to provide peer mentorship. You can watch videos like "Be Your Own Hero," "Own the Room," and "Centered Leadership"—all designed so you can learn a new skill one day and apply it the next. You'll find hundreds of personal stories from women and men all over the world who are leaning in to their lives. You can take inspiration from our posts about trailblazing women as you blaze a trail of your own.

We also welcome all women and men to be part of the the conversation at facebook.com/leaninorg and leanin.tumblr.com.

Come join us!

Acknowledgments

I am grateful to the many people who believed in these ideas and gave so much of themselves to make the publication of *Lean In* possible.

My deepest thanks go to my writing partner Nell Scovell. Nell and I have been working together on speeches, starting with the 2011 Forrestal Lecture at the U.S. Naval Academy, where I first used the phrase "lean in." When I was considering writing this book, I realized that I was willing to do it only if Nell collaborated with me. Nell responded that she was "not just in, but all in," which says everything about her commitment. She took a break from her work as a television writer/producer and journalist to make this a priority. She put in nights, early mornings, weekends, and holidays to accommodate my limited schedule. Most of all, she was insistent that we keep searching until we found the right way to talk about these complicated and emotional issues. Nell's talent with words is matched only by her sense of humor and her unshakable belief that having more women in leadership positions will result in a fairer and better world. I am grateful to her not just for her expertise and complete dedication, but for her friendship, which I have come to cherish. Her heart rings true and clear on this book's every page.

Marianne Cooper also has lived and breathed this book for the past year and a half. As a sociologist at the Clayman Institute for Gender Research at Stanford University and an expert on gender and social inequality, Marianne brought her vast knowledge to bear as this book's lead researcher. She is meticulous in her approach and has an unparalleled talent for synthesizing research so it is concise, understandable, and convincing. I learned a great deal from her clear thinking, deep insight, and analytical rigor.

This Graduates Edition owes a great deal to the unwavering dedication of Jessica Bennett, whose editorial judgment helped bring this project together. Thank you to Mellody Hobson, Mindy Levy, Kim Keating, Kunal Modi, Rachel Simmons, and Rachel Thomas for contributing chapters and sharing their wisdom with graduates everywhere. And thank you to Sara Kurovski, Allison Ye, Nola Barackman, Matthew Slutsky, Ursula Burns, Marie Tueller, Ty-Licia Hooker, Mana Nakagawa, Regina Agyare, Jana Morrelli, and Sindhura Kolli for sharing their stories so that others could learn from their experiences.

This book would not have been written if it were not for Jennifer Walsh. Through the depth of her conviction, the sheer force of her will, and her absolute refusal to take no for an answer, Jennifer convinced me to write this book. She told me that this process would be an important personal journey for me, and she was right. She stayed by my side from beginning to end, providing guidance and encouragement and reminding me at key moments why I was doing this.

My editor, Jordan Pavlin, believed in this project so much that she dedicated many hours over many months before I fully committed. She was instrumental in helping flesh out the initial ideas and turn those ideas into outlines and finally into chapters. Jordan never read an anecdote she did not think could be expanded, and she continually pushed me to share more of my experiences and emotions. I also owe my deepest gratitude to Sonny Mehta, editor in chief of Knopf, whose unflagging support kept this project on the fast track.

David Dreyer and Eric London were indispensable to the writing of this book. As trusted advisors and brilliant craftsmen, they pored over each and every draft from the very first to the very last. They applied their impeccable judgment and communications expertise to all matters, from suggesting sweeping structural changes to honing minute details. They always (*always*) stayed on point, were able to see issues from multiple angles, and delivered their advice with speed and a sense of humor. Elliot Schrage, Debbie Frost, Ashley Zandy, and Elisabeth Diana provided invaluable support and advice.

A dedicated group of women came together to turn this book's message into a global community committed to empowering women to achieve their ambitions. Rachel Thomas, president of LeanIn.Org, has been an extraordinary leader. Gina Bianchini and Debi Hemmeter cofounded LeanIn.Org with us, and their ideas and energy have shaped the organization. Nicole Stiffle, Andrea Saul, Jeanne Reidy, Tessa Lyons-Laing, Ashley Finch, and Nola Barackman come to work every day determined to make the world a more equal place.

If you read this book, you know the importance I place on feedback, and I am especially grateful to the many people who provided it. From the moment I decided to do this, my sister-in-law, Amy Schefler, jumped in to help. She sent detailed thoughts on topics I should cover as I was working on the initial outline, interviewed all her friends, shared her own stories, and read every draft of each chapter multiple times. Her enthusiasm and passion for this project—as well as her love and support—were truly inspiring.

Gloria Steinem has shared her wisdom with me since I was lucky enough to meet her six years ago. My understanding of the challenges that women face owes much to the time she has generously spent with me. No one has thought about women—and all of humanity—more deeply than Gloria. And she considers every issue with humility, humor, and a profound desire to build a just world. As an activist, her efforts continue to move us all toward the goal of true equality. As a writer, her words often provide the best single-sentence summary on any topic, which is why she is quoted so frequently in this book. The phrase "internalize the revolution" comes from her and echoes her book *Revolution from Within*. It is with love and gratitude that I quote her words in these pages.

Arianna Huffington has been a constant source of support in every aspect of my life for many years. She sent comments on drafts from all around the world, adding her insight and deep understanding of cultural trends. Oprah Winfrey encouraged me to focus on my intent for this book. When I was hesitant to share something personal, I heard her voice in my head—or in the text messages she sent—reminding me of the power of being authentic. Gene Sperling is one of the busiest people I know, and yet he found the time to write page after page of key suggestions. His ability to cut to the heart of the matter on issues that concern public policy and the problems that affect people from every life circumstance is matchless.

Mindy Levy, my childhood friend, was visiting with her family when I roped her into looking at a chapter. She turned out to be a master of structure and organization, which she then applied to future drafts. Mellody Hobson encouraged me to speak from the heart with conviction and confidence. She sets the example of what it means to be a woman, unapologetically. Karen Kehela Sherwood helped crystallize several key ideas, including the "aha" moment of realizing that how women are perceived when negotiating can be used as a negotiation tool. And just as she did for so many of my papers for so many years, my college room-mate Carrie Weber stayed up many late nights line editing every sentence. She helped in ways that only someone who is both a dear friend and an accomplished author could.

Many others generously read drafts and offered thoughts, sometimes under demanding deadlines. Deep thanks to Stephanie Flanders, Molly Graham, Larry Summers, Bill McKibben, Tina Bennett, Scott and Clia Tierney, Amanda

McCall, Jami Passer, Michelle Ebersman, Stephen Paul, Diana Farrell, Adam Freed, Phil Deutch, Marne Levine, Joel Kaplan, Eric Antonow, Lorna Borenstein, Marcus Buckingham, Michael Grimes, Anna Fieler, Kim Scott, Kim Jabal, Carole Geithner, Don Graham, Zander Lurie, and Michael Balaoing.

Many people contributed to the research that underpins this book. Shelley Correll and Lori Mackenzie of the Clayman Institute for Gender Research at Stanford connected me with Marianne, then supported her so that she could dedicate so much time to this project. Mana Nakagawa, a Ph.D. candidate in the International Comparative Education program at Stanford University, did the international research needed to make the book relevant for a global audience. Professor Deborah Gruenfeld of the Stanford Graduate School of Business started educating me on gender issues more than five years ago and has been doing it ever since. Kathleen McCartney, dean of the Harvard Graduate School of Education, explained the NICHD study on early child care and child development. Professor Jennifer Aaker of the Stanford Graduate School of Business shared her research on the importance of setting goals to pursuing happiness. Harvard professor Hannah Riley Bowles interrupted her vacation to spend hours on the phone discussing her work on negotiation. Professor Francis Flynn of the Stanford Graduate School of Business walked me step by step through the findings of his breakthrough Heidi/Howard study. Sharon Meers generously shared all of the research she spent years doing for her book *Getting to 50/50*. Christine Silva, senior director of research at Catalyst, provided important detail on several studies. Kim Parker, senior researcher with the Pew Social & Demographic Trends project, discussed Pew's research report on gender and career aspirations. And special thanks to Phil Garland, vice president of methodology at SurveyMonkey, for his insightful comments on many drafts as well as assistance with statistical analysis.

The team at WME has been on top of every aspect of this book. Ari Emanuel kicked this whole thing off by introducing me to Jennifer, and I am grateful for his friendship as well as his ever-amusing and supportive check-in calls. I am indebted to Tracy Fisher, Theresa Brown, Margaret Riley, Kathleen Nishimoto, and Caitlin Moore for all their efforts. The team at Knopf showed remarkable dedication and enthusiasm in this process: Tony Chirico, Paul Bogaards, Chris Gillespie, Peter Mendelsund, Erinn Hartman, Elizabeth Lindsay, Caroline Bleeke, Katherine Hourigan, Lydia Buechler, Cassandra Pappas, and Lisa Montebello. I further appreciate the contributions of Knopf cover designers Kelly Blair, Chip Kidd, Megan Wilson, Pablo Delcán, Oliver Munday, Christopher Brand, Linda Huang, and Cardon Webb. Many thanks to the team at SurveyMonkey—Jon Cohen, Kalpana Chandrasekhar, Anya McCall, Naiema Din, and Brent Chudoba—for helping us better understand the audience for this book. It was a joy to work closely with Ellen Feldman and Amy Ryan, and I grew to depend on their precision with words, careful attention to detail, and endless patience. Thank you to Divesh Makan of Iconiq for

his organizational and structural help and to Gary Stif-
felman of Ziffren Brittenham for his diligence. I also want
to thank Jill Gillett and Chris Sanagustin for their support
of Nell's work on this project. Much appreciation goes to
Markus Dohle and Madeline McIntosh of Random House
for their steadfast belief in this book.

A special thanks to all the women and men who reached
out to me after my TED Talk and other speeches to share
their stories, struggles, and triumphs. I would not have
kept talking about this subject or written this book had it
not been for their responses and thoughts. When I needed
inspiration, I read and reread their e-mails and letters.

I am also indebted to the many people who have given
me opportunities and guidance over the course of my
career. Larry Summers offered to advise my senior thesis, gave me my first job out of college, and has been an
important part of my life ever since. Lant Pritchett, my
first boss, taught me to look hard at the data and speak
the unvarnished truth. Eric Schmidt, Larry Page, Sergey
Brin, and Omid Kordestani hired me at Google despite
my complete lack of any relevant experience and supported me throughout my many years working for them.
Richard Skolnik, Salim Habayeb, and Maria Clark invited
me to join their team in India at the World Bank. Doug
Elmendorf helped me start a group for women in economics when I was in college and taught me so much over the
course of many years. Don Graham, Pat Mitchell, John
Doerr, Dan Rosensweig, Michael Lynton, Bob Iger, Howard Schultz, and Bob Rubin have all given me key advice

at critical junctures in my career. Fred Kofman shared his insights on leadership, authenticity, and responsibility.

I am lucky to work every day with extraordinary people at Facebook. My colleagues Chris Cox, Mike Schroepfer, Elliot Schrage, David Ebersman, Colin Stretch, Dee Jones, Kelly Hoffman, Charlton Gholson, Libby Leffler, Andrea Besmehn, David Fischer, Lori Goler, and Dan Rose challenge me to live up to their high standards and provide the friendship and support that makes coming to work every day worthwhile. Mark Zuckerberg gave me the opportunity of a lifetime and has continued to inspire and support me ever since. He has taught me by his example to chart my own course and has encouraged me to do what I would do if I were not afraid.

I am blessed to be surrounded by loving friends through this project and all else. I am so grateful for my childhood friends Eve Greenbarg, Mindy Levy, Jami Passer, Beth Redlich, Elise Scheck, Pam Srebrenik, Brook Rose, Merle Saferstein, and Amy Trachter; and my closest adulthood friends Carrie Weber, Marne Levine, Phil Deutch, Katie and Scott Mitic, Craig and Kirsten Nevill-Manning, Adam Freed, Joel Kaplan, Clia and Scott Tierney, Kim Jabal, Lorna Borenstein, David Lawee, Chamath Palihapitiya, Zander Lurie, Kim Keating, Diana Farrell, Scott Pearson, Lori Talingting, and Larry Brilliant.

The boundless support of my family has been the foundation of my life. My deepest gratitude and love to my parents Adele and Joel Sandberg, my brother David Sandberg, my sister Michelle Sandberg, my mother-in-law Paula

Goldberg, my siblings-in-law Amy Schefler, Marc Bodnick, and Rob and Leslye Goldberg, and my goddaughter Elise Geithner.

This book does not just recommend true partnership; it is a product of several true partnerships. Colin Summers, Nell's husband, slowed down his architecture career to become the primary caregiver for their children. In twenty years, his encouragement of her career has never faltered. His contributions to this mission included reading many drafts of this book, discussing its contents over countless meals, and attending several school events alone. Whenever someone suggests that mothers are better suited to raising children, Nell knows in the deepest way possible that fathers can parent with as much love, devotion, and joy.

Scott Saywell, Marianne's husband, encouraged her to take on this project despite her initial reluctance. When my offer came, she had her own book to write and a second baby with food allergies who was not sleeping well. Scott insisted they would figure out a way to make it work, then reorganized his schedule so that it did. He was more than just supportive, he was excited for Marianne.

And finally, I want to thank my truly amazing husband, Dave Goldberg. Dave is my best friend, closest advisor, dedicated coparent, and the love of my life. We both knew that my writing this book would come primarily at the expense of our time together, and so writing *Lean In* was as much his decision as mine. He supported me every step of the way, as he always does, with patience, great insight, humor, and love.

Notes

A LETTER TO GRADUATES

1. For more on this point, see the introduction to this book.

2. See chapter 3 for more about the success-likeability penalty that women experience.

3. Jenifer R. Lightdale and Deborah A. Prentice, "Rethinking Sex Differences in Aggression: Aggressive Behavior in the Absence of Social Roles," *Personality and Social Psychology Bulletin* 20, no. 1 (1994): 34–44.

4. See chapter 2 for information about how women tend to underestimate their abilities and attribute their success to external factors.

5. Bureau of Labor Statistics, *Employment Characteristics of Families Summary* (April 2012), http://www.bls.gov/news.release/famee.nr0 .htm; and Sarah Jane Glynn, *The New Breadwinners: 2010 Update*, Center for American Progress (April 2012), http://www.americanprogress .org/issues/labor/report/2012/04/16/11377/the-new-breadwinners-2010 -update/.

INTRODUCTION. INTERNALIZING THE REVOLUTION

1. International Labour Organization, *ILO Global Estimates of Forced Labour, Results and Methodology* (Geneva: ILO Publications, 2012), 13–14, http://www.ilo.org/wcmsp5/groups/public/—ed_norm/—declaration/ documents/publication/wcms_182004.pdf.

2. Caroline Wyatt, "What Future for Afghan Woman Jailed for Being Raped?," BBC News, South Asia, January 14, 2012, http://www .bbc.co.uk/news/world-south-asia-16543036.

3. According to the U.S. State Department, there are 195 independent states in the world. See U.S. Department of State, *Independent States in the World*, fact sheet (January 2012), http://www.state.gov/ s/inr/rls/4250.htm#note3. The calculation for the number of independent states led by women, defined as women serving as president or prime minister or other executive role, was derived from the most

recent information released by the CIA prior to publication. See Central Intelligence Agency, *Chiefs of State & Cabinet Members of Foreign Governments* (October 2013), https://www.cia.gov/library/publications/world-leaders-1/pdfs/October2013ChiefsDirectory.pdf. However, the calculation includes two electoral changes not reflected in the CIA information: the election of Michelle Bachelet, who will be president of Chile in March 2014, and the election of Catherine Samba-Panza as president of the Central African Republic. Elections vary from country to country in terms of when and how often they are held. Thus, the total number of women chiefs of state or heads of government will change as countries go through their next election cycle.

4. Inter-Parliamentary Union, *Women in National Parliaments* (2013), http://www.ipu.org/wmn-e/world.htm.

5. Claudia Goldin, Lawrence F. Katz, and Ilyana Kuziemko, "The Homecoming of American College Women: The Reversal of the College Gender Gap," *Journal of Economic Perspectives* 20, no. 4 (2006): 133.

6. Catalyst, *Targeting Inequity: The Gender Gap in U.S. Corporate Leadership* (September 2010), http://www.jec.senate.gov/public/index.cfm?a=Files.Serve&File_id=90f0aade-d9f5-43e7-8501-46bbd1c69bb8.

7. The calculation of women CEOs of Fortune 500 companies was drawn from the most recent information released by Catalyst prior to publication. See Catalyst, *Women CEOs of the Fortune 1000* (January 2014), http://www.catalyst.org/knowledge/women-ceos-fortune-1000.

8. Catalyst, *2013 Catalyst Census: Fortune 500 Women Executive Officers and Top Earners* (December 2013), http://www.catalyst.org/knowledge/2013-catalyst-census-fortune-500-women-executive-officers-and-top-earners. Catalyst defines an "executive officer" as one who is "appointed and elected by the board directors," including the "CEO and up to two reporting levels below," and individuals who are "listed as executive officers in SEC filings"; see appendix 1, Methodology Section, 2009 Catalyst Census: Fortune 500, http://www.catalyst.org/knowledge/2009-catalyst-census-methodology; Catalyst, *2013 Catalyst Census: Fortune 500 Women Board Directors* (December 2013), http://www.catalyst.org/knowledge/2013-catalyst-census-fortune-500-women-board-directors; and Center for American Women and Politics, *Women in the U.S. Congress 2014* (January 2014), fact sheet, http://www.cawp.rutgers.edu/fast_facts/levels_of_office/documents/cong.pdf.

9. U.S. Equal Employment Opportunity Commission, 2012 Job Patterns for Minorities and Women in Private Industry, 2012 EEO-1 National Aggregate Report (2012), http://www1.eeoc.gov/eeoc/statistics/employment/jobpat-eeo1/index.cfm. The EEOC's definition of top corporate jobs includes executive and senior level officers as well as managers; Catalyst, *2013 Catalyst Census: Fortune 500 Women Board Directors*, and Center for American Women and Politics, *Women of Color in Elec-*

tive Office 2013 (November 2013), fact sheet, http://www.cawp.rutgers
.edu/fast_facts/levels_of_office/documents/color.pdf. See also Catalyst,
Women of Color Executives: Their Voices, Their Journeys (June 2001), http://
www.catalyst.org/publication/54/women-of-color-executives-their
-voices-their-journeys.

10. Ariane Hegewisch, Claudia Williams, and Anlan Zhang, *The
Gender Wage Gap: 2011*, fact sheet (March 2012), http://www.iwpr.org/
publications/pubs/the-gender-wage-gap-2011; and Carmen DeNavas-
Walt, Bernadette D. Proctor, and Jessica C. Smith, *Income, Poverty,
and Health Insurance Coverage in the United States: 2010*, U.S. Census
Bureau, Current Population Reports, P60–239 (Washington, D.C.:
U.S. Government Printing Office, 2011), 12, http://www.census.gov/
prod/2011pubs/p60–239.pdf. Statistics cited are drawn from calculations of the gender pay gap based on median annual earnings. According to Dr. Pamela Coukos, a senior program advisor at the Department
of Labor's Office of Federal Contract Compliance Programs, the most
commonly cited estimate of the gender pay gap is based upon the difference between men's and women's median annual earnings. Another
widely used estimate of the gender pay gap is based upon the difference between men's and women's median weekly earnings. Some scholars believe weekly earnings are more accurate because they can better
account for differences in the total number of hours worked, and since
men often work more hours than women, this difference can account
for some of the pay gap. Other scholars argue that the median annual
earnings figure is preferable because it includes more types of compensation (such as bonuses, pensions, etc.). Importantly, both approaches
find that women earn less than men. According to recent median annual
earnings, women earn seventy-six and a half cents for every dollar men
earn. According to recent median weekly earnings, women earn eighty-
one cents for every dollar men earn. See Ariane Hegewisch and Claudia Williams, *The Gender Wage Gap: 2012*, fact sheet (September 2013),
http://www.iwpr.org/publications/pubs/the-gender-wage-gap-2012-1.
There are several components that account for the gender wage gap,
including differences in the types of occupations men and women go
into, differences in human capital (experience, education, etc.), and differences in the number of hours men and women work; these components explain some, but not all, of the gender wage gap. For example, a
study examining the hourly wages of men and women found that even
after controlling for human capital, women earned only 81 percent of
what men earned, and after additionally controlling for occupational
and industrial differences, women still earned only 91 percent of what
men earned. See Francine D. Blau and Lawrence M. Kahn, "The U.S.
Gender Pay Gap in the 1990s: Slowing Convergence," *Industrial &
Labor Relations Review* 60, no. 1 (2006): 45–66.

11. Marlo Thomas, "Another Equal Pay Day? Really?," *The Huffington Post*, April 12, 2011, http://www.huffingtonpost.com/marlo-thomas/equal-pay-day_b_847021.html.

12. Sociologist Arlie Russell Hochschild coined the phrase "the stalled revolution" in her book *The Second Shift* (New York: Avon Books, 1989), 12.

13. It should be noted that not all female leaders are supportive of women's interests. See Nicholas D. Kristof, "Women Hurting Women," *New York Times*, September 29, 2012, http://www.nytimes.com/2012/09/30/opinion/sunday/kristof-women-hurting-women.html?hp. For research and discussion about how all women can benefit when more women are in positions of power, see chapter 11.

14. Joanna Barsh and Lareina Yee, *Special Report: Unlocking the Full Potential of Women in the U.S. Economy*, McKinsey & Company (April 2011), 6, http://www.mckinsey.com/Client_Service/Organization/Latest_thinking/Unlocking_the_full_potential.aspx.

1. THE LEADERSHIP AMBITION GAP: WHAT WOULD YOU DO IF YOU WEREN'T AFRAID?

1. From 1981 to 2005, the opt-out rate for college-educated, married white women with children decreased from 25.2 percent to 21.3 percent, reaching its lowest point in 1993 (16.5 percent). Since the mid-1990s, there has been an uptick in this group deciding to leave the workforce. Still, the rate appears to be stabilizing and has not returned to the rates seen thirty or forty years ago (Stone and Hernandez 2012). This pattern of opting out maps broadly onto trends in women's employment rates since the 1960s. From the 1960s to the 1990s, there was a dramatic increase in women's labor force participation, which peaked in 1999 when 60 percent of women were working. Since 1999, there has been a slow decline in women's employment rates (Bureau of Labor Statistics 2007 and 2011). Mirroring these historical employment patterns among women, opting out reached a low in 1993, the decade that recorded the highest rates of women's labor force participation, and saw its sharpest increase from 1999 to 2002, the same years that marked the beginning of the decline in women's overall employment rates (Stone and Hernandez 2012). Thus, the recent decrease in the employment rates of highly educated mothers needs to be reconciled with employment declines among other groups, including declines for nonmothers and men. All are likely linked in part to a weak labor market (Boushey 2008). Despite this dip in employment, college-educated women have the highest labor force participation rates of all mothers (Stone and Hernandez 2012). According to recent research from the U.S. Census Bureau, young, less-educated, and Hispanic women are more likely to be stay-at-home mothers (Kreider

and Elliott 2010). For studies on opting out and women's labor force participation rates, see Pamela Stone and Lisa Ackerly Hernandez, "The Rhetoric and Reality of 'Opting Out,' " in *Women Who Opt Out: The Debate over Working Mothers and Work-Family Balance*, ed. Bernie D. Jones (New York: New York University Press, 2012), 33–56; Heather Boushey, " 'Opting Out?' The Effect of Children on Women's Employment in the United States," *Feminist Economics* 14, no. 1 (2008): 1–36; Rose M. Kreider and Diana B. Elliott, "Historical Changes in Stay-at-Home Mothers: 1969–2009," paper presented at the Annual Meeting of the American Sociological Association, Atlanta, GA, August 2010, http://www.census.gov/population/www/socdemo/ASA2010_Kreider _Elliott.pdf; Bureau of Labor Statistics, "Changes in Men's and Women's Labor Force Participation Rates," The Editor's Desk, January 10, 2007, http://www.bls.gov/opub/ted/2007/jan/wk2/art03.htm; and Bureau of Labor Statistics, *Women in the Labor Force: A Datebook*, report 1034 (December 2011), http://www.bls.gov/cps/wlf-databook-2011.pdf.

While the vast majority of women and mothers are working, when compared to their male counterparts, a sizable employment gap emerges. Surveys of highly educated men and women find that the postgraduation rates of employment and hours of employment are higher for men than for women, especially among those who have children. A survey of three cohorts of Harvard students from 1969 to 1972, 1979 to 1982, and 1989 to 1992 found that fifteen years after graduation, about 90 to 94 percent of the men were employed full-time, full year compared to around 60 to 63.5 percent of the women. The full-time, full-year employment rate among women graduates with two children was even lower, ranging from 41 to 47 percent (Goldin and Katz 2008). A survey of the graduating classes from the University of Chicago Booth School of Business from 1990 to 2006 found that in every year following graduation, between 92 and 94 percent of the men are employed full-time, full year. Upon graduation, 89 percent of the women are employed full-time, full year. Yet, over time, this percentage decreases, such that at six years out, 78 percent of women are employed full-time, full year. At nine years out, the percentage goes down to 69 percent. At ten or more years out, only 62 percent of the women are employed full-time, full year. The percentage is even lower for women with children. Ten or more years out, only about half of women with one or more children are employed full-time, full year. In any given year since graduation, no more than 1 percent of the men are not working, and only between 2 and 4 percent of the men are working part-time. In contrast, the share of women not working or working part-time increases with years since graduation, such that by ten or more years out, 17 percent of the women are not working and 22 percent are working part-time. The remaining small percentages of men and women worked fewer than fifty-two weeks per year. The survey also found that women with children worked 24 percent fewer hours per week than the average man and women without children worked 3.3 percent fewer hours (Bertand, Goldin, and Katz 2010).

Another survey published in 2000 of graduates from the top twelve MBA programs from 1981 to 1995 found that 95 percent of the men, but only 71 percent of the women, worked full-time. The further out from graduation, the lower the full-time employment rate of women (Catalyst, Center for the Education of Women at the University of Michigan, University of Michigan Business School, 2000). For more on these surveys, see Claudia Goldin and Lawrence F. Katz, "Transitions: Career and Family Life Cycles of the Educational Elite," *American Economic Review: Papers & Proceedings* 98, no. 2 (2008): 363–69; Marianne Bertrand, Claudia Goldin, and Lawrence F. Katz, "Dynamics of the Gender Gap for Young Professionals in the Financial and Corporate Sectors," *American Economic Journal: Applied Economics* 2, no. 3 (2010): 228–55; and Catalyst, Center for the Education of Women at the University of Michigan, University of Michigan Business School, *Women and the MBA: Gateway to Opportunity* (2000).

2. Judith Rodin, in discussion with the author, May 19, 2011.

3. National Center for Education Statistics, "Table 283: Degrees Conferred by Degree-Granting Institutions, by Level of Degree and Sex of Student: Selected Years, 1869–70 Through 2021–22," *Digest of Education Statistics* (2012), http://nces.ed.gov/programs/digest/dl2/tables/dt12_283.asp.

4. Hanna Rosin, *The End of Men: And the Rise of Women* (New York: Riverhead Books, 2012).

5. Debra Myhill, "Bad Boys and Good Girls? Patterns of Interaction and Response in Whole Class Teaching," *British Educational Research Journal* 28, no. 3 (2002): 350.

6. The four thousand survey respondents were employees of fourteen companies, almost all of which were Fortune 500 companies or companies of similar size. See Joanna Barsh and Lareina Yee, *Unlocking the Full Potential of Women at Work*, McKinsey & Company (April 2012), 7, http://www.mckinsey.com/careers/women/~/media/Reports/Women/2012%20WSJ%20Women%20in%20the%20Economy%20white%20paper%20FINAL.ashx.

Most surveys on aspirations to senior levels find a gender gap between men and women, with more men than women aspiring to these top management positions. A 2003 survey by the Family and Work Institute, Catalyst, and the Center for Work & Family at Boston College of high-level executives found that 19 percent of the men compared to just 9 percent of the women set their sights on becoming CEO or managing partner. The same survey found that 54 percent of the men and only 43 percent of the women hope to join the ranks of senior management. Also, of the executives who said they had reduced their aspirations (25 percent), women did so more than men (34 percent of women compared to 21 percent of men). The most frequently cited reason for reducing aspiration was the same for both men and women—67 percent said a very important reason was "the sacrifices I would have to make in my personal or family life." It's also important to note that women who think little progress has been made in breaking through the glass ceiling are more likely to have reduced their aspirations than women who think progress has occurred. See Families and Work Institute, Catalyst, Center for Work & Family at Boston College, *Leaders in a Global Economy: A Study of Executive Women and Men* (January 2003), 4, http://www.catalyst.org/knowledge/leaders -global-economy-study-executive-women-and-men.

A 2003 study examining the career aspirations of business students found that 81 percent of the men but only 67 percent of the women aspire to top management positions. See Gary N. Powell and D. Anthony Butterfield, "Gender, Gender Identity, and Aspirations to Top Management," *Women in Management Review* 18, no. 1 (2003): 88–96.

A 2007 study of employed managers and professionals enrolled in master's degree programs also found that the women had relatively weaker aspirations to senior management. See Barrie Litzky and Jeffrey Greenhaus, "The Relationship Between Gender and Aspirations to Senior Management," *Career Development International* 12, no. 7 (2007): 637–59. A survey of graduates from the top twelve MBA programs from 1981 to 1995 found that only 44 percent of women strongly agreed or agreed that they had a "desire to advance to a senior position" compared to 60 percent of men who strongly agreed or agreed. See Catalyst, Center for the Education of Women at the University of Michigan, and University of Michigan Business School, *Women and the MBA*. A McKinsey & Company report found that as women age, their desire to advance decreases more quickly than men's desire. The report concluded that at every age, "more men want to take on more responsibility in their organizations and have greater control over results." See Joanna Barsh and Lareina Yee, *Special Report: Unlocking the Full Potential of Women in the U.S. Economy*, McKinsey & Company (April 2011), 6, http:// www.mckinsey.com/Client_Service/Organization/Latest_thinking/ Unlocking_the_full_potential.aspx.

While most surveys find that more men than women aspire to top positions, a notable exception is a 2004 Catalyst survey of about 700 female senior leaders and 250 male senior leaders working in Fortune 1000 companies. This survey found comparable aspirations to reach the CEO level among women and men (55 percent of women and 57 percent of men). The survey also found that among those in line and staff positions, more women than men aspired to the CEO level. See Catalyst, *Women and Men in U.S. Corporate Leadership: Same Workplace, Different Realities?* (2004),

14–16, http://www.catalyst.org/publication/145/women-and-men-in-us -corporate-leadership-same-workplace-different-realities.

There are several explanations offered as to why women have lower aspirations than men, including that women feel there is a lack of fit between themselves (their personal characteristics) and senior leadership positions, which are often characterized in highly masculine terms; women feel there are too many obstacles to overcome; women do not want to prioritize career over family; women place less importance than do men on job characteristics common to senior roles, such as high pay, power, and prestige; gender role socialization influences girls' and women's attitudes and choices about occupational achievement; and women are more often located in jobs that lack opportunities for advancement and they lower their aspirations in response to this disadvantageous structural position. For a review of some of these explanations, see Litzsky and Greenhaus, "The Relationship Between Gender and Aspirations to Senior Management," 637–59. For an analysis of women's educational and occupational choices, see Jacquelynne S. Eccles, "Understanding Women's Educational and Occupational Choices: Applying the Eccles et al. Model of Achievement-Related Choices," *Psychology of Women Quarterly* 18, no. 4 (1994): 585–609. For analysis of how structural position shapes aspirations, see Naomi Casserir and Barbara Reskin, "High Hopes: Organizational Position, Employment Experiences, and Women's and Men's Promotion Aspirations," *Work and Occupations* 27, no. 4 (2000): 438–63; and Rosabeth Moss Kanter, *Men and Women of the Corporation*, 2nd ed. (New York: Basic Books, 1993).

7. Alison M. Konrad et al., "Sex Differences and Similarities in Job Attribute Preferences: A Meta-Analysis," *Psychological Bulletin* 126, no. 4 (2000): 593–641; and Eccles, "Understanding Women's Educational and Occupational Choices," 585–609. A survey of highly qualified women found that only 15 percent of them selected "a powerful position" as an important career goal. See Sylvia Ann Hewlett and Carolyn Buck Luce, "Off-Ramps and On-Ramps: Keeping Talented Women on the Road to Success," *Harvard Business Review* 83, no. 3 (2005): 48. Studies on job attribute preferences find that more men than women prefer jobs characterized by challenging work, power and influence over others, high levels of responsibility, risk taking, opportunities for achievement and advancement, and high prestige. Women tend to prefer jobs that are characterized as work that helps others, enables them to develop their skills and abilities, and allows them to spend time with family. For a recent review of research on this topic, see Erica S. Weisgram, Lisa M. Dinella, and Megan Fulcher, "The Role of Masculinity/Femininity, Values, and Occupational Value Affordances in Shaping Young Men's and Women's Occupational Choices," *Sex Roles* 65, nos. 3–4 (2011): 243–58.

8. Linda Schweitzer et al., "Exploring the Career Pipeline: Gender

Differences in Pre-Career Expectations," *Relations Industrielles* 66, no. 3 (2011): 422–44. This survey of 23,413 Canadian postsecondary students found that reaching a managerial level within three years of graduating was a major career priority for 10 percent of the men but only 5 percent of the women.

9. Hewlett and Luce, "Off-Ramps and On-Ramps," 48. This study of highly qualified women and men found that close to half the men described themselves as "extremely ambitious" or "very ambitious" in comparison to about a third of the women. Notably, the proportion of women describing themselves as "very ambitious" was higher among women in business (43 percent) and law and medicine (51 percent).

10. Eileen Patten and Kim Parker, *A Gender Reversal on Career Aspirations*, Pew Research Center (April 2012), http://www.pewsocialtrends .org/2012/04/19/a-gender-reversal-on-career-aspirations/. The finding that young women place more emphasis on career success than do young men does not hold when controlling for education. Among college graduates under age forty, there is not a significant difference between men and women in the share placing a high emphasis on career success. There is a significant gender difference among non–college graduates under age forty. These findings are based on small sample sizes and should be interpreted with caution.

11. The millennial generation is typically defined as those born between 1980 and 2000.

12. This survey of millennial adults found that 36 percent of men, but only 25 percent of women, said that the sentence "I aspire to a leadership role in whatever field I ultimately work" applies to them "very well." See Darshan Goux, *Millennials in the Workplace*, Bentley University Center for Women and Business (2012), 17–25, http://www.bentley.edu/ centers/sites/www.bentley.edu.centers/files/centers/cwb/millennials -report.pdf.

Another survey, conducted in 2008 by the Girl Scouts, found no difference between girls and boys in terms of their likelihood to have leadership aspirations and to think of themselves as leaders. The survey did find that girls are more concerned about social backlash. One-third of the girls who reported not wanting to be leaders attributed their lack of desire to "fear of being laughed at, making people mad at them, coming across as bossy, or not being liked by people." See Girl Scout Research Institute, *Change It Up: What Girls Say About Redefining Leadership* (2008), 19, http://www.girlscouts.org/research/pdf/change_it_up _executive_summary_english.pdf.

13. Samantha Ettus, "Does the Wage Gap Start in Kindergarten?," *Forbes*, June 13, 2012, http://www.forbes.com/sites/samantha ettus/2012/06/13/kindergarten-wage-gap/.

14. A study of accomplished men and women with the credentials

to run for political office found that 62 percent of men versus 46 percent of women had considered running. The study found that 22 percent of the men versus 14 percent of the women were interested in running for office in the future. The men also were almost 60 percent more likely than the women to think that they were "very qualified" to run. See Jennifer L. Lawless and Richard L. Fox, *Men Rule: The Continued Under-Representation of Women in U.S. Politics* (Washington, D.C.: Women & Politics Institute, American University School of Public Affairs, January 2012), http://www.american.edu/spa/wpi/upload/2012 -Men-Rule-Report-final-web.pdf.

15. A survey of more than four thousand middle and high school students found that only 22 percent of girls but 37 percent of boys said that "being in charge of other people" was "extremely important" or "very important" to them in a future job. The survey also found that 37 percent of girls compared to 51 percent of boys said that "being my own boss" was "extremely important" or "very important" to them in a future job. See Deborah Marlino and Fiona Wilson, *Teen Girls on Business: Are They Being Empowered?*, The Committee of 200, Simmons College School of Management (April 2003), 21, http://www.simmons.edu/ som/docs/centers/TGOB_report_full.pdf.

16. Jenna Johnson, "On College Campuses, a Gender Gap in Student Government," *Washington Post*, March 16, 2011, http://www .washingtonpost.com/local/education/on-college-campuses-a-gender -gap-in-student-government/2011/03/10/ABim1Bf_story.html.

17. For research on how aggressive women violate social norms, see Madeline E. Heilman and Tyler G. Okimoto, "Why Are Women Penalized for Success at Male Tasks? The Implied Communality Deficit," *Journal of Applied Psychology* 92, no. 1 (2007): 81–92; Madeline E. Heilman et al., "Penalties for Success: Reactions to Women Who Succeed at Male Gender-Typed Tasks," *Journal of Applied Psychology* 89, no. 3 (2004): 416–27; Alice H. Eagly and Steven J. Karau, "Role Congruity Theory of Prejudice Toward Female Leaders," *Psychological Review* 109, no. 3 (2002): 573–98; and Madeline E. Heilman, "Description and Prescription: How Gender Stereotypes Prevent Women's Ascent up the Organizational Ladder," *Journal of Social Issues* 57, no. 4 (2001): 657–74.

18. Gayle Tzemach Lemmon, "We Need to Tell Girls They Can Have It All (Even If They Can't)," *The Atlantic*, June 29, 2012, http:// www.theatlantic.com/business/archive/2012/06/we-need-to-tell-girls -they-can-have-it-all-even-if-they-cant/259165/.

19. For reviews of research, see May Ling Halim and Diane Ruble, "Gender Identity and Stereotyping in Early and Middle Childhood," in *Handbook of Gender Research in Psychology: Gender Research in General and Experimental Psychology*, vol. 1, ed. Joan C. Chrisler and Donald R. McCreary (New York: Springer, 2010), 495–525; Michael S. Kimmel

and Amy Aronson, eds., *The Gendered Society Reader*, 3rd ed. (Oxford: Oxford University Press, 2008); and Campbell Leaper and Carly Kay Friedman, "The Socialization of Gender," in *Handbook of Socialization: Theory and Research*, ed. Joan E. Grusec and Paul D. Hastings (New York: Guilford Press, 2007), 561–87.

20. Melissa W. Clearfield and Naree M. Nelson, "Sex Differences in Mother's Speech and Play Behavior with 6, 9, and 14-Month-Old Infants," *Sex Roles* 54, nos. 1–2 (2006): 127–37. Studies have found that parents tend to talk more with daughters than with sons. Further, mothers have more emotionally complex conversations and use a more conversational and supportive style of communication with their daughters than with their sons. For reviews of research, see Clearfield and Nelson, "Sex Differences in Mother's Speech and Play Behavior," 127–37; and Gretchen S. Lovas, "Gender and Patterns of Language Development in Mother-Toddler and Father-Toddler Dyads," *First Language* 31, no. 1 (2011): 83–108.

21. Emily R. Mondschein, Karen E. Adolph, and Catherine S. Tamis-Le Monda, "Gender Bias in Mothers' Expectations About Infant Crawling," *Journal of Experimental Child Psychology* 77, no. 4 (2000): 304–16.

22. Clearfield and Nelson, "Sex Differences in Mother's Speech and Play Behavior," 127–37. Another study observing close to eight hundred families in four different public venues found that in three of the four locations, a larger percentage of male toddlers were allowed to walk by themselves than were female toddlers. See G. Mitchell et al., "Reproducing Gender in Public Places: Adults' Attention to Toddlers in Three Public Places," *Sex Roles* 26, nos. 7–8 (1992): 323–30.

23. Emma Gray, "Gymboree Onesies: 'Smart Like Dad' for Boys, 'Pretty Like Mommy' for Girls," *The Huffington Post*, November 16, 2011, http://www.huffingtonpost.com/2011/11/16/gymboree -onesies_n_1098435.html.

24. Andrea Chang, "JC Penney Pulls 'I'm Too Pretty to Do Homework' Shirt," *Los Angeles Times* blog, August 31, 2011, http://latimesblogs .latimes.com/money_co/2011/08/jcpenney-pulls-im-too-pretty-to-do -homework-shirt.html.

25. Over the last forty years, gender bias and gender differences in the classroom have been studied extensively. On balance, studies find that teachers give more attention to boys than girls. Boys also tend to have a more dominant presence in the classroom. Still, depending on the methodology employed (such as the age of students, the subject area being taught, and the achievement level of the students), some studies have found few differences in teacher interactions and behavior in the classroom between boys and girls. Notably, very few studies have documented instances in which girls receive more attention from teachers

than do boys. For reviews of the research, see Robyn Beaman, Kevin Wheldall, and Carol Kemp, "Differential Teacher Attention to Boys and Girls in the Classroom," *Educational Review* 58, no. 3 (2006): 339–66; Susanne M. Jones and Kathryn Dindia, "A Meta-Analytic Perspective on Sex Equity in the Classroom," *Review of Educational Research* 74, no. 4 (2004): 443–71; Ellen Rydell Altermatt, Jasna Javanovic, and Michelle Perry, "Bias or Responsivity? Sex and Achievement-Level Effects on Teachers' Classroom Questioning Practices," *Journal of Educational Psychology* 90, no. 3 (1998): 516–27; Myra Sadker, David Sadker, and Susan Klein, "The Issue of Gender in Elementary and Secondary Education," *Review of Research in Education* 17 (1991): 269–334; and Roberta M. Hall and Bernice R. Sandler, *The Classroom Climate: A Chilly One for Women?* (Washington, D.C.: Association of American Colleges, 1982).

26. Riley Maida, "4 Year Old Girl Questions Marketing Strategies," YouTube video, 1:12 minutes, posted by Neuroticy2, December 28, 2011, http://www.youtube.com/watch?v=P3mTTloB_0c.

27. Kelly Danaher and Christian S. Crandall, "Stereotype Threat in Applied Settings Re-Examined," *Journal of Applied Social Psychology* 38, no. 6 (2008): 1639–55. Based on their analysis of gender, stereotype threat, and performance on the AP calculus test, Danaher and Crandall estimate that if the demographic gender question was moved to the end of the test, 4,763 more young women would pass. For more research about how stereotype threat decreases women's performance, see Catherine Good, Joshua Aronson, and Jayne Ann Harder, "Problems in the Pipeline: Stereotype Threat and Women's Achievement in High-Level Math Courses," *Journal of Applied and Developmental Psychology* 29, no. 1 (2008): 17–28.

Stereotypes of all kinds, ranging from "white men can't jump" to "Asians are better at math" have been shown to influence performance as well as the evaluation of performance. See Jeff Stone, Zachary W. Perry, and John M. Darley, " 'White Men Can't Jump': Evidence for the Perceptual Confirmation of Racial Stereotypes Following a Basketball Game," *Basic and Applied Social Psychology* 19, no. 3 (1997): 291–306; Jeff Stone et al., "Stereotype Threat Effects on Black and White Athletic Performance," *Journal of Personality and Social Psychology* 77, no. 6 (1999): 1213–27; and Margaret Shih, Todd L. Pittinsky, and Nalini Ambady, "Stereotype Susceptibility: Identity Salience and Shifts in Quantitative Performance," *Psychological Science* 10, no. 1 (1999): 80–83.

28. Jenessa R. Shapiro and Amy M. Williams, "The Role of Stereotype Threats in Undermining Girls' and Women's Performance and Interest in STEM Fields," *Sex Roles* 66, nos. 3–4 (2011): 175–83.

29. Goux, *Millennials in the Workplace*, 32.

30. Sarah Jane Glynn, *The New Breadwinners: 2010 Update,* Center for American Progress (April 2012), 2, http://www.americanprogress .org/issues/labor/report/2012/04/16/11377/the-new-breadwinners -2010-update/. In 2009, 41.4 percent of mothers were breadwinners for their families and another 22.5 percent were co-breadwinners.

31. Heather Boushey, "The New Breadwinners," in *The Shriver Report: A Woman Nation Changes Everything,* ed. Heather Boushey and Ann O'Leary, A Report by Maria Shriver and the Center for American Progress (October 2009), 34, http://www.americanprogress.org/issues/ women/report/2009/10/16/6789/the-shriver-report/.

32. Mark Mather, *U.S. Children in Single-Mother Families,* Population Reference Bureau, Data Brief (May 2012).

33. Human Rights Watch, *Failing Its Families: Lack of Paid Leave and Work-Family Supports in the US* (February 2011), http://www.hrw.org/ sites/default/files/reports/us0211webwcover.pdf.

34. Ellen Bravo, " 'Having It All?'—The Wrong Question for Most Women," *Women's Media Center,* June 26, 2012, http://www.womens mediacenter.com/feature/entry/having-it-all-the-wrong-question-for -most-women.

35. Sharon Meers and Joanna Strober, *Getting to 50/50: How Working Couples Can Have It All by Sharing It All* (New York: Bantam Books, 2009).

36. Rosalind Chait Barnett, "Women and Multiple Roles: Myths and Reality," *Harvard Review of Psychology* 12, no. 3 (2004): 158–64; Rosalind Chait Barnett and Janet Shibley Hyde, "Women, Men, Work, and Family: An Expansionist Theory," *American Psychologist* 56, no. 10 (2001): 781–96; and Rosalind Chait Barnett and Caryl Rivers, *She Works/He Works: How Two-Income Families Are Happy, Healthy, and Thriving* (Cambridge, MA: Harvard University Press, 1998).

37. Cheryl Buehler and Marion O'Brian, "Mothers' Part-Time Employment: Associations with Mother and Family Well-Being," *Journal of Family Psychology* 25, no. 6 (2011): 895–906; Rebekah Coley et al., "Maternal Functioning, Time, Money: The World of Work and Welfare," *Children and Youth Services Review* 29, no. 6 (2007): 721–41; Leslie Bennetts, *The Feminine Mistake: Are We Giving Up Too Much?* (New York: Hyperion, 2007); Lynne P. Cook, " 'Doing' Gender in Context: Household Bargaining and the Risk of Divorce in Germany and the United States," *American Journal of Sociology* 112, no. 2 (2006): 442–72; and Barnett, "Women and Multiple Roles," 158–64.

38. This phrase was first used by Spencer Johnson in his 1998 book, *Who Moved My Cheese?.* See Spencer Johnson, *Who Moved My Cheese? An Amazing Way to Deal with Change in Your Work and in Your Life* (New York: Putnam, 1998), 48.

2. SIT AT THE TABLE

1. Peggy McIntosh, "Feeling Like a Fraud," Wellesley Centers for Women working paper no. 18 (Wellesley, MA: Stone Centers Publications, 1985).

2. Early research on the impostor syndrome in the late 1970s suggested it was more prevalent among high-achieving women. Subsequent studies in the 1980s and 1990s were equivocal, with some studies agreeing and others finding that men were sometimes vulnerable to these kinds of fears too, at comparable rates. Recently, studies that focused on college students, doctoral students, and family medicine residents have again found the syndrome to be more prevalent among women than men. Most research and discussion about the impostor syndrome argues that women are more limited by it because they experience it more frequently and with more intensity than do men. For a discussion, see Gina Gibson-Beverly and Jonathan P. Schwartz, "Attachment, Entitlement, and the Impostor Phenomenon in Female Graduate Students," *Journal of College Counseling* 11, no. 2 (2008): 120–21; and Shamala Kumar and Carolyn M. Jagacinski, "Imposters Have Goals Too: The Imposter Phenomenon and Its Relationship to Achievement Goal Theory," *Personality and Individual Differences* 40, no. 1 (2006): 149. For other recent studies, see Gregor Jöstl et al., "When Will They Blow My Cover? The Impostor Phenomenon Among Austrian Doctoral Students," *Zeitschrift für Psychologie* 220, no. 2 (2012): 109–20; Loretta Neal McGregor, Damon E. Gee, and K. Elizabeth Posey, "I Feel Like a Fraud and It Depresses Me: The Relation Between the Imposter Phenomenon and Depression," *Social Behavior and Personality* 36, no. 1 (2008): 43–48; and Kathy Oriel, Mary Beth Plane, and Marlon Mundt, "Family Medicine Residents and the Impostor Phenomenon," *Family Medicine* 36, no. 4 (2004): 248–52. For the original study, see Pauline Rose Clance and Suzanne Ament Imes, "The Impostor Phenomenon in High Achieving Women: Dynamics and Therapeutic Intervention," *Psychotherapy: Theory, Research and Practice* 15, no. 3 (1978): 241–47.

3. "Tina Fey—From Spoofer to Movie Stardom," *The Independent*, March 19, 2010, http://www.independent.co.uk/arts-entertainment/films/features/tina-fey—from-spoofer-to-movie-stardom-1923552.html.

4. S. Scott Lind et al., "Competency-Based Student Self-Assessment on a Surgery Rotation," *Journal of Surgical Research* 105, no. 1 (2002): 31–34.

5. Jennifer L. Lawless and Richard L. Fox, *Men Rule: The Continued Under-Representation of Women in U.S. Politics* (Washington, D.C.: Women & Politics Institute, American University School of Public

Affairs, January 2012), http://www.american.edu/spa/wpi/upload/2012 -Men-Rule-Report-final-web.pdf.

6. Working Group on Student Experiences, *Study on Women's Experiences at Harvard Law School* (Cambridge, MA: Working Group on Student Experiences, February 2004), http://www.law.harvard.edu/ students/experiences/FullReport.pdf. A higher percentage of male law students than female law students ranked themselves in the top quintile of their class in the following categories: legal reasoning (33% vs. 15%), quantitative reasoning (40% vs. 11%), quick on feet (28% vs. 17%), brief writing (23% vs. 18%), oral argument (24% vs. 13%), research (20% vs. 11%), building consensus (27% vs. 21%), and persuading others (20% vs. 12%). In only one skill, ethical issues, did a slightly higher percentage of female students (26%) than male students (25%) rank themselves in the top quintile of their class.

7. For studies on how women estimate their abilities in front of others, see Kimberly A. Daubman, Laurie Heatherington, and Alicia Ahn, "Gender and the Self-Presentation of Academic Achievement," *Sex Roles* 27, nos. 3–4 (1992): 187–204; Laurie Heatherington et al., "Two Investigations of 'Female Modesty' in Achievement Situations," *Sex Roles* 29, nos. 11–12 (1993): 739–54; and Laurie Heatherington, Laura S. Townsend, and David P. Burroughs, " 'How'd You Do on That Test?' The Effects of Gender on Self-Presentation of Achievement to Vulnerable Men," *Sex Roles* 45, nos. 3–4 (2001): 161–77. For a review and analysis of how women judge themselves on masculine tasks, see Sylvia Beyer, "The Effects of Gender, Dysphoria, and Performance Feedback on the Accuracy of Self-Evaluations," *Sex Roles* 47, nos. 9–10 (2002): 453–64.

8. Sylvia Beyer, "Gender Differences in Causal Attributions by College Students of Performance on Course Examinations," *Current Psychology* 17, no. 4 (1998): 346–58. Research has documented the tendency for girls and women to underestimate their skills, abilities, and performance relative to boys and men, especially in regard to masculine tasks. Yet depending on the specific methodology used, some studies have found that women give more accurate appraisals of their performance, while men overestimate their performance. Several explanations have been advanced to explain why women tend to lower their self-assessments, including low self-confidence; "feminine modesty," which holds that to act in accordance with gender role stereotypes and/or to avoid the negative consequences of female immodesty, girls and women present themselves in a more humble manner; and concern with protecting the self-esteem of others. From this relational perspective, women want to preserve a sense of equality and compatibility in their personal relationships, and thus they lower their self-assessments so as to avoid being perceived as bragging or to avoid making someone else, who may

have performed worse, feel badly. The gender of the person to whom women make a self-assessment has sometimes been found to affect the degree to which they underestimate themselves, with some evidence finding that women lower their self-assessments in the presence of vulnerable male partners, for example, by lowering estimates of their GPA in front of a male partner who is worried about his grades. However, studies on this specific topic are inconsistent. For a review of these explanations, see Heatherington, Townsend, and Burroughs, " 'How'd You Do on That Test?,' " 161–77; and Laurie Heatherington, Andrea B. Burns, and Timothy B. Gustafson, "When Another Stumbles: Gender and Self-Presentation to Vulnerable Others," *Sex Roles* 38, nos. 11–12 (1998): 889–913.

9. Tomi-Ann Roberts and Susan Nolan-Hoeksema, "Sex Differences in Reactions to Evaluative Feedback," *Sex Roles* 21, nos. 11–12 (December 1989): 725–47; and Maria Johnson and Vicki S. Helgeson, "Sex Differences in Response to Evaluative Feedback: A Field Study," *Psychology of Women Quarterly* 26, no. 3 (2002): 242–51.

10. Sylvia Beyer, "Gender Differences in Causal Attributions by College Students of Performance on Course Examinations," *Current Psychology* 17, no. 4 (1998): 354. For a review of consequences from negative self-evaluation, including depression and lower aspirations, see Sylvia Beyer and Edward M. Bowden, "Gender Differences in Self-Perception: Convergent Evidence from Three Measures of Accuracy and Bias," *Personality and Social Psychology Bulletin* 23, no. 2 (1997): 169.

11. Nicole Perlroth and Claire Cain Miller, "The $1.6 Billion Woman, Staying on Message," *New York Times*, February 4, 2012, http://www.nytimes.com/2012/02/05/business/sheryl-sandberg-of-facebook-staying-on-message.html?pagewanted=all.

12. Dana R. Carney, Amy J. C. Cuddy, and Andy J. Yap, "Power Posing: Brief Nonverbal Displays Affect Neuroendocrine Levels and Risk Tolerance," *Psychological Science* 21, no. 10 (2010): 1363–68.

13. Bianca Bosker, "Cisco Tech Chief Outlines the Advantages of Being a Woman in Tech," *The Huffington Post*, October 27, 2011, http://www.huffingtonpost.com/2011/10/27/cisco-chief-technology-officer-woman-in-tech_n_1035880.html.

14. Claire Cain Miller, "For Incoming I.B.M. Chief, Self-Confidence Is Rewarded, *New York Times*, October 27, 2011, http://www.nytimes.com/2011/10/28/business/for-incoming-ibm-chief-self-confidence-rewarded.html.

15. Caroline Howard, "The World's 100 Most Powerful Women: This Year It's All About Reach," *Forbes*, August 24, 2011, http://www.forbes.com/sites/carolinehoward/2011/08/24/the-worlds-100-most-powerful-women-this-year-its-all-about-reach/.

3. SUCCESS AND LIKEABILITY

1. A description and analysis of the study were provided by Professor Francis J. Flynn in discussion with the author, June 22, 2011.

2. To read the case study, see Kathleen McGinn and Nicole Tempest, *Heidi Roizen*, Harvard Business School Case Study #9–800–228 (Boston: Harvard Business School Publishing, 2009).

3. Madeline E. Heilman and Tyler G. Okimoto, "Why Are Women Penalized for Success at Male Tasks?: The Implied Communality Deficit," *Journal of Applied Psychology* 92, no. 1 (2007): 81–92; Madeline E. Heilman et al., "Penalties for Success: Reactions to Women Who Succeed at Male Gender-Typed Tasks," *Journal of Applied Psychology* 89, no. 3 (2004): 416–27; and Madeline E. Heilman, Caryn J. Block, and Richard F. Martell, "Sex Stereotypes: Do They Influence Perceptions of Managers?" *Journal of Social Behavior and Personality* 10, no. 6 (1995): 237–52. For helpful reviews of relevant issues, see Alice H. Eagly and Steven J. Karau, "Role Congruity Theory of Prejudice Toward Female Leaders," *Psychological Review* 109, no. 3 (2002): 573–98; Madeline E. Heilman, "Description and Prescription: How Gender Stereotypes Prevent Women's Ascent up the Organizational Ladder," *Journal of Social Issues* 57, no. 4 (2001): 657–74; and Cecilia L. Ridgeway, "Gender, Status, and Leadership," *Journal of Social Issues* 57, no. 4 (2001): 637–55. It should be noted that successful women pay a likeability penalty specifically in arenas considered to be male domains.

4. Cyndi Kernahan, Bruce D. Bartholow, and B. Ann Bettencourt, "Effects of Category-Based Expectancy Violation on Affect-Related Evaluations: Toward a Comprehensive Model," *Basic and Applied Social Psychology* 22, no. 2 (2000): 85–100; and B. Ann Bettencourt et al., "Evaluations of Ingroup and Outgroup Members: The Role of Category-Based Expectancy Violation," *Journal of Experimental Social Psychology* 33, no. 3 (1997): 244–75. Research on this topic, known as "expectancy theory," finds that we tend to evaluate people based upon stereotypes about the groups to which they belong. When people act in ways that violate our preconceived expectations, we take notice and evaluate them more extremely and intensely than we would otherwise.

5. Shankar Vedantam, " 'Nicer Sex' Image at Play in Politics," *Chicago Tribune*, November 13, 2007, http://articles.chicagotribune.com/2007-11-13/news/0711120690_1_female-leaders-women-and-leadership-social-psychologist.

6. Ken Auletta, "A Woman's Place: Can Sheryl Sandberg Upend Silicon Valley's Male-Dominated Culture?," *The New Yorker*, July 11, 2012, http://www.newyorker.com/reporting/2011/07/11/110711fa_fact_auletta?currentPage=all.

7. Professor Deborah H. Gruenfeld, discussion with the author, June 22, 2012.

8. A study by Madeline E. Heilman et al. (2004) found that among competent employees, those who were less liked received fewer organizational reward recommendations (such as getting put on the fast track, salary increases) than employees who were liked. See Heilman et al., "Penalties for Success," 416–27.

9. Laurie A. Rudman, "Self-Promotion as a Risk Factor for Women: The Costs and Benefits of Counterstereotypical Impression Management," *Journal of Personality and Social Psychology* 74, no. 3 (1998): 629–45; Laurie A. Rudman and Peter Glick, "Feminized Management and Backlash Toward Agentic Women: The Hidden Costs to Women of a Kinder, Gentler Image of Middle Managers," *Journal of Personality and Social Psychology* 77, no. 5 (1999): 1004–10; and Laurie A. Rudman and Peter Glick, "Prescriptive Gender Stereotypes and Backlash Toward Agentic Women," *Journal of Social Issues* 57, no. 4 (2001): 743–62.

10. Professor Francis J. Flynn, discussion with the author, June 22, 2011.

11. Madeline E. Heilman and Julie J. Chen, "Same Behavior, Different Consequences: Reactions to Men's and Women's Altruistic Citizenship Behaviors," *Journal of Applied Psychology* 90, no. 3 (2005): 431–41.

12. Catalyst, *The Double-Bind Dilemma for Women in Leadership: Damned if You Do, Doomed if You Don't* (July 2007), 1, http://www.catalyst.org/knowledge/double-bind-dilemma-women-leadership-damned-if-you-do-doomed-if-you-dont-o.

13. Linda Babcock and Sara Laschever, *Women Don't Ask* (New York: Bantam Books, 2007), 1–4; Linda Babcock et al., "Gender Differences in the Propensity to Initiate Negotiations," in *Social Psychology and Economics*, ed. David De Cremer, Marcel Zeelenberg, and J. Keith Murnighan (Mahwah, NJ: Lawrence Erlbaum, 2006), 239–59; and Fiona Greig, "Propensity to Negotiate and Career Advancement: Evidence from an Investment Bank That Women Are on a 'Slow Elevator,'" *Negotiation Journal* 24, no. 4 (2008): 495–508. In general, studies find that men negotiate more than women and tend to reap more rewards from their efforts. However, these trends depend on the context in which the negotiation occurs. Small et al. (2007) found that the gender difference in initiating a negotiation disappears if the situation is characterized as an opportunity to "ask" as opposed to an opportunity to "negotiate." And Bowles et al. (2005) found that women's performance dramatically improves if they are negotiating for others and not for themselves. See Deborah A. Small et al., "Who Goes to the Bargaining Table? The Influence of Gender and Framing on the Initiation of Negotiation," *Journal of Personality and Social Psychology* 93, no. 4 (2007): 600–613; and Hannah Riley Bowles et al.,

"Constraints and Triggers: Situational Mechanics of Gender in Negotiation," *Journal of Personality and Social Psychology* 89, no. 6 (2005): 951–65.

14. Babcock and Laschever, *Women Don't Ask*, 1–2.

15. Emily T. Amanatullah and Catherine H. Tinsley, "Punishing Female Negotiators for Asserting Too Much . . . or Not Enough: Exploring Why Advocacy Moderates Backlash Against Assertive Female Negotiators," *Organizational Behavior and Human Decision Processes* 120, no. 1 (2013): 110–22; and Hannah Riley Bowles, Linda Babcock, and Lei Lai, "Social Incentives for Gender Differences in the Propensity to Initiate Negotiations: Sometimes It Does Hurt to Ask," *Organizational Behavior and Human Decision Processes* 103, no. 1 (2007): 84–103.

16. Emily T. Amanatullah and Michael W. Morris, "Negotiating Gender Roles: Gender Differences in Assertive Negotiating Are Mediated by Women's Fear of Backlash and Attenuated When Negotiating on Behalf of Others," *Journal of Personality and Social Psychology* 98, no. 2 (2010): 256–67; and Bowles et al., "Constraints and Triggers," 951–65.

17. Bowles, Babcock, and Lai, "Social Incentives for Gender Differences," 84–103.

18. Hannah Riley Bowles and Linda Babcock, "How Can Women Escape the Compensation Negotiation Dilemma? Relational Accounts Are One Answer," *Psychology of Women Quarterly*, article in press (2012), 2, http://dx.doi.org/10.1177/0361684312455524.

19. Ibid., 1–17.

20. Cecilia L. Ridgeway, "Status in Groups: The Importance of Motivation," *American Sociological Review* 47, no. 1 (1982): 76–88. In male group situations, women were found to be more influential when they made group-oriented statements (for example, "I think it's important that we cooperate").

21. Bowles and Babcock, "How Can Women Escape the Compensation Negotiation Dilemma?" 1–17.

22. Linda Babcock and Sara Laschever, *Ask for It: How Women Can Use the Power of Negotiation to Get What They Really Want* (New York: Bantam Dell, 2008), 253.

23. For more information and advice about how to be "relentlessly pleasant," see ibid., 251–66.

24. E. B. Boyd, "Where Is the Female Mark Zuckerberg?," *San Francisco*, December 2011, http://www.modernluxury.com/san-francisco/story/where-the-female-mark-zuckerberg.

25. Jessica Valenti, "Sad White Babies with Mean Feminist Mommies," Jessica Valenti blog, June 19, 2012, http://jessicavalenti.tumblr.com/post/25465502300/sad-white-babies-with-mean-feminist-mommies-the.

4. IT'S A JUNGLE GYM, NOT A LADDER

1. Bureau of Labor Statistics, *Number of Jobs Held, Labor Market Activity, and Earnings Growth Among the Youngest Baby Boomers: Results from a Longitudinal Study* (July 2012), http://www.bls.gov/news.release/pdf/nlsoy.pdf. This report found that the average person born between 1957 and 1964 had 11.3 jobs between the ages of eighteen and forty-six, with almost half of these jobs being held between the ages of eighteen and twenty-four.

2. For reviews of the research on women tending to be more risk averse than men, see Marianne Bertrand, "New Perspectives on Gender," in *Handbook of Labor Economics*, vol. 4B, ed. Orley Ashenfelter and David Card (Amsterdam: North Holland, 2010), 1544–90; Rachel Croson and Uri Gneezy, "Gender Differences in Preferences," *Journal of Economic Literature* 47, no. 2 (2009): 448–74; and Catherine C. Eckel and Phillip J. Grossman, "Men, Women, and Risk Aversion: Experimental Evidence," in *Handbook of Experimental Economics Results*, vol. 1, ed. Charles R. Plott and Vernon L. Smith (Amsterdam: North Holland, 2008), 1061–73.

3. Centers for Disease Control and Prevention, *Drowning Risks in Natural Water Settings*, http://www.cdc.gov/Features/dsDrowning Risks/.

4. Karen S. Lyness and Christine A. Schrader, "Moving Ahead or Just Moving? An Examination of Gender Differences in Senior Corporate Management Appointments," *Gender & Organization Management* 31, no. 6 (2006): 651–76. This study examined 952 announcements in *The Wall Street Journal* about senior management appointments. Analysis of the announcements found that compared to their male counterparts, women's new roles were more similar to their previous roles and women were less likely to switch to new companies. Among those in managerial staff positions, women were less likely than men to move into a line position or into a new functional area. These differences suggest that women's job changes may offer fewer career benefits than the benefits men receive for their job moves.

5. Londa Schiebinger, Andrea Davies, and Shannon K. Gilmartin, *Dual-Career Academic Couples: What Universities Need to Know*, Clayman Institute for Gender Research, Stanford University (2008), http://gender.stanford.edu/sites/default/files/DualCareerFinal_0.pdf; Kimberlee A. Shauman and Mary C. Noonan, "Family Migration and Labor Force Outcomes: Sex Differences in Occupational Context," *Social Forces* 85, no. 4 (2007): 1735–64; and Pam Stone, *Opting Out? Why Women Really Quit Careers and Head Home* (Berkeley: University of California Press, 2007).

6. Irene E. De Pater et al., "Challenging Experiences: Gender

Differences in Task Choice," *Journal of Managerial Psychology* 24, no.1 (2009): 4–28. In this study, the authors surveyed close to one hundred business school students about their internship experience. The survey found that in conditions of "higher decision latitude," where interns had more control over the things they did during their internship, women reported having fewer challenging experiences. In Irene E. De Pater et al., "Individual Task Choice and the Division of Challenging Tasks Between Men and Women," *Group & Organization Management* 34, no. 5 (2009): 563–89, researchers found that when pairs of men and women negotiated over the assignment of tasks, men ended up with the more challenging ones. For findings that suggest that gendered beliefs such as "women need protection" (benevolent sexism) impede women's access to challenging tasks, see Eden B. King et al., "Benevolent Sexism at Work: Gender Differences in the Distribution of Challenging Developmental Experiences," *Journal of Management* 38, no. 6 (2012): 1835–66.

7. Georges Desvaux, Sandrine Devillard-Hoellinger, and Mary C. Meaney, "A Business Case for Women," *The McKinsey Quarterly* (September 2008): 4, http://www.womenscolleges.org/files/pdfs/Business CaseforWomen.pdf.

8. Lloyds TSB found that their female employees tended not to put themselves up for promotion despite being 8 percent more likely to meet or surpass performance standards than their male colleagues. See Desvaux, Devillard-Hoellinger, and Meaney, "A Business Case for Women," 4. Studies on gender and promotion mostly at the university level in England and Australia also find that women are hesitant to put themselves up for promotion, often because they undervalue their skills, abilities, and work experience. See Anne Ross-Smith and Colleen Chesterman, " 'Girl Disease': Women Managers' Reticence and Ambivalence Towards Organizational Advancement," *Journal of Management & Organization* 15, no. 5 (2009): 582–95; Liz Doherty and Simonetta Manfredi, "Women's Progression to Senior Positions in English Universities," *Employee Relations* 28, no. 6 (2006): 553–72; and Belinda Probert, " 'I Just Couldn't Fit It In': Gender and Unequal Outcomes in Academic Careers," *Gender, Work and Organization* 12, no. 1 (2005): 50–72.

9. Hannah Seligson, "Ladies, Take off Your Tiara!," *The Huffington Post*, February 20, 2007, http://www.huffingtonpost.com/hannah -seligson/ladies-take-off-your-tiar_b_41649.html.

5. ARE YOU MY MENTOR?

1. Mentors provide advice, support, and feedback to their mentee. Sponsors hold senior positions and use their influence and power to advocate on behalf of their mentee, such as pushing to get the mentee a stretch assignment or a promotion. For a discussion of the differences

between mentoring and sponsoring, see Herminia Ibarra, Nancy M. Carter, and Christine Silva, "Why Men Still Get More Promotions than Women," *Harvard Business Review* 88, no. 9 (2010): 80–85; and Sylvia Ann Hewlett et al., *The Sponsor Effect: Breaking Through the Last Glass Ceiling*, a *Harvard Business Review* Research Report (December 2010): 5–7.

2. Studies have found that people who are mentored and sponsored report having more career success (such as higher compensation, a greater number of promotions, greater career and job satisfaction, and more career commitment). See Tammy D. Allen et al., "Career Benefits Associated with Mentoring for Protégés: A Meta-Analysis," *Journal of Applied Psychology* 89, no. 1 (2004): 127–36. A study of several thousand white-collar workers with at least a bachelor's degree found that sponsorship seemed to encourage both men and women to ask for a stretch assignment and a pay increase. Among the men surveyed who had a sponsor, 56 percent were likely to ask for a stretch assignment and 49 percent were likely to ask for a pay raise. In contrast, among the men surveyed without a sponsor, only 43 percent were likely to ask for a stretch assignment and 37 percent were likely to ask for a pay raise. Among the women surveyed who had a sponsor, 44 percent were likely to ask for a stretch assignment and 38 percent were likely to ask for a pay raise. In contrast, among the women surveyed without a sponsor, only 36 percent were likely to ask for a stretch assignment and only 30 percent were likely to ask for a pay raise. See Hewlett et al., *The Sponsor Effect*, 9–11.

3. For a discussion of the difficulties women can have with mentorship, see Kimberly E. O'Brien et al., "A Meta-Analytic Investigation of Gender Differences in Mentoring," *Journal of Management* 36, no. 2 (2010): 539–40. In general, men and women receive similar amounts of mentoring, yet not all mentoring provides the same types of benefits and rewards. For example, mentors who have more power and sway in their organizations (typically white men) can provide better career opportunities to their protégés than can mentors who have less power (often women and minorities). Research indicates that men, particularly white men, tend to have more influential mentors than women (or minority men) have. A Catalyst study found that while 78 percent of the male business professionals were mentored by a CEO or another senior executive, only 69 percent of the female professionals were mentored by those at the highest levels. This difference disadvantages women because mentees with more senior mentors reported faster career progression. See Ibarra, Carter, and Silva, "Why Men Still Get More Promotions than Women," 80–85. Also see George F. Dreher and Taylor H. Cox Jr., "Race, Gender, and Opportunity: A Study of Compensation Attainment

and the Establishing of Mentoring Relationships," *Journal of Applied Psychology* 81, no. 3 (1996): 297–308.

4. The survey by Hewlett et al. of educated white-collar workers found that 19 percent of men reported having sponsors as compared to 13 percent of women. See Hewlett et al., *The Sponsor Effect*, 8–11. A 2010 study of high-potential men and women found that in comparison to their male counterparts, women were "overmentored and undersponsored." See Ibarra, Carter, and Silva, "Why Men Still Get More Promotions than Women," 80–85.

5. Romila Singh, Belle Rose Ragins, and Phyllis Tharenou, "Who Gets a Mentor? A Longitudinal Assessment of the Rising Star Hypothesis," *Journal of Vocational Behavior* 74, no. 1 (2009): 11–17; and Tammy D. Allen, Mark L. Poteet, and Joyce E. A. Russell, "Protégé Selection by Mentors: What Makes the Difference?," *Journal of Organizational Behavior* 21, no. 3 (2000): 271–82.

6. Alvin W. Gouldner, "The Norm of Reciprocity: A Preliminary Statement," *American Sociological Review* 25, no. 2 (1960): 161–78.

7. Tammy D. Allen, Mark L. Poteet, and Susan M. Burroughs, "The Mentor's Perspective: A Qualitative Inquiry and Future Research Agenda," *Journal of Vocational Behavior* 51, no. 1 (1997): 86.

8. Hewlett et al., *The Sponsor Effect*, 35.

9. Ibarra, Carter, and Silva, "Why Men Still Get More Promotions than Women," 80–85.

6. SEEK AND SPEAK YOUR TRUTH

1. Denise L. Loyd et al., "Expertise in Your Midst: How Congruence Between Status and Speech Style Affects Reactions to Unique Knowledge," *Group Processes & Intergroup Relations* 13, no. 3 (2010): 379–95; and Lawrence A. Hosman, "The Evaluative Consequences of Hedges, Hesitations, and Intensifiers: Powerful and Powerless Speech Styles," *Human Communication Research* 15, no. 3 (1989): 383–406. For a review of how power shapes behavior, see Dacher Keltner, Deborah H. Gruenfeld, and Cameron Anderson, "Power, Approach, Inhibition," *Psychological Review* 110, no. 2 (2003): 265–84. For a review of gender and speech, see Cecilia L. Ridgeway and Lynn Smith-Lovin, "The Gender System and Interaction," *Annual Review of Sociology* 25, no. 1 (1999): 202–3.

2. Bell Leadership Institute, *Humor Gives Leaders the Edge* (2012), http://www.bellleadership.com/humor-gives-leaders-edge/.

3. Research by Kimberly D. Elsbach, professor of management at the University of California at Davis, and her colleagues found that most of the time when women cry at work, they receive negative reactions from colleagues and coworkers, unless the crying is related to a serious

personal issue such as a death in the family or a divorce. Crying during a meeting or because of professional pressures or a disagreement is viewed as "unprofessional," "disruptive," "weak," and even "manipulative." For further description of Professor Elsbach's findings, see Jenna Goudreau, "Crying at Work, a Woman's Burden," *Forbes*, January 11, 2011, http://www.forbes.com/sites/jennagoudreau/2011/01/11/crying-at-work-a-womans-burden-study-men-sex-testosterone-tears-arousal/.

4. Marcus Buckingham, "Leadership Development in the Age of the Algorithm," *Harvard Business Review* 90, no. 6 (2012): 86–94; and Bill George et al., "Discovering Your Authentic Leadership," *Harvard Business Review* 85, no. 2 (2007): 129–38.

7. DON'T LEAVE BEFORE YOU LEAVE

1. In general, research on this topic finds that although young women often report having a strong commitment to both their future career and their future families, they anticipate that combining the two will be difficult and require trade-offs. Janelle C. Fetterolf and Alice H. Eagly, "Do Young Women Expect Gender Equality in Their Future Lives? An Answer from a Possible Selves Experiment," *Sex Roles* 65, nos. 1–2 (2011): 83–93; Elizabeth R. Brown and Amanda B. Diekman, "What Will I Be? Exploring Gender Differences in Near and Distant Possible Selves," *Sex Roles* 63, nos. 7–8 (2010): 568–79; and Linda Stone and Nancy P. McKee, "Gendered Futures: Student Visions of Career and Family on a College Campus," *Anthropology & Education Quarterly* 31, no. 1 (2000): 67–89.

2. Lesley Lazin Novack and David R. Novack, "Being Female in the Eighties and Nineties: Conflicts Between New Opportunities and Traditional Expectations Among White, Middle Class, Heterosexual College Women," *Sex Roles* 35, nos. 1–2 (1996): 67. Novack and Novack found that if forced to choose between getting married or having a career, 18 percent of the male students and 38 percent of the female students in their study would choose getting married. They also found that 67 percent of the male students and 49 percent of the female students would choose having a career over getting married. Notably, about 22 percent of the men and 15 percent of the women declined to answer this "marriage or career" question, with the majority creating their own response of having both marriage and career. The authors state that "many men found the choice of marriage or career unacceptable, likely because historically they have been able to experience both options." A recent survey by the Pew Research Center found that among young people ages eighteen to thirty-four, the percentage of women stating that "having a successful marriage" is "one of the most important things" in their lives has increased among young women but decreased among young men since 1997. See Eileen Patten and Kim Parker, *A Gender*

Reversal on Career Aspirations, Pew Research Center (April 2012), http://www.pewsocialtrends.org/2012/04/19/a-gender-reversal-on-career-aspirations/. Another recent study of young people aged eighteen to thirty-one found that women had a higher "drive to marry" than men. See Judith E. Owen Blakemore, Carol A. Lawton, and Lesa Rae Vartanian, "I Can't Wait to Get Married: Gender Differences in Drive to Marry," *Sex Roles* 53, nos. 5–6 (2005): 327–35. For a notable exception, see Mindy J. Erchull et al., "Well . . . She Wants It More: Perceptions of Social Norms About Desires for Marriage and Children and Anticipated Chore Participation," *Psychology of Women Quarterly* 34, no. 2 (2010): 253–60, which surveyed college students and found no difference between men and women in their self-reported level of desire to marry.

3. For reviews of studies about job satisfaction and turnover, see Petri Böckerman and Pekka Ilmakunnas, "Job Disamenities, Job Satisfaction, Quit Intentions, and Actual Separations: Putting the Pieces Together," *Industrial Relations* 48, no. 1 (2009): 73–96; and Brooks et al., "Turnover and Retention Research: A Glance at the Past, a Closer Review of the Present, and a Venture into the Future," *The Academy of Management Annals* 2, no. 1 (2008): 231–74.

4. Caroline O'Connor, "How Sheryl Sandberg Helped Make One Entrepreneur's Big Decision," *Harvard Business Review* Blog Network, September 26, 2011, http://blogs.hbr.org/cs/2011/09/how_sheryl _sandberg_helped_mak.html.

5. Approximately 80 percent of women without children are in the workforce. Of women with children, that number drops to 70.6 percent. For men, having children increases workforce participation. About 86 percent of men without children and 94.6 percent of men with children are in the workforce. These labor force participation rates are based on the employment rates of men and women aged twenty-five to forty-four, with and without children under the age of eighteen. Bureau of Labor Statistics, "Table 6A: Employment Status of Persons by Age, Presence of Children, Sex, Race, Hispanic or Latino Ethnicity, and Marital Status, Annual Average 2011," Current Population Survey, Employment Characteristics, unpublished table (2011).

6. Sylvia Ann Hewlett and Carolyn Buck Luce, "Off-Ramps and On-Ramps: Keeping Talented Women on the Road to Success," *Harvard Business Review* 83, no. 3 (2005): 44.

7. David Cotter, Paula England, and Joan Hermsen, "Moms and Jobs: Trends in Mothers' Employment and Which Mothers Stay Home," in *Families as They Really Are*, ed. Barbara J. Risman (New York: W. W. Norton, 2010), 416–24. Women whose husbands earn the least (in the bottom quarter of male earnings) are the group of women most likely to stay at home, followed by women whose husbands are in the top 5 percent of male earners.

8. The National Association of Child Care Resource & Referral Agencies, *Parents and the High Cost of Child Care: 2010 Update* (2010), 1, http://eyeonkids.ca/docs/files/cost_report_073010-final.pdf.

9. Child Care Aware of America, *Parents and the High Cost of Child Care: 2012 Report* (2012), 7, http://www.naccrra.org/sites/default/files/default_site_pages/2012/cost_report_2012_final_081012_0.pdf.

10. Youngjoo Cha, "Reinforcing Separate Spheres: The Effect of Spousal Overwork on Men's and Women's Employment in Dual-Earner Households," *American Sociological Review* 75, no. 2 (2010): 318. This study also found that the odds of quitting among professional mothers whose husbands work sixty hours or more a week is 112 percent greater than those of professional mothers whose husbands work less than fifty hours a week.

11. Findings from the 2007 survey of Harvard Business School (HBS) alumni were provided by the Career and Professional Development Office at Harvard Business School to the author on October 15, 2012. Another survey of graduates with two or more children of HBS classes of 1981, 1985, and 1991 showed that more than 90 percent of male graduates were in full-time careers compared with only 38 percent of female graduates. Finding provided by Myra M. Hart, professor emeritus of Harvard Business School, e-mail message to researcher, September 23, 2012. The results from these HBS surveys may be influenced by the disproportionately low response rate for women relative to men. Also, these surveys were not designed to allow respondents to explain what they are doing if they are not employed in a full-time capacity for pay. When respondents indicate that they are not working full-time, they could still be actively involved in nonprofits and community organizations or sitting on boards. It should be noted that women are more likely than men to have career interruptions linked with having children, prioritizing personal goals, and meeting family responsibilities. For more on women's nonlinear career paths, see Lisa A. Mainiero and Sherry E. Sullivan, "Kaleidoscope Careers: An Alternate Explanation for the 'Opt-Out' Revolution," *The Academy of Management Executive* 19, no. 1 (2005): 106–23.

Other research has found that the employment participation rates of women vary across professions. A study of women from the Harvard graduating classes of 1988 to 1991 found that fifteen years after graduation, married women with children who had become M.D.s had the highest labor force participation rate (94.2%), while married women with children who went on to get other degrees had much lower labor force participation rates: Ph.D.s (85.5%), J.D.s (77.6%), MBAs (71.7%). These findings suggest professional cultures play a role in women's rates of employment. See Jane Leber Herr and Catherine Wolfram, "Work

Environment and 'Opt-Out' Rates at Motherhood Across Higher-Education Career Paths" (November 2011), http://faculty.haas.berkeley.edu/wolfram/Papers/OptOut_ILRRNov11.pdf.

12. This survey of Yale alumni from the classes of 1979, 1984, 1989, and 1994 was conducted in 2000 as cited in Louise Story, "Many Women at Elite Colleges Set Career Path to Motherhood," *New York Times*, September 20, 2005, http://www.nytimes.com/2005/09/20/national/20women.html?pagewanted=all.

13. Amy Sennett, "Work and Family: Life After Princeton for the Class of 2006" (July 2006), http://www.princeton.edu/~paw/archive_new/PAW05–06/15–0719/features_familylife.html.

14. Hewlett and Luce, "Off-Ramps and On-Ramps," 46.

15. Stephen J. Rose and Heidi I. Hartmann, *Still a Man's Labor Market: The Long-Term Earnings Gap*, Institute for Women's Policy Research (2004), 10, http://www.aecf.org/upload/publicationfiles/fes3622h767.pdf.

16. Ibid.

17. Hewlett and Luce, "Off-Ramps and On-Ramps," 46.

8. MAKE YOUR PARTNER A REAL PARTNER

1. Melissa A. Milkie, Sara B. Raley, and Suzanne M. Bianchi, "Taking on the Second Shift: Time Allocations and Time Pressures of U.S. Parents with Preschoolers," *Social Forces* 88, no. 2 (2009): 487–517.

2. Scott S. Hall and Shelley M. MacDermid, "A Typology of Dual Earner Marriages Based on Work and Family Arrangements," *Journal of Family and Economic Issues* 30, no. 3 (2009): 220.

3. Between 1965 and 2000, the amount of time per week that married fathers spent on child care almost tripled and the amount of time married fathers spent on housework more than doubled. In 1965, married fathers spent 2.6 hours per week on child care. In 2000, married fathers spent 6.5 hours per week on child care. Most of this increase occurred after 1985. In 1965, married fathers spent about 4.5 hours per week on housework. In 2000, married fathers spent almost 10 hours per week on housework. The largest increase in the time spent on housework took place between 1965 and 1985. The amount of time married fathers spend each week doing housework has not increased much since 1985. See Suzanne M. Bianchi, John P. Robinson, and Melissa A. Milkie, *Changing Rhythms of American Family Life* (New York: Russell Sage Foundation, 2006). Analysis done by Hook (2006) of twenty countries found that between 1965 and 2003, employed, married fathers increased the amount of unpaid domestic work they performed by about six hours per week. See Jennifer L. Hook, "Care in Context: Men's Unpaid Work

in 20 Countries, 1965–2003," *American Sociological Review* 71, no. 4 (2006): 639–60.

4. Letitia Anne Peplau and Leah R. Spalding, "The Close Relationships of Lesbians, Gay Men, and Bisexuals," in *Close Relationships: A Sourcebook*, ed. Clyde A. Hendrick and Susan S. Hendrick (Thousand Oaks, CA: Sage, 2000), 111–24; and Sondra E. Solomon, Esther D. Rothblum, and Kimberly F. Balsam, "Money, Housework, Sex, and Conflict: Same-Sex Couples in Civil Unions, Those Not in Civil Unions, and Heterosexual Married Siblings," *Sex Roles* 52, nos. 9–10 (2005): 561–75.

5. Lynda Laughlin, *Who's Minding the Kids? Child Care Arrangements: Spring 2005 and Summer 2006*, U.S. Census Bureau, Current Population Reports, P70–121 (August 2010), 1. For a commentary, see K. J. Dell'Antonia, "The Census Bureau Counts Fathers as 'Child Care,'" *New York Times*, February 8, 2012, http://parenting.blogs.nytimes.com/2012/02/08/the-census-bureau-counts-fathers-as-child-care/.

6. Laughlin, *Who's Minding the Kids?*, 7–9.

7. Maria Shriver, "Gloria Steinem," *Interview*, July 15, 2011, http://www.interviewmagazine.com/culture/gloria-steinem/.

8. For a review of studies on maternal gatekeeping, see Sarah J. Schoppe-Sullivan et al., "Maternal Gatekeeping, Coparenting Quality, and Fathering Behavior in Families with Infants," *Journal of Family Psychology* 22, no. 3 (2008): 389–90.

9. Sarah M. Allen and Alan J. Hawkins, "Maternal Gatekeeping: Mothers' Beliefs and Behaviors That Inhibit Greater Father Involvement in Family Work," *Journal of Marriage and Family* 61, no. 1 (1999): 209.

10. Richard L. Zweigenhaft and G. William Domhoff, *The New CEOs: Women, African American, Latino and Asian American Leaders of Fortune 500 Companies* (Lanham, MD: Rowman & Littlefield, 2011), 28–29.

11. James B. Stewart, "A C.E.O.'s Support System, a k a Husband," *New York Times*, November 4, 2011, http://www.nytimes.com/2011/11/05/business/a-ceos-support-system-a-k-a-husband.html?pagewanted=all.

12. Pamela Stone, *Opting Out? Why Women Really Quit Careers and Head Home* (Berkeley: University of California Press, 2007), 62.

13. Stewart, "A C.E.O.'s Support System."

14. For a thorough review, see Michael E. Lamb, *The Role of the Father in Child Development* (Hoboken, NJ: John Wiley & Sons, 2010); and Anna Sarkadi et al., "Fathers' Involvement and Children's Developmental Outcomes: A Systematic Review of Longitudinal Studies," *Acta Paediatrica* 97, no. 2 (2008): 153–58.

15. Elisabeth Duursma, Barbara Alexander Pan, and Helen Raikes, "Predictors and Outcomes of Low-Income Fathers' Reading with Their Toddlers," *Early Childhood Research Quarterly* 23, no. 3 (2008): 351–65;

Joseph H. Pleck and Brian P. Masciadrelli, "Paternal Involvement in U.S. Residential Fathers: Levels, Sources, and Consequences," in *The Role of the Father in Child Development*, ed. Michael E. Lamb (Hoboken, NJ: John Wiley & Sons, 2004): 222–71; Ronald P. Rohner and Robert A. Veneziano, "The Importance of Father Love: History and Contemporary Evidence," *Review of General Psychology* 5, no. 4 (2001): 382–405; W. Jean Yeung, "Fathers: An Overlooked Resource for Children's Educational Success," in *After the Bell—Family Background, Public Policy, and Educational Success*, ed. Dalton Conley and Karen Albright (London: Routledge, 2004), 145–69; and Lois W. Hoffman and Lise M. Youngblade, *Mothers at Work: Effects on Children's Well-Being* (Cambridge: Cambridge University Press, 1999).

16. For a review of studies on the impact of fathers on children's emotional and social development, see Rohner and Veneziano, "The Importance of Father Love," 392.

17. Robin J. Ely and Deborah L. Rhode, "Women and Leadership: Defining the Challenges," in *Handbook of Leadership Theory and Practice*, ed. Nitin Nohria and Rakesh Khurana (Boston: Harvard Business School Publishing, 2010), 377–410; and Deborah L. Rhode and Joan C. Williams, "Legal Perspectives on Employment Discrimination," in *Sex Discrimination in the Workplace: Multidisciplinary Perspectives*, ed. Faye J. Crosby, Margaret S. Stockdale, and S. Ann Ropp (Malden, MA: Blackwell, 2007), 235–70. A survey of fifty-three Fortune 100 companies found that 73.6 percent offered mothers paid family or disability leave, but only 32.1 percent offered fathers paid family leave. See Joint Economic Committee of the U.S. Congress, *Paid Family Leave at Fortune 100 Companies: A Basic Standard but Still Not a Gold Standard* (March 2008), 6.

18. The five states that have short-term disability insurance programs that provide paid medical leave for birth mothers are California, Hawaii, New Jersey, New York, and Rhode Island. California and New Jersey also provide six weeks of paid leave that can be used by either the mother or the father. The state of Washington has passed a paid parental leave law but has been unable to implement it due to budgetary constraints. See National Partnership for Women & Families, *Expecting Better: A State-by-State Analysis of Laws That Help New Parents* (May 2012).

19. A survey of nearly one thousand fathers working in white-collar jobs for large companies found that about 75 percent of them took only one week off or less when their partners had a baby and 16 percent didn't take any time off at all. See Brad Harrington, Fred Van Deusen, and Beth Humberd, *The New Dad: Caring, Committed and Conflicted*, Boston College, Center for Work & Family (2011): 14–15. A report on California's new paid family leave policy found that fathers who made use of

the policy took a median of three weeks off to care for and bond with their babies. See Eileen Applebaum and Ruth Milkman, *Leaves That Pay: Employer and Worker Experiences with Paid Family Leave in California*, Center for Economic and Policy Research (January 2011), 18.

20. Joan C. Williams and Heather Boushey, *The Three Faces of Work-Family Conflict: The Poor, The Professionals, and the Missing Middle*, Center for American Progress and Center for WorkLife Law (January 2010), 54–55, http://www.americanprogress.org/issues/2010/01/three_faces_report.html.

21. Laurie A. Rudman and Kris Mescher, "Penalizing Men Who Request a Family Leave: Is Flexibility Stigma a Femininity Stigma?," *Journal of Social Issues* 69, no. 2 (2013): 322–40.

22. Jennifer L. Berdahl and Sue H. Moon, "Workplace Mistreatment of Middle-Class Workers Based on Sex, Parenthood, and Caregiving," *Journal of Social Issues* 69, no. 2 (2013): 341–66; Adam B. Butler and Amie Skattebo, "What Is Acceptable for Women May Not Be for Men: The Effect of Family Conflicts with Work on Job-Performance Ratings," *Journal of Occupational and Organization Psychology* 77, no. 4 (2004): 553–64; Julie Holliday Wayne and Bryanne L. Cordeiro, "Who Is a Good Organizational Citizen? Social Perception of Male and Female Employees Who Use Family Leave," *Sex Roles* 49, nos. 5–6 (2003): 233–46; and Tammy D. Allen and Joyce E. A. Russell, "Parental Leave of Absence: Some Not So Family-Friendly Implications," *Journal of Applied Social Psychology* 29, no. 1 (1999): 166–91.

23. In 2012, fathers made up 3.46 percent of stay-at-home parents. See U.S. Census Bureau, "Table SHP-1 Parents and Children in Stay-at-Home Parent Family Groups: 1994 to Present," America's Families and Living Arrangements, Current Population Survey, Annual Social and Economic Supplement (2012), http://www.census.gov/hhes/families/data/families/html. For a review of research about the social isolation of stay-at-home fathers, see Brad Harrington, Fred Van Deusen, and Iyar Mazar, *The New Dad: Right at Home*, Boston College, Center for Work & Family (2012), 6.

24. A study of 207 stay-at-home fathers found that about 45 percent of them reported receiving a negative comment or judgmental reaction from another adult. The source of the vast majority of these derogatory comments and reactions was stay-at-home mothers. See Aaron B. Rochlen, Ryan A. McKelley, and Tiffany A. Whittaker, "Stay-at-Home Fathers' Reasons for Entering the Role and Stigma Experiences: A Preliminary Report," *Psychology of Men & Masculinity* 11, no. 4 (2010): 282.

25. In 2011, wives earned more than their husbands in 28.1 percent of families in which both wives and husbands had earnings. See Bureau of Labor Statistics, *Wives Who Earn More Than Their Husbands, 1987–*

2011, 1988–2012, Annual Social and Economic Supplements to the Current Population Survey, http://www.bls.gov/cps/wives_earn_more.htm.

26. The Cambridge Women's Pornography Cooperative, *Porn for Women* (San Francisco: Chronicle Books, 2007).

27. For a review see Scott Coltrane, "Research on Household Labor: Modeling and Measuring Social Embeddedness of Routine Family Work," *Journal of Marriage and Family* 62, no. 4 (2000): 1208–33.

28. Lynn Price Cook, " 'Doing' Gender in Context: Household Bargaining and Risk of Divorce in Germany and the United States," *American Journal of Sociology* 112, no. 2 (2006): 442–72.

29. Scott Coltrane, *Family Man: Fatherhood, Housework, and Gender Equality* (Oxford: Oxford University Press, 1996).

30. For a discussion of earnings and bargaining power in the household, see Frances Woolley, "Control Over Money in Marriage," in *Marriage and the Economy: Theory and Evidence from Advanced Industrial Societies*, ed. Shoshana A. Grossbard-Shechtman and Jacob Mincer (Cambridge: Cambridge University Press, 2003), 105–28; and Leora Friedberg and Anthony Webb, "Determinants and Consequences of Bargaining Power in Households," NBER Working Paper 12367 (July 2006), http://www.nber.org/papers/w12367. For research on employment mitigating the financial consequences of divorce for women, see Matthew McKeever and Nicholas H. Wolfinger, "Reexamining the Economic Costs of Marital Disruption for Women," *Social Science Quarterly* 82, no. 1 (2001): 202–17. For a discussion of women, longevity, and financial security, see Laura L. Carstensen, *A Long Bright Future: An Action Plan for a Lifetime of Happiness, Health, and Financial Security* (New York: Broadway Books, 2009).

31. Constance T. Gager and Scott T. Yabiku, "Who Has the Time? The Relationship Between Household Labor Time and Sexual Frequency," *Journal of Family Issues* 31, no. 2 (2010): 135–63; Neil Chethik, *VoiceMale: What Husbands Really Think About Their Marriages, Their Wives, Sex, Housework, and Commitment* (New York: Simon & Schuster, 2006); and K. V. Rao and Alfred DeMaris, "Coital Frequency Among Married and Cohabitating Couples in the United States," *Journal of Biosocial Science* 27, no. 2 (1995): 135–50.

32. Sanjiv Gupta, "The Consequences of Maternal Employment During Men's Childhood for Their Adult Housework Performance," *Gender & Society* 20, no. 1 (2006): 60–86.

33. Richard W. Johnson and Joshua M. Wiener, *A Profile of Frail Older Americans and Their Caregivers*, Occasional Paper Number 8, The Retirement Project, Urban Institute (February 2006), http://www.urban.org/UploadedPDF/311284_older_americans.pdf.

34. Gloria Steinem, "Gloria Steinem on Progress and Women's Rights," interview by Oprah Winfrey, Oprah's Next Chapter, YouTube

video, 3:52 minutes, April 16, 2012, published by Oprah Winfrey Network, http://www.youtube.com/watch?v=orrmWHnFjqI&feature=relmfu.

35. This survey of just over one thousand adults found that 80 percent of men in their forties said that "doing work which challenges me to use my skills and abilities" was very important to them. Among men in their twenties and thirties, the survey found that 82 percent of them said that "having a work schedule which allows me to spend time with my family" was very important to them. See Radcliffe Public Policy Center, *Life's Work: Generational Attitudes Toward Work and Life Integration* (Cambridge, MA: Radcliffe Public Policy Center, 2000).

9. THE MYTH OF DOING IT ALL

1. Sharon Poczter, "For Women in the Workplace, It's Time to Abandon 'Have It All' Rhetoric," *Forbes*, June 25, 2012, http://www.forbes.com/sites/realspin/2012/06/25/for-women-in-the-workplace-its-time-to-abandon-have-it-all-rhetoric/.

2. U.S. Census Bureau, "Table FG1 Married Couple Family Groups, by Labor Force Status of Both Spouses, and Race and Hispanic Origin of the Reference Person," America's Families and Living Arrangements, Current Population Survey, Annual Social and Economic Supplement (2012), http://www.census.gov/hhes/families/data/cps2012.html.

3. U.S. Census Bureau, "Table FG10 Family Groups," America's Families and Living Arrangements, Current Population Survey, Annual Social and Economic Supplement (2012), http://www.census.gov/hhes/families/data/cps2012.html. Calculation derived by focusing on all family groups with children under eighteen.

4. Tina Fey, *Bossypants* (New York: Little, Brown, 2011), 256.

5. Gloria Steinem, "Gloria Steinem on Progress and Women's Rights," interview by Oprah Winfrey, Oprah's Next Chapter, YouTube video, 3:52 minutes, April 16, 2012, published by Oprah Winfrey Network, http://www.youtube.com/watch?v=orrmWHnFjqI&feature=relmfu.

6. Beth Saulnier, "Meet the Dean," *Weill Cornell Medicine Magazine*, Spring 2012, 25.

7. Jennifer Stuart, "Work and Motherhood: Preliminary Report of a Psychoanalytic Study," *The Psychoanalytic Quarterly* 76, no. 2 (2007): 482.

8. Nora Ephron, 1996 commencement address, Wellesley College, http://www.wellesley.edu/events/commencement/archives/1996commencement.

9. Robin J. Ely and Deborah L. Rhode, "Women and Leadership: Defining the Challenges," in *Handbook of Leadership Theory and Practice*, ed. Nitin Nohria and Rakesh Khurana (Boston: Harvard Business School Publishing, 2010), 377–410; Deborah L. Rhode and Joan C.

Williams, "Legal Perspectives on Employment Discrimination," in *Sex Discrimination in the Workplace: Multidisciplinary Perspectives*, ed. Faye J. Crosby, Margaret S. Stockdale, and S. Ann Ropp (Malden, MA: Blackwell, 2007), 235–70; and Ann Crittenden, *The Price of Motherhood: Why the Most Important Job in the World Is Still the Least Valued* (New York: Metropolitan Books, 2001).

10. Pamela Stone, *Opting Out? Why Women Really Quit Careers and Head Home* (Berkeley: University of California Press, 2007); Leslie A. Perlow, "Boundary Control: The Social Ordering of Work and Family Time in a High-Tech Corporation," *Administrative Science Quarterly* 43, no. 2 (1998): 328–57; and Arlie Russell Hochschild, *The Time Bind: When Work Becomes Home and Home Becomes Work* (New York: Metropolitan Books, 1997). Joan Williams, a law professor and founding director of the Center for WorkLife Law at the University of California, Hastings College of the Law, refers to these penalties as "flexibility stigma."

11. Jennifer Glass, "Blessing or Curse? Work-Family Policies and Mother's Wage Growth over Time," *Work and Occupations* 31, no. 3 (2004): 367–94; and Mindy Fried, *Taking Time: Parental Leave Policy and Corporate Culture* (Philadelphia: Temple University Press, 1998). Depending on the type of flexible work practice, women in nonprofessional jobs can pay steep penalties as well. For example, Webber and Williams (2008) examined two groups of mothers (professional and low-wage workers) and found that both groups experienced penalties for working part-time (less pay, demotions, etc.). See Gretchen Webber and Christine Williams, "Mothers in 'Good' and 'Bad' Part-Time Jobs: Different Problems, Same Result," *Gender & Society* 22, no. 6 (2008): 752–77.

12. Nicholas Bloom et al., "Does Working from Home Work? Evidence from a Chinese Experiment" (February 2013), http://www.stanford.edu/~nbloom/WFH.pdf. New research also suggests that work from home practices like telecommuting can have downsides such as increasing work hours and intensifying work demands made upon employees. See Mary C. Noonan and Jennifer L. Glass, "The Hard Truth About Telecommuting," *Monthly Labor Review* 135, no. 6 (2012): 38–45.

13. New research suggests that working long hours reduces productivity. Harvard Business School professor Leslie A. Perlow found that by forcing consultants at the Boston Consulting Group to work less, they became more effective. To enable one scheduled night off per week, Perlow had the work teams engage in open and honest communication so they could divvy up work more efficiently. She also had the work teams devise plans and share information so that the consultants could cover for one another during their nights off. As a result of these relatively small changes, the consultants felt better about both their work and their work-life balance. Consultants and their supervisors evaluated their work more highly. Fewer people quit. Team communication

improved. And a larger share of consultants who took time away from work felt like they were delivering value to their client compared with the share of consultants who continued to work very long hours. See Leslie Perlow, *Sleeping with Your Smartphone: How to Break the 24/7 Habit and Change the Way You Work* (Boston: Harvard Business Review Press, 2012).

14. Colin Powell with Tony Koltz, *It Worked For Me: In Life and Leadership* (New York: HarperCollins, 2012), 40.

15. Joan C. Williams and Heather Boushey, *The Three Faces of Work-Family Conflict: The Poor, The Professionals, and the Missing Middle*, Center for American Progress and Center for WorkLife Law (January 2010), 7, http://www.americanprogress.org/issues/2010/01/three_faces_report .html.

16. Economic Policy Institute, "Chart: Annual Hours of Work, Married Men and Women, 25–54, with Children, 1979–2010, by Income Fifth," *The State of Working America*, http://stateofworkingamerica.org/ chart/swa-income-table-2–17-annual-hours-work-married/. Assuming a fifty-week work year, middle-income married men and women with children worked 428 more hours in 2010 than in 1979, or an average of 8.6 more hours per week.

While some groups of Americans may have too much work to do, other groups, particularly low-wage, less-skilled workers do not have enough. Sociologists refer to this trend as the "growing dispersion" of work hours between more and less educated workers. For more on the dispersion of work hours, see Arne L. Kallenberg, *Good Jobs, Bad Jobs: The Rise of Polarized and Precarious Employment Systems in the United States, 1970s to 2000s* (New York: Russell Sage Foundation, 2011), 152–54; and Jerry A. Jacobs and Kathleen Gerson, *The Time Divide: Work, Family, Gender Inequality* (Cambridge, MA: Harvard University Press, 2004).

17. Peter Kuhn and Fernando Lozano, "The Expanding Workweek? Understanding Trends in Long Work Hours Among U.S. Men, 1979–2006," *Journal of Labor Economics* 26, no. 2 (2008): 311–43; Cynthia Fuchs Epstein and Arne L. Kalleberg, eds., *Fighting for Time: Shifting Boundaries of Work and Social Life* (New York: Russell Sage Foundation, 2004).

18. Sylvia Ann Hewlett and Carolyn Buck Luce, "Extreme Jobs: The Dangerous Allure of the 70-Hour Workweek," *Harvard Business Review* 84, no. 12 (2006): 51.

19. Sarah Perez, "80% of Americans Work 'After Hours,' Equaling an Extra Day of Work Per Week," *Techcrunch*, July 2, 2012, http:// techcrunch.com/2012/07/02/80-of-americans-work-after-hours -equaling-an-extra-day-of-work-per-week/.

20. Bronwyn Fryer, "Sleep Deficit: The Performance Killer," *Harvard Business Review* 84, no. 10 (2006): 53–59, http://hbr.org/2006/10/ sleep-deficit-the-performance-killer. For reviews on the cognitive im-

pact of insufficient sleep, see Paula A. Alhola and Paivi Polo-Kantola, "Sleep Deprivation: Impact on Cognitive Performance," *Neuropsychiatric Disease and Treatment* 3, no. 5 (2007): 553–67; and Jeffrey S. Durmer and David F. Dinges, "Neurocognitive Consequences of Sleep Deprivation," *Seminars in Neurology* 25, no. 1 (2005): 117–29.

21. Suzanne M. Bianchi, John P. Robinson, and Melissa A. Milkie, *The Changing Rhythms of American Family Life* (New York: Russell Sage Foundation, 2006), 74–77. This study of the amount of time parents report taking care of their children finds that in 2000 both employed and nonemployed mothers spent, on average, almost 6.5 more hours per week on caregiving than their counterparts reported in 1975. Findings like these lead the authors to conclude, "It is as if a cultural shift occurred that propelled all mothers toward spending more time with their children" (p. 78). The increase in the amount of time parents spend with their children is largely explained by parents combining caregiving and leisure activities, which means that "either child care has become more oriented toward fun activities, or that parents are more frequently including children in their own leisure activities" (p. 85). This move away from adult-only leisure activities combined with an increase in multitasking while spending free time with children points to a willingness among parents to sacrifice personal time in order to spend more time with their children. A 2009 study found that in comparison to nonemployed mothers, full-time employed mothers spend less time per week in every leisure activity ranging from TV watching to community and socializing activities, resulting in ten less hours of leisure time per week. As opposed to mothers, there is little difference in the amount of leisure time between fathers with wives who work full-time versus fathers with wives who work less than full-time. See Melissa A. Milkie, Sara B. Raley, and Suzanne M. Bianchi, "Taking on the Second Shift: Time Allocations and Time Pressures of U.S. Parents with Preschoolers," *Social Forces* 88, no. 2 (2009): 487–517.

22. Sharon Hays, *The Cultural Contradictions of Motherhood* (New Haven, CT: Yale University Press, 1996).

23. The NICHD Early Child Care Research Network, ed., *Child Care and Child Development: Results from the NICHD Study of Early Child Care and Youth Development* (New York: Guilford, 2005).

24. National Institute of Child Health and Human Development, *Findings for Children up to Age 4½ Years,* The NICHD Study of Early Child Care and Youth Development, NIH Pub. No. 05-4318 (2006), 1, http://www.nichd.nih.gov/publications/pubs/upload/seccyd_06.pdf.

25. Ibid.; see also NICHD Early Child Care Research Network, "Child-Care Effect Sizes for the NICHD Study of Early Child Care and Youth Development," *American Psychologist* 61, no. 2 (2006): 99–116. In some cases, the U.S. study showed that children who spent longer

hours in child care exhibited higher instances of behavioral problems such as temper tantrums or talking back. These problems arose less often in high-quality child-care settings and largely subsided by the sixth grade. As Kathleen McCartney, dean of the Harvard Graduate School of Education and a principal investigator of the study, noted, "The child care hours effect is small by any standard. Any risks associated with more hours in child care need to be weighed against the benefits of maternal employment, including decreased maternal depression and more family income" (e-mail to author, February 26, 2012). For a discussion of these findings and issues, see Kathleen McCartney et al., "Testing a Series of Causal Propositions Relating Time in Child Care to Children's Externalizing Behavior," *Development Psychology* 46, no. 1 (2010): 1–17. For a meta-analysis of maternal employment and children's achievement, see Wendy Goldberg et al., "Maternal Employment and Children's Achievement in Context: A Meta-Analysis of Four Decades of Research," *Psychological Bulletin* 134, no. 1 (2008): 77–108.

Scholars have noted that while the preponderance of evidence shows that maternal employment has no adverse effect on young children's development, maternal employment in the first year of life has been linked with lower cognitive development and behavior issues for some children. Several factors moderate these findings, ranging from the level of parental sensitivity to the quality of the care babies receive. See Jane Waldfogel, "Parental Work Arrangements and Child Development," *Canadian Public Policy* 33, no. 2 (2007): 251–71.

Whether care is provided by a parent or another caregiver, studies consistently find that it is the quality of the caretaking that matters most. Children need to receive care that is sensitive and responsive to their particular needs. For a discussion, see Jane Waldfogel, *What Children Need* (Cambridge, MA: Harvard University Press, 2006).

26. National Institute of Child Health and Human Development, *Findings for Children up to Age 4½ Years*; National Institute of Child Health and Human Development Early Child Care and Research Network, "Fathers' and Mothers' Parenting Behavior and Beliefs as Predictors of Children's Social Adjustment and Transition to School," *Journal of Family Psychology* 18, no. 4 (2004): 628–38.

27. NICHD Early Child Care and Research Network, "Child-Care Effect Sizes," 113.

28. A UK study of eleven thousand children revealed that the children who demonstrated the highest measures of well-being came from families in which both parents worked outside the home. Controlling for maternal education and household income, children from two-job families, especially girls, had the fewest number of behavioral difficulties, such as being hyperactive or feeling unhappy and worried. See Anne McMunn et al., "Maternal Employment and Child Socio-Emotional

Behavior in the UK: Longitudinal Evidence from the UK Millennium Cohort Study," *Journal of Epidemiology & Community Health* 66, no. 7 (2012): 1–6.

29. Robin W. Simon, "Gender, Multiple Roles, Role Meaning, and Mental Health," *Journal of Health and Social Behavior* 36, no. 2 (1995): 182–94.

30. Marie C. Wilson, *Closing the Leadership Gap: Add Women, Change Everything* (New York: Penguin, 2007), 58.

31. Melanie Rudd, Jennifer Aaker, and Michael I. Norton, "Leave Them Smiling: How Small Acts Create More Happiness than Large Acts," working paper (2011), http://faculty-gsb.stanford.edu/aaker/pages/documents/LeaveThemSmiling_RuddAakerNorton12–16–11.pdf.

32. Mary C. Curtis, "There's More to Sheryl Sandberg's Secret," *Washington Post*, April 4, 2012, http://www.washingtonpost.com/blogs/she-the-people/post/theres-more-to-sheryl-sandbergs-secret/2012/04/04/gIQAGhZsvS_blog.html.

10. LET'S START TALKING ABOUT IT

1. Gloria Steinem, "In Defense of the 'Chick-Flick,'" *Alternet*, July 6, 2007, http://www.alternet.org/story/56219/gloria_steinem%3A_in_defense_of_the_'chick_flick'.

2. Marianne Cooper, "The New F-Word," *Gender News*, February 28, 2011, http://gender.stanford.edu/news/2011/new-f-word.

3. Susan Faludi, *Backlash: The Undeclared War Against American Women* (New York: Crown, 1991).

4. Richard H. Thaler and Cass R. Sunstein, *Nudge: Improving Decisions About Health, Wealth, and Happiness* (New Haven, CT: Yale University Press, 2008).

5. Corinne A. Moss-Racusin et al., "Science Faculty's Subtle Gender Biases Favor Male Students," *Proceedings of the National Academy of Sciences of the United States of America* 109, no. 41 (2012): 16474–79.

6. For a study on job applicants, see Rhea E. Steinpreis, Katie A. Anders, and Dawn Ritzke, "The Impact of Gender on the Review of Curricula Vitae of Job Applicants and Tenure Candidates: A National Empirical Study," *Sex Roles* 41, nos. 7–8 (1999): 509–28. For a study on gender bias and scholarships, see Christine Wennerås and Agnes Wold, "Nepotism and Sexism in Peer Review," *Nature* 387 (1997): 341–43. For the study on bias in orchestra tryouts, see Claudia Goldin and Cecilia Rouse, "Orchestrating Impartiality: The Impact of 'Blind' Auditions on Female Musicians," *The American Economic Review* 90, no. 4 (2000): 715–41.

7. Economists Claudia Goldin and Cecilia Rouse examined the hiring practices among top orchestras in the United States and found that

changing to blind auditions, in which judges could hear but not see the applicant, reduced discrimination against women. They estimate that the switch to blind auditions accounts for 30 percent of the increase in the proportion of women among new hires. See Goldin and Rouse, "Orchestrating Impartiality," 715–41.

8. Emily Pronin, Thomas Gilovich, and Lee Ross, "Objectivity in the Eye of the Beholder: Divergent Perceptions of Bias in Self Versus Others," *Psychological Review* 111, no. 3 (2004): 781–99; Emily Pronin, Daniel Y. Lin, and Lee Ross, "The Bias Blind Spot: Perceptions of Bias in Self Versus Others," *Personality and Social Psychology Bulletin* 28, no. 3 (2002): 369–81.

9. Eric Luis Uhlmann and Geoffrey L. Cohen, "Constructed Criteria: Redefining Merit to Justify Discrimination," *Psychological Science* 16, no. 6 (2005): 474–80. Overall, this study found that when a man possessed a particular characteristic or trait, then that quality was rated as a more important hiring criterion than when he did not possess that quality. Even typically female qualities such as "being family oriented" or "having children" were rated as more important hiring criteria when a man had these qualities than when he did not. This kind of favoritism was not shown toward the female applicant. In fact, when it came to possessing a strong educational record, the study found a trend toward the reverse in that when a female applicant had a strong educational record that quality was rated as a less important hiring criterion then when she did not possess a strong educational record. However, this reversal trend did not reach statistical significance.

This study found that evaluators redefine hiring criteria for gender-stereotypical jobs to match the specific experiences and credentials that a candidate of the desired gender happens to possess. For the stereotypically male job of police chief, the male candidate was favored. But when the authors conducted the same kind of experiment for a stereotypically female job of women's studies professor, the female applicant got a boost. In this case, having a strong record of public advocacy on women's issues was rated an important hiring criterion when the female candidate had the strong record and not important when the female candidate did not have a strong record. No such favoritism was extended to the male candidate. Other research supports the idea that evaluators can subtly shift the criteria they base their hiring decision upon to the detriment of gender- or racial-atypical candidates. For example, a 2008 study by Phelan et al. examined the hiring criteria used to evaluate male and female agentic (highly competent, confident, ambitious) or communal (modest, sociable) managerial job applicants. The results found that evaluators "weighed competence more heavily than social skills for all applicants, with the exception of agentic women, whose social skills were given more weight than competence." The authors conclude that "evaluators shifted the job criteria away from agentic women's strong suit (competence) and toward their perceived deficit (social skills) to justify discrimination."

Uhlmann and Cohen report that in the police chief experiment the pro-male bias was driven largely by the male evaluators. While both male and female evaluators tended to construct hiring criteria favorable to the male candidate, men exhibited this bias more. When it came to hiring evaluations, male evaluators gave more positive evaluations to the male applicant than to the identical female applicant, while women gave equivalent evaluations. In the women's studies professor experiment the bias was driven by the female evaluators. It was the female evaluators, not the male evaluators, who redefined hiring criteria to the female applicant's benefit and who favored the female candidate over the male candidate in hiring evaluations. Importantly, this study found that when evaluators were asked to commit to the hiring criteria that were important for a job before learning about the applicant's gender, neither men nor women showed gender bias in their hiring evaluations. This finding suggests that to reduce discrimination, unambiguous standards of merit should be agreed upon prior to the review of job candidates.

This study illustrates that people can shift hiring criteria so that they fit with the experiences and credentials of the person (male or female) they would like to hire, particularly for gender-stereotypical jobs, thereby using "merit" to justify discrimination. Since those who felt most confident about their powers of objectivity showed the most bias in the police chief experiment, the authors suggest that this group may have felt "that they had chosen the right man for the job, when in fact they had chosen the right job criteria for the man" (p. 478). Due to time constraints, the authors did not assess self-perceived measures of objectivity in the women's studies professor experiment. Also see Julie E. Phelan, Corinne A. Moss-Racusin, and Laurie A. Rudman, "Competent Yet Out in the Cold: Shifting Criteria for Hiring Reflect Backlash Toward Agentic Women," *Psychology of Women Quarterly* 32, no. 4 (2008): 406–13. For more research showing that belief in one's objectivity is linked with an increase in gender discrimination, see Eric Luis Uhlmann and Geoffrey L. Cohen, " 'I Think It, Therefore It's True': Effects of Self-Perceived Objectivity on Hiring Discrimination," *Organizational Behavior and Human Decision Processes* 104, no. 2 (2007): 207–23.

10. Sreedhari D. Desai, Dolly Chugh, and Arthur Brief, "Marriage Structure and Resistance to the Gender Revolution in the Workplace," Social Science Research Network (March 2012). http://papers.ssrn.com/sol3/papers.cfm?abstract_id=2018259. This study also found that like

men in traditional marriages, men in neotraditional marriages (men married to women who work part-time) were more likely than men in modern marriages to hold negative attitudes and beliefs about women in the workplace.

11. For a discussion of benevolent sexism, see Peter Glick and Susan T. Fiske, "The Ambivalent Sexism Inventory: Differentiating Hostile and Benevolent Sexism," *Journal of Personality and Social Psychology* 70, no. 3 (1996): 491–512.

12. Melissa Korn, "Choice of Work Partner Splits Along Gender Lines," *Wall Street Journal*, June 6, 2012, http://online.wsj.com/article/ SB10001424052702303506404577448652549105934.html.

13. A 2012 report by Dow Jones found that successful, venture-backed start-ups have a higher median proportion of female executives (7.1 percent) compared to unsuccessful start-ups (3.1 percent). Likewise, Herring (2009) found that racial and gender diversity in business organizations were associated with positive performance outcomes like increased sales revenue and greater relative profits. However, Kochan et al. (2003) found no significant direct effects of gender or racial diversity on business outcomes. Since diverse teams have access to different perspectives, skill sets, and ways of approaching problems, they have the potential to outperform less diverse groups. Yet studies have found that this potential is often thwarted by issues of group process such as communication breakdowns, for example, the hesitancy among those in the minority to voice an opinion that differs from the majority. Thus, in order for diverse teams to thrive, organizations need to create environments that foster trust, social cohesion, and a tolerance for divergent viewpoints among team members. See Jessica Canning, Maryam Haque, and Yimeng Wang, *Women at the Wheel: Do Female Executives Drive Start-Up Success?*, Dow Jones and Company (September 2012), http://www.dowjones.com/collateral/files/WomenPE_report_final .pdf; Cedric Herring, "Does Diversity Pay? Race, Gender, and the Business Case for Diversity," *American Sociological Review* 74, no. 2 (2009): 208–24; Elizabeth Mannix and Margaret A. Neale, "What Difference Makes a Difference? The Promise and Reality of Diverse Teams in Organizations," *Psychological Science in the Public Interest* 6, no. 2 (2005): 31–55; and Thomas Kochan et al., "The Effects of Diversity on Business Performance: Report of the Diversity Research Network," *Human Resource Management* 42, no. 1 (2003): 3–21.

14. Cynthia C. Hogan, e-mail message to the author, March 30, 2012.

15. Information about Harvard Business School's efforts to create a more inclusive learning environment was provided to the author in discussions during a visit there on May 23, 2012.

16. Sean Alfano, "Poll: Women's Movement Worthwhile," CBS

News, February 11, 2009, http://www.cbsnews.com/2100-500160_162
-965224.html.

11. WORKING TOGETHER TOWARD EQUALITY

1. For analysis of the "rhetoric of choice," or the pervasive belief that
women, but not men, freely choose whether or not to work in spite of
ideological, familial, and institutional obstacles that can prevent them
from successfully combining work and family life, see David Cotter,
Joan M. Hermsen, and Reeve Vanneman, "The End of the Gender Revolution? Gender Role Attitudes from 1977 to 2008," *American Journal
of Sociology* 117, no. 1 (2011): 259–89; Pamela Stone, *Opting Out? Why
Women Really Quit Careers and Head Home* (Berkeley: University of California Press, 2007); and Joan Williams, *Unbending Gender: Why Family
and Work Conflict and What to Do About It* (Oxford: Oxford University
Press, 2000).

2. Professor Deborah H. Gruenfeld, discussion with the author,
June 26, 2012.

3. Patricia Sellers, "New Yahoo CEO Mayer is Pregnant," CNN-
Money, July 16, 2012, http://postcards.blogs.fortune.cnn.com/2012/07/
16/mayer-yahoo-ceo-pregnant/.

4. "German Family Minister Slams Yahoo! CEO Mayer," *Spie-
gel* Online International, August 1, 2012, http://www.spiegel.de/inter
national/germany/german-government-official-criticizes-yahoo-exec
-for-short-maternity-leave-a-847739.html.

5. Kara Swisher, "Kara Swisher at Garage Geeks," YouTube video,
9:33 minutes, posted by ayeletknoff, August 1, 2012, http://www
.youtube.com/watch?v=jFtdsRx2frI&feature=youtube.

6. For a discussion of how individual women are seen as represen-
tative of all women and how female scarcity leads to stereotyping, see
Rosabeth Moss Kanter, *Men and Women of the Corporation*, 2nd ed. (New
York: Basic Books, 1993).

7. The article "Sheryl Sandberg Is the Valley's 'It' Girl—Just Like
Kim Polese Once Was" can be found at the end of Eric Jackson, "Apology
to Sheryl Sandberg and to Kim Polese [Updated]," *Forbes*, May 23, 2012,
http://www.forbes.com/sites/ericjackson/2012/05/23/apology-sheryl
-sandberg-kim-polese/.

8. Kim Polese, "Stop Comparing Female Execs and Just Let Sheryl
Sandberg Do Her Job," *Forbes*, May 25, 2012, http://www.forbes.com/
sites/carolinehoward/2012/05/25/stop-comparing-female-execs-and
-just-let-sheryl-sandberg-do-her-job/.

9. Jackson, "Apology to Sheryl Sandberg and to Kim Polese
[Updated]."

10. For a review of research related to the queen bee syndrome, see

Belle Derks et al., "Gender-Bias Primes Elicit Queen Bee Behaviors in Senior Policewomen," *Psychological Science* 22, no. 10 (2011): 1243–49; and Belle Derks et al., "Do Sexist Organizational Cultures Create the Queen Bee?," *British Journal of Social Psychology* 50, no. 3 (2011): 519–35.

11. Elizabeth J. Parks-Stamm, Madeline E. Heilman, and Krystle A. Hears, "Motivated to Penalize: Women's Strategic Rejection of Successful Women," *Personality and Social Psychology Bulletin* 34, no. 2 (2008): 237–47; Rocio Garcia-Retamero and Esther López-Zafra, "Prejudice Against Women in Male-Congenial Environments: Perceptions of Gender Role Congruity in Leadership," *Sex Roles* 55, nos. 1–2 (2006): 51–61; David L. Mathison, "Sex Differences in the Perception of Assertiveness Among Female Managers," *Journal of Social Psychology* 126, no. 5 (1986): 599–606; and Graham L. Staines, Carol Tavris, and Toby E. Jayaratne, "The Queen Bee Syndrome," *Psychology Today* 7 (1974): 55–60.

12. Naomi Ellemers et al., "The Underrepresentation of Women in Science: Differential Commitment or the Queen Bee Syndrome?" *British Journal of Social Psychology* 43, no. 3 (2004): 315–38. Female professors from older generations, who rose to the top when there were more barriers to women's advancement, held the most gender bias toward their female students. This finding suggests that queen bee behaviors are a consequence of gender discrimination.

13. Katherine Stroebe et al., "For Better or for Worse: The Congruence of Personal and Group Outcomes on Targets' Responses to Discrimination," *European Journal of Social Psychology* 39, no. 4 (2009): 576–91.

14. Madeleine K. Albright, Women in the World Summit, March 8, 2012, http://www.thedailybeast.com/articles/2012/03/09/women-in-the -world-highlights-angelina-jolie-madeline-albright-more-video.html.

15. Derks et al., "Do Sexist Organizational Cultures Create the Queen Bee?," 519–35; Robert S. Baron, Mary L. Burgess, and Chuan Feng Kao, "Detecting and Labeling Prejudice: Do Female Perpetrators Go Undetected?," *Personality and Social Psychology Bulletin* 17, no. 2 (1991): 115–23.

16. Sarah Dinolfo, Christine Silva, and Nancy M. Carter, *High Potentials in the Leadership Pipeline: Leaders Pay It Forward*, Catalyst (2012), 7, http://www.catalyst.org/publication/534/42/high-potentials-in -the-pipeline-leaders-pay-it-forward.

17. Janet Aschkenasy, "How a 'Good Old Girls' Network at Merrill Advanced the Careers of Four Women," Wall Street Technology Association, July 16, 2012, http://news.efinancialcareers.com/us-en/106965/ how-a-good-old-girls-network-at-merrill-advanced-the-careers-of -four-women/.

18. Kunal Modi, "Man Up on Family and Workplace Issues: A

Response to Anne-Marie Slaughter," *The Huffington Post*, July 12, 2012, http://www.huffingtonpost.com/kunal-modi/.

19. Joan Williams, "Slaughter vs. Sandberg: Both Right," *The Huffington Post*, June 22, 2012, http://www.huffingtonpost.com/joan-williams/ann-marie-slaughter_b_1619324.html.

20. Debora Spar, "Why Do Successful Women Feel So Guilty?," *The Atlantic*, June 28, 2012, http://www.theatlantic.com/business/archive/2012/06/why-do-successful-women-feel-so-guilty/259079/.

21. Institute for Women's Policy Research, *Women and Paid Sick Days: Crucial for Family Well-Being*, fact sheet, February 2007.

22. Lynda Laughlin, *Maternity Leave and Employment Patterns of First-Time Mothers: 1961–2008*, U.S. Census Bureau, Current Population Reports, P70–128 (October 2011), 9, http://www.census.gov/prod/2011pubs/p70–128.pdf.

23. Human Rights Watch, *Failing Its Families: Lack of Paid Leave and Work-Family Supports in the US* (2011), http://www.hrw.org/sites/default/files/reports/us0211webwcover.pdf.

24. Ellen Bravo, " 'Having It All?'—The Wrong Question to Ask for Most Women," Women's Media Center, June 26, 2012, http://www.womensmediacenter.com/feature/entry/having-it-all-the-wrong-question-for-most-women.

25. Nicholas D. Kristof, "Women Hurting Women," *New York Times*, September 29, 2012, http://www.nytimes.com/2012/09/30/opinion/sunday/kristof-women-hurting-women.html?_r=0.

26. A study of panel data from the EEOC of more than twenty thousand firms from 1990 to 2003 found that an increase in the percentage of top women managers is associated with a subsequent rise in the percentage of females in midlevel managerial roles within firms. This study also found that while women at the top have a positive influence on the advancement of lower-level women, this influence diminished over time. See Fiden Ana Kurtulus and Donald Tomaskovic-Devey, "Do Female Top Managers Help Women to Advance? A Panel Study Using EEO-1 Records," *The Annals of the American Academy of Political and Social Science* 639, no. 1 (2012): 173–97. A study of more than eight hundred U.S. firms found that when more women sat on the executive compensation committee of the board, the gender gap in executive pay was smaller. This study found, however, that having a female CEO was not associated with a reduction in the gender gap in pay. See Taekjin Shin, "The Gender Gap in Executive Compensation: The Role of Female Directors and Chief Executive Officers," *The Annals of the American Academy of Political and Social Science* 639, no. 1 (2012): 258–78. A study of seventy-two large U.S. corporations found that having a higher proportion of lower-level female managers in the 1980s and early 1990s was positively associated

with having more work-life HR policies in 1994 and with having a larger share of senior management roles held by women in 1999. See George F. Dreher, "Breaking the Glass Ceiling: The Effects of Sex Ratios and Work-Life Programs on Female Leadership at the Top," *Human Relations* 56, no. 5 (2003): 541–62.

27. *Gloria: In Her Own Words*, HBO documentary, directed by Peter Kunhardt (2011).

12. OWN WHO YOU ARE

1. Francis M. Beal, "Double Jeopardy: To Be Black and Female," in *The Black Woman: An Anthology*, ed. Toni Cade Bambara (New York: Signet, 1970), 90–100; and Kimberle Crenshaw, *Demarginalizing the Intersection of Race and Sex: A Black Feminist Critique of Antidiscrimination Doctrine, Feminist Theory, and Antiracist Politics*, University of Chicago Legal Forum (1989), 139–67.

2. U.S. Department of Education, *The Condition of Education 2012*, table A-47–2, National Center for Education Statistics (2012), http://nces.ed.gov/fastfacts/display.asp?id=72.

3. Ariane Hegewisch and Claudia Williams, *The Gender Wage Gap: 2012*, fact sheet, Institute for Women's Policy Research (September 2013), http://www.iwpr.org/publications/pubs/the-gender-wage-gap-2012-1. For more information regarding the gender wage gap, see note 10 of the introduction to this book.

4. Black Entrepreneur Profile, *African American CEOs of Fortune 500 Companies* (August 2013), http://www.blackentrepreneurprofile.com/fortune-500-ceos/.

5. White men hold 67.9 percent of Fortune 100 board seats and 73.3 percent of Fortune 500 board seats. See Alliance for Board Diversity, *Missing Pieces: Women and Minorities on Fortune 500 Boards* (2013), http://theabd.org/2012_ABD%20Missing_Pieces_Final_8_15_13.pdf; and Derek T. Dingle, "The African Americans Directing America's Largest Corporations," *Black Enterprise*, September 5, 2013, http://www.blackenterprise.com/b-e-exclusives/african-americans-directing-americas-largest-corporations/.

6. Russell Reynolds Associates, *2013 Fortune 250 Diversity Study*, forthcoming.

7. A recent study found that when a leader from a poorly performing company was a black woman, she received more negative evaluations than when that same leader was a white man, a white woman, or a black man. See Ashleigh Shelby Rosette and Robert W. Livingston, "Failure Is Not an Option for Black Women: Effects of Organizational Performance on Leaders with Single Versus Dual-Subordinate Identities," *Journal of Experimental Social Psychology* 48, no. 5 (2012): 1162–67.

8. Michael I. Norton and Evan P. Apfelbaum, "The Costs of Racial 'Color Blindness,'" *Harvard Business Review* 91, nos. 7–8 (2013): 22.

13. MAN UP AND LEAN IN

1. Center for American Women and Politics, *Women in the U.S. Congress 2013*, fact sheet (April 2013), http://www.cawp.rutgers.edu/fast_facts/levels_of_office/documents/cong.pdf.

2. *Elle* and the Center for American Progress, *The Big Power Grab* (August 2013), http://www.elle.com/life-love/society-career/power-survey#slide-1.

3. Tammy D. Allen et al., "Career Benefits Associated with Mentoring for Protégés: A Meta-Analysis," *Journal of Applied Psychology* 89, no. 1 (2004): 127–36; and Herminia Ibarra, Nancy M. Carter, and Christine Silva, "Why Men Still Get More Promotions Than Women," *Harvard Business Review* 88, no. 9 (2010): 80–85.

4. Between the mid-1980s and 2000, the percentage of all children who lived in a household where all the adults worked increased from about 60 percent to 70 percent. Suzanne Bianchi, *New Realities of Working Families*, United States Department of Labor (June 1999), http://www.dol.gov/oasam/programs/history/herman/reports/futurework/conference/workingfamilies/workingfamilies_toc.htm; and Joan C. Williams and Heather Boushey, *The Three Faces of Work-Family Conflict: The Poor, The Professionals, and the Missing Middle*, Center for American Progress and Center for WorkLife Law (January 2010), http://www.americanprogress.org/issues/2010/01/three_faces_report.html.

5. Melissa A. Milkie, Sara B. Raley, and Suzanne M. Bianchi, "Taking on the Second Shift: Time Allocations and Time Pressures of U.S. Parents with Preschoolers," *Social Forces* 88, no. 2 (2009): 487–517.

14. LISTEN TO YOUR INNER VOICE

1. Women's Initiative, *Steering Committee's Report*, Duke University (2003), http://universitywomen.stanford.edu/reports/WomensInitiativeReport.pdf.

2. Colleen Walsh, "Winfrey: Failure Is Just Movement," *Harvard Gazette*, May 30, 2013, http://news.harvard.edu/gazette/story/2013/05/winfrey-failure-is-just-movement/.

15. FIND YOUR FIRST JOB

1. Georges Desvaux, Sandrine Devillard-Hoellinger, and Mary C. Meaney, "A Business Case for Women," *The McKinsey Quarterly* (Septem-

ber 2008), 4, http://www.womenscolleges.org/files/pdfs/BusinessCasefor Women.pdf.

2. Cross-Tab Marketing Services, *Online Reputation in a Connected World* (January 2010), 6.

3. National Association of Colleges and Employers, *The Job Outlook for the Class of 2014* (2013), http://www.naceweb.org/uploadedFiles/Pages/MyNACE/grab_and_go/students/job-outlook-2014-student-version.pdf.

4. The success rate of landing a job from open positions listed on a job board or from placing a résumé on a job board is only between 4 and 10 percent. See Mark Emery Bolles and Richard Nelson Bolles, *What Color Is Your Parachute? Guide to Job-Hunting Online* (Berkeley: Ten Speed Press, 2011).

5. Albert Mehrabian, *Nonverbal Communication* (Chicago: Adeline-Atherton, 1972). It should be noted that situational factors can influence the degree to which what someone says, her body language, and her tone of voice shape the impressions that are formed about her.

6. Tomi-Ann Roberts and Susan Nolan-Hoeksema, "Sex Differences in Reactions to Evaluative Feedback," *Sex Roles* 21, nos. 11–12 (December 1989): 725–47; and Maria Johnson and Vicki S. Helgeson, "Sex Differences in Response to Evaluative Feedback: A Field Study," *Psychology of Women Quarterly* 26, no. 3 (2002): 242–51.

7. Sylvia Beyer, "Gender Differences in Causal Attributions by College Students of Performance on Course Examinations," *Current Psychology* 17, no. 4 (1998): 346–58.

8. Joanna Barsh and Lareina Yee, *Unlocking the Full Potential of Women at Work*, McKinsey & Company (2012), http://www.mckinsey.com/careers/women/~/media/Reports/Women/2012%20WSJ%20Women%20in%20the%20Economy%20white%20paper%20FINAL.ashx.

9. Bureau of Labor Statistics, *Number of Jobs Held, Labor Market Activity, and Earnings Growth Among the Youngest Baby Boomers: Results from a Longitudinal Study* (July 2012), http://www.bls.gov/news.release/pdf/nlsoy.pdf. This report found that the average person born between 1957 and 1964 had 11.3 jobs between the ages of eighteen and forty-six, with almost half of these jobs being held between the ages of eighteen and twenty-four.

16. NEGOTIATE YOUR SALARY

1. Ariane Hegewisch and Claudia Williams, *The Gender Wage Gap: 2012*, fact sheet, Institute for Women's Policy Research (September 2013), http://www.iwpr.org/publications/pubs/the-gender-wage-gap-2012-1.

2. National Women's Law Center, *How the Wage Gap Hurts Women and Families*, fact sheet (April 2013), http://www.nwlc.org/sites/default/files/pdfs/factorotherthan_sexfactsheet_5.30.12_final.pdf.

3. Christianne Corbett and Catherine Hill, *Graduating to a Pay Gap: The Earnings of Women and Men One Year After Graduation*, American Association of University Women (October 2012), http://www.aauw.org/files/2013/02/graduating-to-a-pay-gap-the-earnings-of-women-and-men-one-year-after-college-graduation.pdf.

4. Hilary M. Lips, "The Gender Pay Gap: Challenging the Rationalizations, Perceived Equity, Discrimination, and the Limits of the Human Capital Model," *Sex Roles* 68, nos. 3–4 (2013): 169–85; Corbett and Hill, *Graduating to a Pay Gap;* Francine D. Blau and Lawrence M. Kahn, "The Gender Pay Gap: Have Women Gone as Far as They Can?" *Academy of Management Perspectives* 21, no. 1 (2007): 7–23; and Linda Babcock and Sara Laschever, *Women Don't Ask* (New York: Bantam Books, 2007).

5. Hannah Riley Bowles and Linda Babcock, "How Can Women Escape the Compensation Negotiation Dilemma? Relational Accounts Are One Answer," *Psychology of Women Quarterly* 37, no. 1 (2013): 80–96.

6. Roger Dawson, *Secrets of Power Negotiating: Inside Secrets from a Master Negotiator* (Franklin Lakes, NJ: Career Press, 1999).

7. Bowles and Babcock, "How Can Women Escape the Compensation Negotiation Dilemma?"

8. Amanda M. Fairbanks, "5 Ways to Earn What You're Worth," *The Huffington Post*, June 13, 2011, http://www.huffingtonpost.com/2011/06/13/women-salary-job-negotiation_n_875642.html.

17. LET'S LEAN IN TOGETHER

1. Patrick R. Laughlin, Erin C. Hatch, Jonathan S. Silver, and Lee Boh, "Groups Perform Better Than the Best Individuals on Letters-to-Numbers Problems: Effects of Induced Strategies," *Journal of Personality and Social Psychology* 90, no. 4 (2006): 644–51; and Paul Zarnoth and Janet A. Sniezek, "The Social Influence of Confidence in Group Decision Making," *Journal of Experimental Social Psychology* 33, no. 4 (1997): 345–66.

2. Dana R. Carney, Amy J. C. Cuddy, and Andy J. Yap, "Power Posing: Brief Nonverbal Displays Affect Neuroendocrine Levels and Risk Tolerance," *Psychological Science* 21, no. 10 (2010): 1363–68.

Index

Aaker, Jennifer, 175
Abzug, Bella, 199
Addams, Jane, 199
affirmative action, 182, 230
Afghanistan, 5
After School Matters, 240
Agyare, Regina, 296–7
Albright, Madeleine, 207
ambition gap, 19–33, 217,
        348n–52n
    authority figures as silencing
        female voices and, 26
    biological gender differences
        and, 23
    family-work conflict and,
        29–30, 119, 125, 182,
        348n–9n, 350n
    fear as factor in, 31, 32, 33
    female employment dropout
        rates and, 18, 346n–8n
    gender socialization and
        stereotypes as contributing
        to, 21, 24–8, 51, 52, 318–19,
        350n, 351n, 353n–4n
    millennials and, 20–1, 28–9,
        351n
    and political aspirations, 37
    pressure to prioritize marriage
        and, 21–3, 222–4
    race and, 228–9, 271–3
American Express, 188–9

AmeriCorps, 256
Anderson, Cameron, 49–50
Angelou, Maya, 328
anorexia nervosa, 274
Anthony, Susan B., 199, 217–18
Are You My Mother? (Eastman), 81
Ariel Investments, 230, 231–2,
        235, 237, 240
    Black Corporate Directors
        Conference of, 237
Armstrong, Tim, 112
Art of War, The, 233
Atlantic, 22, 211
Auletta, Ken, 52, 197

Bachelet, Michelle, 344n
Barackman, Nola, 241–3
Barnard College, 31, 33, 211
Barnes, Brenda, 127
Barnett, Rosalind Chait, 30
BATNA ("best alternative to a
        negotiated agreement"), 306,
        315
Bay, Willow, 88
"benevolent sexism," 193, 363n
Bennett, Jessica, 298–300
Berkman, Brenda, 329
"bias blind spots," 192, 194, 249
bias training, 253
Biden, Joe, 195

Bodenheimer, George, 238
Bodnick, Marc, 58
Booz Allen Hamilton, 282, 295
Bossypants (Fey), 155
Boston College, Center for Work
    & Family at, 348*n*
Boston Consulting Group,
    375*n*–6*n*
Boston Globe, 298
Bowles, Hannah Riley, 59, 360*n*
Brandeis University, 30
Bravo, Ellen, 29
breast-feeding, pumping, 23–4,
    124, 136, 163, 164
Brin, Sergey, 4, 76, 162
Brokaw, Tom, 102
Brooklyn Polytechnic Institute,
    257
Buckingham, Marcus, 114
Buffett, Warren, 8, 16, 162
Bullock, Sandra, 28
Burnett, Erin, 88
Burns, Ursula, 227, 257–8

Caesars casino, 289–90
California, University of
    at Berkeley, 16
    at Hastings, 210
Callahan, Mike, 197
CareerBuilder, 284
career paths, managing of,
    66–80
    accepting stretch assignments
        in, 79, 119
    eighteen-month plans in,
        74–6
    as jungle gym vs. ladder, 67,
        76–7
    long-term goals in, 68–70, 72
    premature family planning
        and, 116–22
    prioritizing jobs with potential
        for growth in, 73, 77

spousal support as crucial in,
    138–9
taking risks in, 76–9, 80
Carell, Steve, 154
Carnegie Mellon University, 57
Catalyst, 344*n*, 348*n*, 349*n*, 364*n*
Census Bureau, U.S., 346*n*
Center for Work-Life Policy, 91
Chan, Priscilla, 147
Chang, Ruth, 139
Chenault, Ken, 188–9
Chicago, University of, Booth
    School of Business, 347*n*
Chicago Fire Department, 237
Chicago Public Education Fund,
    240
child care, 9, 140
    costs of, 125, 129–30
    done by fathers, 134–5, 369*n*
    rising weekly hours spent by
        parents on, 170, 377*n*
    studies on stay-at-home
        mothering vs. paid, 171–2,
        377*n*–8*n*
    women as primarily responsible
        for, 9–10, 18, 124, 134, 135,
        150, 182, 254–5
China, women in, 222–4
Choksi, Priti, 121
Cinderella Ate My Daughter
    (Orenstein), 117
Cisco, 44
Clark, Andy, 148
Clinton, Bill, 72
Clinton, Hillary, 47, 328
CNN, 88
Cohen, Betsy, 97
Cohen, Geoffrey L., 380*n*–1*n*
Colao, Vittorio, 188
Coleman, Mary Sue, 60
CollegeSpring, 87
Columbia Business School, 49
communication, authentic,
    97–115

building relationships with, 106, 111–12
fostering culture of, 108
humor as tool in, 109
importance of listening in, 101–2
personal and emotional sharing in, 110–15
power dynamics in stifling of, 98–9
recognizing points of view in, 100
simple language in, 100
soliciting feedback in, 102–3, 105–6, 107
taking responsibility for mistakes and, 106–7
tone of voice and body language in, 327, 388*n*
vs. blindly following leaders, 103–4
Congress, U.S., 178
Conscious Business (Kofman), 99
Cooper, Marianne, 179
Cornell University, 153
Coukos, Pamela, 345*n*
Craigslist, 284
Crandall, Christian S., 354*n*
"crouch to conquer," 233–4
crying at work, 110–11, 114, 115, 365*n*–6*n*
Curse of the Good Girl, The (Simmons), 270
Curtis, Mary, 175–6
Customs Service, U.S., 106

Danaher, Kelly, 354*n*
Date Night, 154
dating, 22, 145, 146–7
Decker, Sue, 64
Deloitte, 93
Deloitte Tax, 93
Depression, Great, 15

Dhanani, Sabeen Virani, 186
discrimination laws, 190–1
dispersion of work hours between more and less educated workers, 376*n*
diversity, 235–6, 238
divorce, 22, 149
"doing it all," 19, 154–71, 174
and employed women's fears of falling short as mothers, 170–1, 172–4, 176
extended working hours as national trend and, 166–7
fear of putting family ahead of career and, 161–5
letting go of unattainable standards and, 155–9, 163, 175–6
trade-offs between work and home as inevitable and, 169, 211
Donahoe, John, 157
Dostart, Steve, 213
double bind, 54–5, 56, 92
double standards, 248, 250–1
in accounting for success, 37–8
applied to senior leaders, 209
in maternity and paternity leave, 143
Dow Jones, 382*n*
DreamWorks Animation, 240
driving, 320–2

Early Child Care Research Network, 171–2
Ear Peace: Save Your Hearing, 215
eating disorders, 274–6
eBay, 66, 72, 157
Ebony, 239

education, 5, 15–17, 19, 125
  and gender bias in classroom,
    xi, 26, 353*n*–4*n*
  race and, 227, 271–3
  role of, 272–3
  women as outperforming men
    in, 19, 227
EEOC (Equal Employment
    Opportunity Commission),
    344*n*–5*n*, 385*n*
eighteen-month plans, 74–6
Einhorn, Rosalind, 15–16
Elam, Michele, 179
Elsbach, Kimberly D.,
    365*n*–6*n*
Ely, Robin, 198
employed women
  ambition gap in, xvi, 19–33,
    348*n*–52*n*
  crying at work by, 110–11, 114,
    115, 365*n*–6*n*
  cultural expectation to think
    "communally" in, 56, 59, 61,
    75, 208–9
  discrimination quietly endured
    by, xiii, 182, 185, 187–8
  downplaying of achievements
    by, xiv, 19, 52, 57–8, 64, 219,
    252, 280, 304, 318, 324
  earnings penalties for time out
    of workforce of, 129
  emotional and financial
    benefits of, 30, 149, 378*n*
  employment dropout rates of,
    xii–xiii, 18, 124–6, 139, 182,
    346*n*–8*n*, 367*n*
  family-work conflict of, *see*
    family-work conflict
  fear of speaking honestly in,
    98–9, 115
  "fitting in" as survival
    technique of, 180, 184, 185,
    217

gender bias in hiring of,
    xii–xiii, 191–3, 379*n*–81*n*
gender bias in performance
    evaluations of, 194–5
gender bias perpetuated by, xiv,
    206–7, 208, 324, 384*n*
gender pay gap and, 5, 6–7,
    28, 217, 303–4, 309, 345*n*,
    385*n*–6*n*
housework and child care as
    primarily done by, 9–10, 19,
    124, 134, 150, 182, 254
insecurities and self-doubt in,
    xiv, xv, 9–10, 34–8, 43–8, 52,
    79, 98–9, 162, 170–1, 172–4,
    176, 211, 257–8, 356*n*
in leadership positions,
    see leadership positions,
    women in
learning to withstand criticism
    in, 62–3
limited career options in early
    days of, 16–17
managing career paths and, *see*
    career paths, managing of
marital partnerships of, *see*
    spousal partnerships
maternity leave of, 143–4,
    160–1, 163, 203, 205, 214,
    371*n*
mentorships and, *see* mentors,
    mentorships
negative stereotypes and
    depictions of, 28–9, 61–2,
    220, 248, 251–2, 304
in negotiations, xvi–xvii,
    57–61, 75–6, 298–300,
    301–17, 360*n*, 363*n*
parenthood and, *see* family-
    work conflict; parenting
pregnancy and, 3–4, 10,
    121–2, 123, 132, 143, 202–3,
    205

reasons for leaving workforce of, 125–6, 129, 139, 367*n*

as reluctant in applying for promotions, 80, 187, 363*n*

risk aversion in, 19, 43–4, 45, 77–9, 363*n*

single mothers as, 29, 154

as slower in seizing opportunities, 43–5, 118, 264

speaking out on gender issues of, 183–91, 194–8

speaking up, 231–2, 235, 268, 296, 302–3

spousal support as crucial for, 138–9, 169

success-likeability correlation in, *see* success-likeability correlation

employment/hiring practices

appearance and, 288–9

e-mail/cover letter, 283–7

interview preparation, 287–95

online presence, 278–9, 282

résumés, 279–82

tips for getting a job, 278–95

employment policies

career penalties for making use of flexible, 164, 375*n*

easing work-family conflicts with, 129, 162–3, 189, 214–15

paid parental leave laws and, 371*n*–2*n*

parental leave and, 29, 129, 143–4, 160–1, 163, 203, 205, 214, 371*n*–2*n*

pregnancy parking and, 4, 10, 215

traditional gender roles reinforced by, 143–4, 371*n*

Ephron, Nora, 147, 158–9

Equal Pay Day (2011), 6–7

ESPN, 238

Estée Lauder Companies, 240

Etsy, 146

Ettus, Samantha, 21

"expectancy theory," 359*n*

Facebook, xiv, xv, 7, 13, 28, 34, 38, 44, 45, 47, 55, 66–7, 71, 75, 83, 85, 87, 88, 101, 102, 112, 116, 118, 120, 121, 143, 158, 174, 177, 183, 185, 278, 285, 328

authentic communication at, 98, 104, 106, 108–9, 111

author in career move to, 58–9, 62, 64–5, 77–8, 93–4, 123, 167–9

family-friendly work policies at, 165, 175, 189

risk-taking culture at, 31

Facebook Women, 196–7

Fairbanks, Mabel, 328

Family and Work Institute, 348*n*

Family Values @ Work, 29

family-work conflict, xvii, 18–19, 116–30, 139, 140–1, 154–76, 203, 219–21, 254

ambition gap and, 29–30, 119, 125, 182, 348*n*–9*n*, 350*n*

career opportunities missed due to premature planning for, 117–21, 122, 123–4, 127–8

career penalties for making use of family-friendly work policies and, 129–30, 143–4, 164, 375*n*

child-care costs and, 125, 129–30

"doing it all" and, 19, 154–6, 159–65, 169, 175–6, 211

extended working hours as national trend and, 166–7, 376*n*

family-work conflict *(continued)*
family-friendly employment
policies in easing of, 129,
162–3, 175, 189, 214–15
fear of being seen as favoring
family over career in, 161–5,
196–7
female employment dropout
rates and, 18, 124–6, 129,
139, 182, 367*n*
finding successful balance in,
119, 122–4, 156, 196
guilt over not spending enough
time with children in, 170–1,
172–4, 176, 211
inflexible employment policies
and, 9, 29, 129, 214, 371*n*
letting go of unattainable
standards in, 155–9, 163,
175–6
making efficient use of time at
work in, 163–6, 175
masculine cultural expectations
in, 130, 144–5
"mommy wars" and, 210–11,
212
societal pressures on women to
stay home in, 125–7, 171
taking control of job demands
and schedules in, 159–65,
168–9, 195–7, 375*n*
technology's effect on work
schedules in, 165, 166,
375*n*
trade-offs between work and
home as inevitable in, 169,
196, 211
Farrell, Diana, 64, 207–8
female entrepreneurs, 61
Feminine Mystique, The (Friedan),
150
feminists, feminism, xii, 199–200,
203, 211, 213

negative stigma of, 179, 182,
183, 199–200
see also women's rights, women's
rights movement
Ferraro, Geraldine, 179
Fey, Tina, 36, 154–5, 328
Fieler, Anna, 129–30
Fischer, David, 108, 163
Fitzgerald, Ella, 242
"flexibility stigma," 375*n*
Flynn, Francis, 49–50, 56
Fonda, Jane, 42, 183
Forbes, 204
World's 100 Most Powerful
Women list of, 47
Fortune Most Powerful Women
Summit, 45, 64
Freed, Adam, 110
Free to Be . . . You and Me, 27
Frei, Frances, 198
Friedan, Betty, 150, 205
Frohlinger, Carol, 80

Gandhi, Indira, 51
Gandhi, Sonia, 47
Gbowee, Leymah, 8–9, 214
Geithner, Tim, 34
gender bias, xiii, 189–90, 191–5,
200, 201, 207, 208, 249–51,
254
"blind spots" for, 192, 194,
249
in classroom, xi, 26, 353*n*–4*n*
in domestic responsibilities, 18,
134–5, 139, 219–21
in family-related employment
policies, 143–4, 254
in hiring practices, xii–xiii,
191–3, 379*n*–81*n*
in media, 38
in "modern" vs. "traditional"
husbands, 193, 381*n*–2*n*

in performance evaluations,
194–5
success-likeability correlation
and, *see* success-likeability
correlation
women as perpetuators of, xiv,
206–7, 208, 324, 384*n*
"gender discount" problem, 56
gender discrimination, 10, 182,
185, 186, 187–8, 190–1,
192–3, 206–7, 303–4,
384*n*
see also gender bias; sexism
gender issues, speaking out on,
183–91, 194–200, 204–5
backlash to, 184–5
and bias, 194–5, 200, 250–2
defensiveness of those
scrutinized in, 194
family-work conflict concerns
and, 195–7
female leaders' important role
in, 4, 9, 10, 13, 214–15
institutional changes spurred
on by, 197–9, 200
legal risks as creating barriers
for, 190–1
men's role in, 186–9, 248,
250–2
with potential employers,
195–6
gender pay gap, 5, 6–7, 28, 217,
303–4, 309, 345*n*, 385*n*–6*n*
gender roles, domestic, 134–5,
139, 141, 150–1
flipping of, 135–6
as reinforced by employment
policies, 143–4, 371*n*
gender socialization, 21, 24–8,
54–5, 350*n*, 351*n*, 353*n*–4*n*
gender stereotypes, 27–8, 50,
56–7, 78, 201, 204, 213, 216,
232–5, 248, 318–19

cultural expectations on men
and, 50, 130, 144–5, 304
as discouraging ambitious
traits in females, 24–8, 50–1,
52, 54–5, 223, 251
expectations on women to
think and act "communally"
and, 56, 59, 61, 208–9
introduced in childhood, 24,
27–8
salary negotiations and, xvi,
57–61, 298–9
societal rules of conduct and,
24, 25–7, 50–1, 52, 54–5, 57,
60, 357*n*
"stereotype threat" and, 28,
354*n*
success-likeability correlation
and, 50–65, 360*n*
women doing additional work
without reward due to, 56,
252
"gender wars," 210–11, 212, 213
Germany, 23
Getting to 50/50 (Meers and
Strober), 30, 63, 119
Girl Scouts, 351*n*
Girls Leadership Institute, 262,
270
Giuliani, Rudy, 261
glass ceiling, 7, 349*n*
Gleit, Naomi, 94
Glimcher, Laurie, 156
Goldberg, Dave, 4, 22, 25, 42,
58, 77, 99, 123, 131, 132–4,
140–2, 145, 150, 167, 168,
173, 174
Goldberg, Leslye, 292–3
Goldberg, Mel, 150–1
Goldberg, Paula, 150
Goldfein, Jocelyn, 55–6
Goldin, Claudia, 379*n*–80*n*
Goldman Sachs, 63, 88, 92, 103

Goldstein, Katherine, 323–4
Goler, Lori, 66–7, 75, 196
Goodfriend, Amy, 63
Google, 13, 43, 64, 73, 75, 76, 83,
    85–6, 89, 94, 99, 107, 108,
    110–11, 112, 122, 124, 140,
    168, 169, 177, 183, 187, 208,
    279, 286
  author's maternity leave from,
    160–1
  family-friendly policies at,
    162–3, 165, 215
  pregnancy parking instituted
    at, 3–4, 215
Graham, Don, 85
Graham, Molly, 105
Greene, Chad, 109
Groupon, 240
Gruenfeld, Deborah, 54, 202,
    326–7
Gymboree, 24

Hart, Camille, 47, 64, 162
Hart, Myra M., 368*n*
Harvard Business Review, 91
Harvard Business School (HBS),
    49, 52, 82–3, 125, 139, 198–9,
    200, 368*n*
Harvard Law School, 37, 46
Harvard University, 35, 38–41,
    68, 71, 85, 347*n*, 368*n*
  Kennedy School of
    Government at, 59, 209
"having it all," 153–4
  see also "doing it all"
Hearsay Social, 86
Heidi/Howard study, 49–51, 53,
    194
Heilman, Madeline E., 360*n*
Hemani, Abby, 114
Hemmeter, Debi, 127
Henry Ford Scholars, 51, 53

Hewlett-Packard, 79
Hobson, Mellody, 225–40
Hochschild, Arlie Russell,
    345*n*
Hoffman, Reid, 122
Hogan, Cynthia, 195–6
Holiday, Billie, 242
Holleran, Jen, 147–8
Holley, Derek, 94–5
honest communication, *see*
    communication, authentic
Hook, Jennifer L., 369*n*
Hooker, Ty-Licia, 271–3
household chores, 9–10, 18, 182,
    254–5
  done by fathers, 134, 135–6,
    369*n*
  equal division of, 139–41,
    146–9, 151, 255
Huffington, Arianna, 62
Huffington Post, 44, 62
Hughes, Langston, 241–2
Hurston, Zora Neale, 242

IBM, 45
Icarus, 154
I Don't Know How She Does It, 28
Iliad, The (Homer), 39
impostor syndrome, 35–8, 356*n*
India, 70–1
  patriarchal culture in, 320–2
inner voice, 263–70, 277, 296–7
  self-discovery and, 265
  speaking up and, 235, 259–60,
    265, 268, 296, 302–3
  worst-case scenario and, 269
Innovisor, 193–4
insecurities and self-doubt, xiv,
    xv, 9–10, 34–8, 244–6, 262,
    278, 356*n*–8*n*
  avoiding stretch assignments
    due to, 79

as barrier to seizing
opportunities, xiv, xvi, 43–5,
219, 264
efforts needed in correcting
gender gap in, 46–8
in employed mothers, 170–1,
172–4, 176, 211
faking confidence in
overcoming of, 42–3, 245
in fear of putting family ahead
of career, 162, 164
fear of speaking honestly due
to, 98–9, 268
after graduation, xii, 264–5, 269
impostor syndrome and, 35–8,
356n
listening to your inner voice
and, *see* inner voice
in men vs. women, 38, 40–2, 43
overcoming, 219–21, 245–6
as self-fulfilling prophecy, 42,
79, 216
underestimating own skills
and abilities due to, xiv, 37,
357n–8n, 363n
as way to appear more
likeable, 52
"intensive mothering," 170
and employed mothers' leisure
time, 377n

J. C. Penney, 24
Johns Hopkins University School
of Medicine, 186–7
Johnson, John H., 239
Joyner, Tom, 239

Kanarek, Larry, 159, 160, 168
Kanter, Rosabeth Moss, 139
Keating, Kim, 301–17
Keating Advisors, 303, 317

Kelly, Ray, 106–7
Kennedy, Flo, 199
Keys, Alicia, 328
Kofman, Fred, 99–100, 102
Kolb, Deborah, 80
Kolli, Sindhura, 320–2
Kordestani, Omid, 75, 76,
110–11, 112, 163
Kurovski, Sara, 219–21

labor and childbirth, 131–2
Labor Department, U.S., 345n
Latham, Stephen, 329
Launch Media, 133
leadership positions, women
in, 61–4, 115, 128, 201–10,
216–18, 385n–6n
ambition gap and, 19–33, 217,
348n–52n
external vs. internal barriers to,
xiv, xvi, 9–11, 35
fear at root of barriers to, 31,
32, 33
female coalition of support
needed in promoting of,
202–9
female rivalry, 205–7, 217
inflexible employment policies
as barrier to, 9, 129, 214–15
in instigating solutions to
women's issues, 4, 9, 10, 13,
214–15, 385n–6n
as learning to withstand
criticism, 62–3
male coalition of support
needed in promoting of,
207–10, 216
negative stereotypes and
depictions of, 28, 50–1, 61–2,
204
"queen bee" behaviors of, 206,
208, 384n

leadership positions, women in
      (continued)
   risk aversion in career paths of,
      77–9, 363*n*
   shortage of, 6–8, 183, 203–4,
      210
   spousal support as crucial for,
      138–9, 216
   success-likeability correlation
      and, 50–1, 54–5, 61–2
   trying to fit in, 180
leadership skills, 54–5, 114–15,
      198
   authentic communication in,
      99–100, 114
   sense of humor in, 109
   "work-life balance" in,
      165–6
Leading to WIN Women's
      Initiative, 93
Lean In Circles, xvii, 223, 323,
      325–6
Lean In Community, 328–9
Lean In Education, 326–8
Lehman, William, 178
Leib, Dori Levy, 282
Lemmon, Gayle Tzemach, 22
Levine, Marne, 109
Levy, Mindy, 277–95
Liberia, 8
LIFT, 256
LinkedIn, 122, 279, 280, 285
Lucas, George, 233

Makers video series, 197
Malcolm X, 272
"Man Up on Family and
      Workplace Issues" (Modi),
      209–10
marriage
   ambition gap and social
      pressure to prioritize, 21–3,
      222–4

dual income-earners as
      beneficial to, 30, 149
   "modern" vs. "traditional",
      and gender bias in men, 193,
      381*n*–2*n*
   see also family-work conflict;
      spousal partnerships
"maternal gatekeeping," 137
maternity leave, 29, 143–4,
      160–1, 163, 203, 205, 214,
      222, 371*n*
Mayer, Marissa, 183, 202–3, 205
McCarthy, Joe, 63
McCartney, Kathleen, 378*n*
McGee, Dyllan, 197
McIntosh, Peggy, 35, 36
McKinsey & Company, 71, 94,
      159, 168, 181, 207, 256,
      349*n*
McKinsey Global Institute, 64
McKinsey report (2011), 9
McKinsey survey (2012), 20
Meers, Sharon, 30, 63, 92, 209,
      213–14
Meir, Golda, 51, 179
men
   ambition gap between women
      and, 19–33
   employment participation rates
      of, 368*n*
   gender bias of, in "modern" vs.
      "traditional" marriages, 193,
      381*n*–2*n*
   in marital partnerships, *see*
      spousal partnerships
   masculine cultural expectations
      on, 50, 130, 144–5
   mentorships as more easily
      accessible to, 9, 18, 84, 90,
      364*n*
   as outperformed by women in
      education, 19
   paternal involvement of, *see*
      paternal involvement

as quicker in seizing
opportunities, 43
self-confidence in women vs.,
38, 40–2, 43
women's future progress and
important role of, 186–9,
208–10, 216
mental health issues, 274–6
mentors, mentorships, 38,
81–2, 84–96, 210, 253, 325,
363n–5n
capturing attention of
potential, 86–7, 88–9
efficient use of time in,
89–90
formal programs for, 92–3
men as having easier access to,
9, 18, 84, 90, 364n
misconceptions on searching
for, 81–2, 84–5, 86
peers as, 94–6
qualities sought by, 86
as reciprocal relationship, 88
senior male/junior female
models in, 90–3
Merkel, Angela, 47, 51
Merrill Lynch, 208
Metropolitan Museum of Art,
241
Michigan, University of, 60
Mighty Be Our Powers (Gbowee), 8
millennials, 20–1, 28–9, 351n
Mitchell, Pat, 85, 176, 184
Mitic, Katie and Scott, 135–6
Modern Family, 233
Modi, Kunal, 209–10,
247–56
"mommy wars," 210–11, 212
Mondale, Walter, 179
Moneyline, 88
Monster, 284
Moon, Youngme, 198
Morgan Stanley, 317
Morrelli, Jana, 318–19

Nakagawa, Mana, 276
nannies, 134, 173
National Institute of Child
Health and Human
Development, 171
Naval Academy, U.S., 212
Negotiating Women, Inc., 80
negotiations, 301–17, 363n
in business deals, 75–6
gender differences in, 57–8,
360n
"how to," 303–17
salary, xvi–xvii, 57–61, 223,
298–300, 301–17
tone of voice and body
language in, 327
women and success in, 59–61
Neiman, Garrett, 87
Nevill-Manning, Kirsten, 104
"New F-Word, The" (Cooper),
179
Newkirk, Kyle, 259–60
Newsweek, 298
New York, N.Y., women's
influence in, 241–3
New York *Daily News*, 261
New Yorker, 52
New York Times, 38
New York University, 49
Nixon, Richard, 51
Nobel Peace Prize, 8
Nohria, Nitin, 82–3, 198
Nooyi, Indra, 47
Novack, David R., 366n
Novack, Lesley Lazin, 366n
nudge techniques, 187

Obama, Barack, 226
Obama, Michelle, 47
Obama administration, 109
Ochoa, Ellen, 328
O'Connor, Caroline, 121–2
O'Connor, Sandra Day, 179

Odd Girl Out (Simmons), 270
Odyssey, The (Homer), 39
Office Space, 100
off-ramping, 124, 129
O'Neill, Tip, 178, 199
opportunities, career, 77
    family planning in passing on,
       117–21, 122, 123–4, 127–8,
       219
    self-doubt as barrier to seizing
       of, xvi, 43–5, 219, 264
    skill development and, xvi
Orenstein, Peggy, 117
Osofsky, Justin, 88–9

PACER (Parent Advocacy
    Coalition for Educational
    Rights), 150
Page, Larry, 4, 76, 162
Paley Center, 85
parenting, 131–45, 147–8,
    149–52, 213–14
    benefits of paternal
       involvement in, 142–3, 149,
       171–2
    empowering men's roles in,
       136–8, 151–2, 248
    fathers as primary caregivers
       in, 132, 135–6, 144, 146,
       372*n*
    gender-biased employment
       policies in, 143–4
    "intensive mothering"
       phenomenon in, 170
    letting go of unattainable
       standards in, 155–9
    "maternal gatekeeping" in,
       137
    "mommy wars" in, 210–11, 212
    rising weekly hours spent on
       primary child care and, 170,
       377*n*
    single mothers and, 29, 154

stay-at-home, opting out of
    workforce for, 119, 120, 130,
    144, 149–50, 372*n*
stay-at-home, society as
    undervaluing work of, 212
stay-at-home, studies on
    paid child care vs., 171–2,
    377*n*–8*n*
women's lopsided role in, 9–10,
    18, 124, 134–5
    see also family-work conflict;
       paternal involvement
Parikh, Jay, xiv–xv
Parker, Sarah Jessica, 28
paternal involvement, 132,
    135–45, 148, 149, 152, 174,
    214
    benefits of, 142–3, 149,
       171–2
    empowering men's parental
       roles and, 136–8, 151–2
    inflexible employment policies
       as barrier to, 143–4, 371*n*
    and men as primary caregivers,
       132, 135–6, 144, 146, 372*n*
    rising weekly hours spent on,
       369*n*
    societal expectations in
       hindering of, 130, 144–5,
       372*n*
    stay-at-home, 130, 144, 218,
       372*n*
paternity leave, 143–4, 371*n*–2*n*
Paul, Alice, 199
Paul, Stephen, 52
pay raises, 84, 323, 364*n*
    see also promotions
Pennsylvania, University of, 16
Pepsi-Cola North America,
    127
performance evaluations, gender
    bias in, 194–5
Perlow, Leslie A., 375*n*–6*n*
Perry, Vicki, 46

Pew Research Center, 20, 366*n*
Phi Beta Kappa, 35, 40
Playdom, 330
Poczter, Sharon, 153–4
Poe, Edgar Allan, 241
Polese, Kim, 204
Porn for Women (Anderson), 146
posture, 43
Powell, Colin, 165–6
pregnancy, pregnant women,
    3–4, 97, 121–2, 123, 132, 143,
    202–3, 205
  reserved parking for, 4, 10, 215
Princeton University, 126
Pritchett, Lant, 71, 79
Probasco, John, 186–7
Procter & Gamble, 287
promotions, xiii, 10, 190, 193,
    206, 296, 299, 303
  gender-based requirements
    for, xiii
  mentorships as aiding in, 91,
    93, 363*n*
  women as reluctant in applying
    for, 80, 187, 363*n*
Proposal, The, 28
Pynchon, Victoria, 314

"queen bee" behaviors, 206, 208,
    384*n*

race, racism, xiii, 225–40, 386*n*
  achievement gap and, 227
  ambition gap and, 228–9,
    271–3
  education and, 227, 271–3
  embracing diversity and,
    235–6, 238
  female advancement and, 225,
    230
  salary and employment
    statistics, 227

stereotypes and, 227, 232–5,
    236–7, 386*n*
  as taboo issue, 226
  "unapologetically black" and,
    239–40
Radcliffe College, 35
Rainbow PUSH, 236
Rangan, Kash, 71
Rao, Shailesh, 75
rape, 5, 8, 259–60
Rhodes Scholarship, 261–2, 263,
    270
Ride, Sally, 179
Ridgeway, Cecilia L., 361*n*
Riley (four-year-old girl), 27
Rockefeller Foundation, 18
Rodin, Judith, 18
Roebling, Emily, 242
Rogers, John, 230, 231–2, 236
Roizen, Heidi, 49
Rometty, Virginia "Ginni," 45
Rose, Dan, 44
Rouse, Cecilia, 379*n*–80*n*
Rousseff, Dilma, 47
Rubin, Robert, 103

salary negotiations, xvi–xvii,
    57–61, 223, 298–300,
    301–17
Salen, Kristina, 146, 152
Samba-Panza, Catherine, 344*n*
Sandberg, Adele, 16–17, 21, 69,
    101–2, 131, 146–7, 166, 170,
    212, 215–16
Sandberg, David, 25–6, 40–1, 70,
    74, 138, 142
Sandberg, Joel, 17, 21, 69, 131,
    142, 215
Sandberg, Michelle, 25–6, 70,
    101–2, 131–2, 169
Sanford, Margery, 69
San Francisco, 61
Santiago, José, 237

Sara Lee, 127
Scheck, Elise, 123
Schefler, Amy, 114, 138, 163–5
Schmidt, Eric, 73–4, 76, 110
Schreier, Bryan, 85–6
Schroepfer, Mike, 196
Schultz, Howard, 115
Scott, Kim Malone, 183–4
self-confidence, 38, 318–19
    correcting gender gap in, xv,
        46–8
    faking of, 42–3
    mastering the art of, 47
    see also insecurities and self-
        doubt
self-doubt, *see* insecurities and
    self-doubt
Sellers, Pattie, 64, 67
Senate Judiciary Committee, 195
separation anxiety, 172
Sequoia Capital, 86
sexism, 9, 178, 180, 204, 207, 226,
    249–50
    "benevolent," 193, 363n
sex trade, 5
sexual harassment, xiii, 9, 190
She Negotiates, 314
Shih, Clara, 86–7
Simmons, Rachel, 261–70
single mothers, 29, 154
Skipper, John, 238
sleep, 166–7, 211
Slutsky, Matthew, 244–6
Small, Deborah A., 360n
social media, 86, 184, 197
Soronko Solutions, 297
South Africa, 91
Soviet Jewry, 212
Spar, Debora, 31, 211
sponsors, sponsorships, 9, 82, 84,
    90–3, 94, 210, 363n–5n
    see also mentors, mentorships
spousal partnerships, 132–52,
    202, 211, 215, 369n

benefits of equal roles in,
    148–9, 151
caring for aging parents and,
    151, 215
empowering men's domestic
    roles in, 136–8, 151–2,
    202
equalizing division of
    household labor in, 139–41,
    146–9, 151, 369n
finding supportive potential
    mates for, 145–6, 152
lopsided gender roles in, 18,
    134–5, 139, 150, 182
strain of more professionally
    successful wives in, 145
support of career as important
    in, 138–9, 169, 216
    see also parenting
Standard Oil Company, 5
Stanford University, 54, 87, 276
    Institute of Design at, 121
Starbucks, 86, 115, 240
Star Wars, 233
stay-at-home mothers, 17, 18, 119,
    120, 149–50, 155, 170, 171
    average weekly hours spent on
        primary child care by, 170,
        377n
    in "mommy wars," 210–11, 212
    society as undervaluing work
        of, 212
    studies on paid child care vs.,
        171–2, 377n–8n
Steel, Bob, 92
Steinem, Gloria, 136, 151, 155,
    177, 183, 205, 217–18, 241
Steiner, Josh, 87
"stereotype threat," 28, 354n
Strober, Joanna, 30, 119
Stuart, Jennifer, 158
*Study on Women's Experiences at
    Harvard Law School*, 357n
Submarine Force, U.S., 212–13

success-likeability correlation,
xiii, 49–65, 194–5, 251,
360*n*
  as double bind, 54–5
  Heidi/Howard study on,
49–51, 53, 194
  learning to withstand criticism
and, 62–3
  salary negotiations and, 57–61,
360*n*
  as starting in grade school,
53–5
  women as downplaying
achievements due to, 52–5,
57–8, 64, 280
Sudan, 5
Summers, Anita, 5
Summers, Larry, xvi, 5, 22, 46,
70–2, 79, 85, 91, 106–7, 113
Summer Success and Leadership
Academy, 273
SurveyMonkey, 140
Swisher, Kara, 203

TaskRabbit, 327–8
Taylor, Maureen, 76
Taylor, Robert, 95–6
Teach for America, 256, 317
TED Talk, 35, 139, 176, 184–8
TEDWomen, 184
Thatcher, Margaret, 51
Thomas, Corin, 327
Thomas, Marlo, 6–7, 63
Thomas, Rachel, 281, 323–30
"Tiara Syndrome," 80
tokenism, 206
Treasury Department, U.S.,
71–2, 87, 91, 103, 106, 108,
113, 162, 181, 185
Truth, Sojourner (graffiti artist),
242
Tueller, Marie, 259–60
Twitter, 286

Uhlmann, Eric Luis, 380*n*–1*n*
USA Today, 127

Valenti, Jessica, 62
Vedantam, Shankar, 51
Village Voice, 298
Vodafone, 188

Walker, Alice, 80
Wall Street Journal, 23, 362*n*
Walt Disney Company, 88
Warrior, Padmasree, 44–5
Washington, George, 241
Washington Post, 175–6
Washington Post Company, 85
Washington state, 371*n*
Weaver, Sigourney, 28
Weber, Carrie, 36, 41
Wellesley Centers for Women, 35
Wellesley College, 158
When Harry Met Sally, 147
White, Emily, 85, 86
White House Project, 174
Whitman, Meg, 72
Williams, Joan, 210–11, 375*n*
Wilson, Marie, 174
Winfrey, Oprah, 82, 151, 270
Witherspoon, Reese, 329
Wojcicki, Susan, 162–3, 183
women
  downplaying of achievements
by, xiv, 19, 52–5, 57–8, 64,
219, 252, 280, 304, 318, 324
  education of, 5, 15–17, 19
  in government, 6, 343*n*–4*n*
  higher education of, 6, 19,
125
  in history, 241–3
  insecurities and self-doubt in,
see insecurities and self-doubt
  "leftover," 222–4
  in navy, 212–13

women *(continued)*
  pressure to prioritize marriage
    for, 21–3, 222–4
  as primary caregivers for aging
    parents, 151, 215
  race and, *see* race, racism
  social rules of conduct for, 24,
    25–7, 50–1, 52, 54–5, 56, 60,
    214, 349*n*
  as stay-at-home mothers, *see*
    stay-at-home mothers
  success-likeability correlation
    in, *see* success-likeability
    correlation
  see also employed women
Women@Google, 183
Women in Consulting panel, 167
Women's Media Center, 183
women's rights, women's rights
    movement, 5, 6, 150, 155,
    179, 183, 199, 211, 217–18
  female coalition of support
    needed in, 202–9, 213
  in foreign countries, 5, 48
  gender pay gap and, 5, 6–7, 217,
    309, 345*n*, 385*n*–6*n*
  male coalition of support
    needed in, 207–10
  speaking out on, *see* gender
    issues, speaking out on
  stalled progress in, 6–8, 11, 18,
    216, 248–9
  see also feminists, feminism

Wood, Chet, 93
work hours
  dispersion of, 376*n*
  husband's, and women's odds of
    quitting job, 125–6, 368*n*
  increases in, 166–7
  long hours and productivity,
    375*n*
Working Girl, 28
Working Group on Student
    Experiences, 357*n*
"work-life balance," 29–30,
    165–6, 375*n*
  see also family-work conflict
World Bank, xvi, 46, 70–1, 79
Wu, Abe, 94–5
Wurtele Center for Work and
    Life, 270

Xerox, 227, 258

Yahoo, 4, 64, 99, 133, 140, 197,
    202–3
Yale University, 125, 158
Ye, Allison, 222–4

Zuckerberg, Mark, 58–9, 64–5,
    68, 83, 98, 101, 104, 106,
    109, 111, 123, 147, 168,
    175–6

A NOTE ABOUT THE AUTHOR

SHERYL SANDBERG is chief operating officer at Facebook. Prior to working at Facebook, she was vice president of Global Online Sales and Operations at Google and chief of staff at the United States Treasury Department. Before that, she worked as a consultant at McKinsey & Company and as a research assistant at the World Bank. Sheryl serves on the boards of Facebook, The Walt Disney Company, Women for Women International, V-Day, and ONE, and chairs the board of LeanIn.Org. She received a B.A. in economics from Harvard University and an MBA from the Harvard Business School. Sheryl lives in Northern California with her husband, Dave Goldberg, and their two children.

A NOTE ON THE TYPE

This book was set in Janson, a typeface long thought to have been made by the Dutchman Anton Janson, who was a practicing typefounder in Leipzig during the years 1668–1687. However, it has been conclusively demonstrated that these types are actually the work of Nicholas Kis (1650–1702), a Hungarian, who most probably learned his trade from the master Dutch typefounder Dirk Voskens. The type is an excellent example of the influential and sturdy Dutch types that prevailed in England up to the time William Caslon (1692–1766) developed his own incomparable designs from them.

Composed by North Market Street Graphics,
Lancaster, Pennsylvania

Printed and bound by Berryville Graphics,
Berryville, Virginia

Designed by Cassandra J. Pappas